SIMON SAYS

S I M O N   S A Y S

A true story of boys, guns, and murder

KATHRYN EASTBURN

Da Capo Press
A Member of the Perseus Books Group

Designed by Timm Bryson
Set in 11 point Dante by the Perseus Books Group

Cataloging-in-Publication data for this book is available from the Library of Congress.

ISBN-13: 978-0-306-81552-2
ISBN-10: 0-306-81552-4

Published by Da Capo Press
A Member of the Perseus Books Group
http://www.dacapopress.com

Da Capo Press books are available at special discounts for bulk purchases in the U.S. by corporations, institutions, and other organizations. For more information, please contact the Special Markets Department at the Perseus Books Group, 2300 Chestnut Street, Suite 200, Philadelphia, PA, 19103, or call (800) 255-1514, or e-mail special.markets@perseusbooks.com.

To my mother, Bettye Carpenter, who taught me to love fiction
and always reminded me that truth is stranger.

In memory of Theodore Albert Waterman III (1981–2007),
who left us suddenly but still guides us.

ACKNOWLEDGMENTS

Deepest gratitude to Charles Dutcher, Donna and Robin Grimes, Cathie Cumming, Glen Urban, Kathy Creech, and Bonnie Matheny for helping me piece together a story that grabbed me early on and never lost its grip. Respects are also due to Nadia Sue and Jennifer Vandresar. Thanks to investigator Leonard Post for helping me get it right.

I would not have completed the first half of the book if not for my colleagues and mentors at the Spalding University M.F.A. program. Blessings to you.

Agent Paul Cirone enthusiastically agreed to represent the project, and my editor, Wendy, shepherded it through. Thanks to both of you for your confidence, patience, and encouragement.

My four wonderful children inspire and sustain me. Eternal gratitude to them and to my sisters, Karen and Kim, for their faith and love.

"That is the bitterest of all,
to bear the yoke of your own wrongdoing."
—*George Eliot*

SIMON SAYS is a traditional American children's game in which a leader issues orders, one by one, to players lined up on a starting line. A command should be obeyed only if it is preceded by the words "Simon says." Players who follow commands according to the game's rule move forward. Those who follow commands not prefaced with the words "Simon says," lose their turns and must return to the starting line. The winner is the first to follow orders correctly and consistently, thus crossing the finish line first.

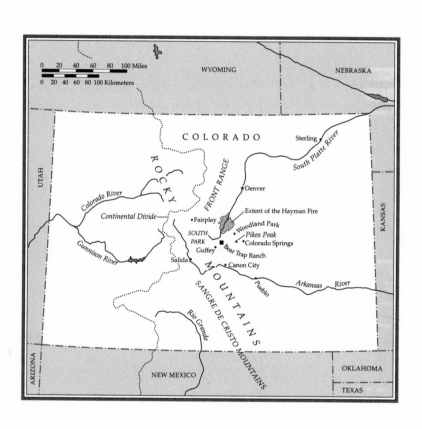

INTRODUCTION

July 2004

On a Sunday night, the sanctuary of the Ascension Lutheran Church in Colorado Springs is packed. The church is a low-rise 1960s building with stained glass in abstract lines and swirls, light wood pews, and indoor-outdoor carpeting to soften the echoes of voices and footsteps in the concrete vestibule. The congregation is composed of middle-class Caucasians, average age forty, eyes searching the front of the sanctuary attentively on this hot summer night.

Tonight's subject is murder and redemption. The speakers are Donna and Robin Grimes, longtime church members whose son Isaac, now eighteen, is serving a sixty-year sentence in adult prison for his part in a triple murder committed in the early hours of the first day of January 2001, on an icy Colorado mountainside.

Donna Grimes is petite and pretty, her face birdlike with fine bones and a thin nose. Rob is bulky and thick and moves carefully to protect his back, the site of two major surgeries in the past few years, including one just four days after Isaac was arrested. Rob speaks with a flat midwestern accent betraying his Kansas upbringing. Donna is articulate and smiles painfully, her eyes wrinkling then widening in a wet stare, when she speaks of their son.

They speak as "we": "We had a kid we thought we knew so well. We never took into consideration that Isaac could lie to us without us knowing."

On New Year's Eve, winter break of his sophomore year at Palmer High School, Isaac Grimes left his job at Carl's Jr. fast-food restaurant with coworker and friend Jonathan Matheny. At some point that evening, Jon and Isaac allegedly drove fifty miles west to Guffey, a tiny, unincorporated mountain village, and continued into the mountains to the home of Carl and JoAnna Dutcher, a retired Vietnam veteran and his wife. The Dutchers' grandson Tony, fifteen, was camping in a lean-to on a rocky ridge about four hundred yards above the house.

As the events of that night were later pieced together by lawyers and police, and by investigators aided by Isaac Grimes's confession, Tony Dutcher's throat was cut and his life ended as he camped out in a sleeping bag on the hill high above his grandparents' home. Carl and JoAnna were shot to death inside their trailer home. Isaac Grimes and Jon Matheny returned to Colorado Springs in the early morning of January 1 and, a few days later, returned to Palmer High School, where they attended classes until March 8. With the help of two other friends, Simon Sue and Glen Urban, they conspired to destroy the murder weapons before Grimes confessed to Tony Dutcher's murder and named Matheny as the gunman who shot down Tony's grandparents. Both boys were arrested, and five weeks later Urban and Sue were taken into custody and charged as accomplices.

Isaac became a suspect because Tony Dutcher had formerly been his best friend and had invited him up to his grandparents' place for New Year's Eve.

The bodies of Carl, JoAnna, and Tony were discovered on January 3. On January 9, Isaac attended Tony Dutcher's funeral.

Donna and Robin Grimes don't talk much about the night of the murders, but they speak often about the months leading up to that night. At the Ascension Lutheran Church, Donna tells her fellow congregants, "What we've learned is that evil is subtle; it grabs and torments its victims."

Donna and Rob recount how at the beginning of ninth grade, Isaac was in Latin class with his former best friend Tony Dutcher and a boy two years older, Simon Sue, a slight young man with dark hair and eyes and an outgoing personality. Donna and Rob recount how Simon keyed in on Isaac's loneliness and awkwardness, how Simon knew that Isaac was looking for a place to belong, so he invited him to the school's chess club.

They tell how Simon and Jon Matheny became Isaac's new best friends, how they were polite and prompt and never got Isaac home late. How on Wednesday nights, the boys said they were going to the community center to play chess.

They recall how they missed the signs that something was going wrong in Isaac's life.

"Sometimes we'd look into his eyes and Isaac wasn't there," said Rob.

Isaac insisted he needed a job. He started doing his own laundry. His room was as orderly as an army barracks. He spent hours staring into the computer screen. He was withdrawn and noncommunicative. He waited up nervously every night until his mother returned from her night shift job.

None of these things indicated to Donna and Robin Grimes that their son was anything other than a normal teenager struggling to forge an identity. Their family was going through a rough time; Rob was out of work and in constant pain.

They never suspected that Isaac was being trained as part of a paramilitary organization dreamed up by his friend Simon Sue, that on Wednesdays he was learning how to take apart and reassemble semiautomatic weapons, that he was learning guerrilla fighting tactics.

On a summer day when the Grimeses returned from Rob's annual company picnic and found Simon and Jon waiting on their front porch, Simon draped in a Guyanan flag, they thought little of it. Simon had just returned from a trip to Guyana with his parents, who were natives of that South American country and visited there often. They didn't know that when Simon and Jon joined Isaac in his bedroom and shut the door behind them, Simon pulled out an M-16 rifle from beneath the flag, put it to Isaac's head, and told Isaac he'd use it on him, his parents, his older sister, and his little brothers if he didn't follow orders. At least that's what Isaac told them later.

They didn't know that later that year Isaac would help plan and carry out the murder of his former best friend, Tony Dutcher. They didn't know that in the days preceding the murder and for weeks afterward, Isaac vomited so frequently the enamel wore off his teeth, a discovery made when his braces were removed in late February.

Robin and Donna Grimes believe their son was the victim of mind control. They regret ever telling him he had to tell the police the truth the first time he was questioned. They are disillusioned with the judicial system that offered him a plea bargain, then sentenced him to sixty years in adult prison. They want their son to receive real therapy instead of the occasional and piecemeal mental health care he has received within the prison system; they believe in his capacity to be rehabilitated. They go to therapy themselves and take medications that allow them to live with the knowledge that their son killed a boy who was once his friend.

They believe many crimes related to the case remain unsolved.

They believe in God and in their son's basic goodness.

"Isaac is a decent kid with a moral heart," Donna tells the rapt congregation of Ascension Lutheran Church. "Satan took what was very good and twisted it for his own evil purposes."

Because of Isaac's youthful looks and tender mental state, the seriousness of his crime, the publicity surrounding the case, and the fact that he turned state's witness and is now widely known among other inmates as a "snitch," Isaac lives in seclusion in the San Carlos correctional facility in Pueblo, Colorado, locked down twenty-three hours a day. He gets one one-hour visit a week from behind a Plexiglas barrier. He spends his time reading about organic farming, taking classes by mail, and writing letters to embassies around the world, explaining and complaining about the American judicial system.

He can have no physical contact with anyone, including his parents, because of prison rules applied to prisoners held in administrative segregation.

"I haven't touched him in two years," Donna tells the congregation of Ascension Lutheran Church, her eyes dark and wounded by what she has just said.

Robin takes her hand and she smiles that pained smile. They will continue to fight and pray for an ending to this nightmare story that will restore meaning to their son's life and to theirs. They will pray for forgiveness. They will wonder over and over what they could have done to stop this evil from happening. They will tell themselves that their son killed because he believed his family would be killed if he didn't.

They will never, for one minute, forget Tony Dutcher and his grandparents, the horrible thing Isaac did, or the incomprehensible things Simon said.

PART ONE

Sights Unseen

CHAPTER 1

Wednesday, January 3, 2001

Guffey, Colorado, is the kind of place the word *hamlet* was invented to describe. Not quite a village, it is a tiny pocket of civilization nestled among the craggy, scrub oak- and pine-strewn wilds of the Colorado Rockies. Mountain lions feast on deer in this country, and men feast on solitude.

In Guffey and in other tiny communities scattered throughout these mountains, espresso shops rub elbows with rough bars. Old hippies settle in search of cheaper land and a simpler life, opening massage studios amid snowmobile dealerships, antique shops, and land title companies housed in dusty wooden buildings, their creaky plank porches bordered by old-time hitching posts.

Turning off State Highway 9 into Guffey, the road quickly changes from asphalt to gravel and packed dirt. A series of log buildings—some old, others designed to look old—lines the road, laid out in a winding circular formation. There's Peaceful Henry's restaurant, where folks can find a good vegetarian dish as well as a fat hamburger, and where an occasional guitar strummer takes the stage to play a few Dead tunes. There's a grocery store that doubles as a post office and a day spa offering therapeutic baths and massage. Old barns have been turned into rented storage spaces. Pickaxes, shovels, and images of gold nuggets invoke Guffey's origins as a way station between mining towns like Cripple Creek and Central City, once havens for working men's dreams of striking it rich, now casino towns with little left of their boomtown glory.

Businesses change hands frequently in these parts when lowlanders find they can't take the isolation of a community like Guffey, a couple of hours and a mind-numbing drive away from the nearest big city, Colorado Springs.

The town of Guffey is unincorporated, and most people who call themselves Guffey residents actually live miles away in the woods surrounding the town center, in broken-up ranches turned into communities with names that evoke wildlife and Old West ways—Wolf Creek, Coyote Acres, Bear Trap Ranch. Some folks retire here to keep a few horses, some to disappear into the landscape, most to escape the noise and lights of the city.

Guffey is so small that there's no official population count—you'll rarely see a person as you're driving through—and so remote from the population centers of the state that the Colorado Department of Transportation misspelled its name—G-u-f-f-y—on the single mileage sign leading to it from points north.

The town has been in the news over the years for having cats and dogs elected as mayor. When the first feline mayor, Paisley, passed away, she was succeeded by three other cats that either disappeared mysteriously or died of natural causes. Eventually Shanda, a golden retriever, was elected mayor and served happily from her post at the Guffey General Store until she died in 2001 at the age of twelve.

Oprah Winfrey once declared Guffey the third best small town in America. Besides that brush with celebrity, the most serious news to come out of Guffey in recent years was the increase in bear encounters at dumpsters behind restaurants, and mountain lion sightings at the local elementary school.

That was, until January 3, 2001, when all hell broke loose in Guffey and the surrounding hillsides.

On the third day of the new year, bitter cold but bright and sunny, the sleepy town of Guffey found itself with ambulances racing through, police cars kicking up gravel and dust, and four dead bodies on its hands—one in town and three at neighboring Bear Trap Ranch.

Across the street from the Freshwater Grocery and Saloon at about 12:30 p.m., shots rang out from the home of Aaron Mandel, a local cook and bartender, ending a long feud with an enraged neighbor. Mandel had bought a gun after calling the sheriff's office to ask how he could legally protect himself from William Wainer, who was still mad four months after the two had been involved in a dispute over a car wreck.

When Wainer came storming into Mandel's house at noon on January 3, a loaded Ruger handgun in his pocket, Mandel first told him to back off, grabbing his own gun. When Wainer didn't back off, Mandel warned him again, then reached for his pocket and lurched forward. He shot Wainer once, then shot him seven more times, then ran across the street to the Freshwater Saloon and announced to its startled patrons, "Call 911. I just shot a man."

Shooting a man who was waving a gun at you in your own house might have made sense to most Guffey folks, but what they heard a few hours later didn't register as any sort of logical event.

At Bear Trap Ranch, just a few miles up the road, locals Carl and JoAnna Dutcher had been found shot to death inside their trailer home. Up the hill from the house, on a rocky overlook, their grandson Tony lay dead in a sleeping bag, his throat cut to the spine.

Investigators from the Park County Sheriff's Office, the Eleventh Judicial District Attorney's Office, and the Colorado Bureau of Investigation, along with family members of the Dutchers, would soon determine that Carl, JoAnna, and Tony had been lying frozen and dead for three days. Some time between the end of the New Year's Eve fireworks and the dark early hours of New Year's Day, grandfather, grandmother, and grandson had been systematically murdered in one of the most brutal slayings these parts had seen since miners and cowboys left the land and city dwellers moved in, looking for the peaceful life.

•◆•

Park County Sheriff Fred Wegener had known Carl Dutcher only vaguely over the past ten years. Dutcher was a loner who pretty much kept to himself at his remote, rural homestead surrounded by ponderosa pine forests and granite cliffs. Carl had twenty-one acres, a pond, a trailer home, a big metal garage, a good wife, peace and quiet, and solitude: everything a man needed at his home on Apache Trail in Bear Trap Ranch.

Driving toward the Dutcher place, Wegener didn't know what he'd find. Carl Dutcher's son James, down in Colorado Springs, had called the Teller County Sheriff's office a couple hours ago, asking an officer to go by and check on his parents, whose phone had been ringing with no answer for several days. A Teller County deputy answered the call and had now summoned Wegener to the scene, which lay barely within Park County jurisdiction, as the eastern boundary of the Dutchers' property marked the dividing line between the two counties.

Wegener and his deputies knew Carl Dutcher as a gruff military veteran, a gun collector, and an arms dealer licensed by the federal government to sell weapons and explosives. This was a serious and potentially lucrative business in a part of the country where weapons were valued, even necessary for folks living away from streetlights and patrol cars, out in the country where bear, mountain lions, and coyotes roamed.

Carl and JoAnna had moved to Guffey and Bear Trap Ranch in 1991 after Carl retired from government service down in Colorado Springs. Carl stayed close to home while JoAnna worked part time at a store down in Divide, a small settlement twenty miles east of Guffey. She was popular with customers and with the other women who worked there.

The couple had known each other since they were children in Kansas and had married in 1964. Carl had served three tours in Vietnam while JoAnna raised their three little boys, Charles, Ty, and James, in Colorado Springs. Dad's retirement from active duty in 1972 was followed by thirteen years of work in civil service.

Carl and JoAnna had come to this rural outpost to enjoy some quiet days and to escape the city, but things hadn't been easy. Youngest son Ty, who lived in Georgia now, had racked up convictions for drugs, robbery, and un-counted numbers of traffic offenses. He'd spent enough time in jail to make law enforcement officials like Wegener well aware of his presence whenever he came west for a visit.

Middle son James had done jail time and time in the state mental hospital. And eldest son Charles had been arrested several times, passing two years in prison for a drug charge back in the early 1990s.

James had told the dispatcher that Charles's boy, Tony—Carl and JoAnna's oldest grandchild—was spending the Christmas holiday with his grandparents up at Bear Trap Ranch, and he hadn't been heard from for a few days either. Wegener accelerated as he turned onto the rough county road leading to the Dutchers' place, hoping for the best but preparing for the worst.

•◆•

Deputy Henry Hasler of the Teller County Sheriff's Office was dispatched to the Dutcher property just a little past noon, following James Dutcher's call. When he arrived he discovered the trailer home, mounted on a perma-nent foundation, sitting midway back from the road at the midpoint of a semicircular gravel driveway. A small white pickup truck with Park County plates stood parked outside. Hasler ran the plate numbers and confirmed that the truck belonged to the residents of the house, Carl and JoAnna Dutcher. He notified his dispatcher and asked that she call the Park County Sheriff's Office and have a deputy come to the location as soon as possible.

Hasler knocked loudly on the front door. "I'm with the sheriff's office," he called out, but no one answered. He walked to the back, noticing that all the windows were covered by shades; he couldn't see in. He could hear the high-pitched bark of a small dog from inside.

Hasler walked down the driveway to a large metal garage and noticed that a small entryway on the side was not closed all the way. He walked into the garage and saw three vehicles, including a black car the Dutchers' son James had described to the dispatcher.

Hasler called his office again and asked the dispatcher to find Clay Briggs, security officer for the Bear Trap Ranch subdivision. Briggs might know whether the Dutchers were away on vacation. When Briggs received the call, he drove straight to the Dutcher house from his own house less than a mile away. He knew that Carl and JoAnna didn't take vacations, and if they weren't going to be around for any amount of time, they would have asked him to keep an eye on the house.

When he arrived at the Dutchers', Briggs told Hasler he was a good friend and he felt certain something was wrong. But Carl often took a nap this time of day, he added hopefully. If both the truck and the black car were at the house, Briggs said, then the Dutchers might possibly be here.

Hasler decided to enter the house. He and Briggs found the back door unlocked. Upon entering the cramped kitchen, they saw bare feet sticking out from the hallway to the right. Looking closer, they saw a man dressed in a blue-and-white bathrobe, sprawled across the narrow hallway, his skin unnaturally white with a gray cast. Hasler stepped over the body he assumed was Carl Dutcher's, pulled his revolver from the holster on his belt, and moved forward to check out the rest of the house. Briggs stared disbelievingly at his friend.

Through the first door on the right, Hasler saw a woman in a blue flannel, floral-printed nightgown. She sat wedged against the bathtub, her feet reaching toward the door, surrounded by a great deal of dried blood. Hasler quickly searched the other rooms of the house, looking for Tony Dutcher, the boy reported missing by his uncle, but found no trace of him. In the bedroom at the far back corner of the house, shattered glass covered the bed, the top of the dresser, and the floor.

In the living room, a tiny toy poodle cowered beside the sofa, shivering.

Hasler raced outside, a shaken Clay Briggs following him, and called dispatch again, this time urging Park County sheriffs to get to the house immediately. Park County assured him that Sheriff Wegener and others were on their way, but their hands were full. They'd had to check out another shooting in Guffey just an hour earlier.

Hasler stretched a piece of barrier tape between the rails of the back porch, then walked around front with Briggs and asked him if he would drive his truck down to one end of the semicircular driveway and stay there until more law enforcement arrived. Hasler parked at the other end of the driveway and sat waiting, watching the front entrance to the house. A quiet pond, about the same size as the house's footprint, lay gray and still in the depression of earth that separated Hasler's vehicle from Briggs's. Along its muddy banks, juncos and starlings pecked and preened.

A little past two, Teller County Sheriff's Detective Cindy Shengle and Park County Deputy Mike Valdez arrived on the scene. Hasler and the other two officers walked through the house and garage to make sure the scene was properly cleared. Soon after, Detective Bob Horn and Sergeant Don Anthony, both of Park County, arrived, and Hasler turned the case over to them since the case lay within their jurisdiction.

Inside the Dutcher home, Shengle, Horn, and Anthony took a closer look. Above the head of the man now positively determined to be Carl Dutcher, the wood paneling on the wall was ripped open in a four-inch-long tear. A picture had been shot off the wall and lay face down, the glass shattered, above Carl's head, near the bathroom door. Late afternoon light streamed through what appeared to be bullet holes in the wall of the far end of the trailer. In the living room, a stack of clothes stood next to the couch, and a pile of red-and-white-striped candy canes littered the coffee table.

The dog whimpered.

"Somebody take that poor dog outside and feed it," said Horn. "But don't touch anything but the dog food."

Outside, Sheriff Wegener and Leonard Post, an investigator from the Eleventh Judicial District Attorney's Office, had arrived at the now crowded scene. Wegener pointed up the mountain and told Deputy Valdez he'd noticed some type of fort up on the rocks behind the house as he was driving in. He asked him to check it out. The house was closed, and Wegener ordered it sealed off until lab technicians could be brought up to sweep the scene for evidence.

Valdez and Shengle inched their way up the rocky mountainside to the encampment. Around 4:15, as the midwinter sun began to wane, they found a dugout fort with low timber walls and a plastic tarp covering. Inside was the bluish body of a boy who looked to be about fourteen years old, his hair mussed. He lay face down in a military-type sleeping bag, his head turned to the side. Some blood had pooled and frozen around his head, and there also appeared to be blood on a rolled-up sleeping bag just a few feet away.

DA's investigator Post was quickly called to the top of the hill where Tony Dutcher lay. Post was a barrel-chested man with a thick head of gray hair and light blue eyes that turned down slightly at the corners. Gently, he knelt and reached to turn the boy's body onto its right side while the others, chatting in the January cold, watched from a distance. Nervously, they joked about how many dead bodies were dumped in their county. Post had to rise to a squat and tug hard on Tony Dutcher's shoulders to turn the boy over.

Post noted a large pool of frozen blood on the piece of plastic directly underneath the boy and his sleeping bag. He unzipped the sleeping bag. The boy's shoes were parked near his head and his feet were wrapped with blankets. Post reached inside the sleeping bag and scanned the length of it for a weapon, but his large, weathered hand came back empty. A knife lay nearby, but the blade was clean. A long cut just below the boy's chin opened a dark chasm that separated his head from the rest of his body. His hands, frozen in rigor mortis, reached up toward his neck, his palms resting against his upper chest. Post made notes as the daylight disappeared and the other officers shuffled about and shivered on the rocky hillside.

Down Ute Pass, in Colorado Springs, the local daily newspaper, the *Gazette,* rushed reporters up the mountain to report the deadliest day in modern Park County history.

"A lot of folks move from the city to get away from this sort of thing," Sheriff Wegener told the *Gazette.* "The big city's coming to the small rural area."

As locals gathered outside the Dutcher home in the last minutes of daylight on January 3, the knowledge sunk in that Carl, JoAnna, and Tony had been lying in the house and up on the hill for days. Sheriff Wegener told them he was sure the murders were an isolated incident. He said it looked as if the Dutchers were targeted specifically. This comforted neighbor Bobby Cole, even though the investigation had just begun.

"We don't need a whole bunch of people packing guns up here," he told the *Gazette.* "That's what this could have turned into."

Wegener decided it would be better for all involved if the bodies were secured overnight and processed the following day. Officers would take shifts outside, watching over Tony Dutcher's body to make sure varmints and other intruders stayed away.

Wegener and his deputies prepared to tell family members the terrible news: Carl, JoAnna, and Tony Dutcher hadn't merely failed to answer the phone. They were dead and probably had been since just after the last time they were heard from on New Year's Eve.

CHAPTER 2

Wednesday Evening, January 3, 2001

Tony Dutcher's mother, Jenny Vandresar, dropped the cordless telephone onto her bed and grabbed a pair of jeans from a nearby chair. Her hands shook as she pulled on the jeans and a black Tommy Hilfiger sweatshirt. She swept her thick hair up into a quick ponytail, then sat on the edge of the bed and dialed her sister's number.

Kathy Creech answered on the second ring.

"Kathy, I need your help," said Jenny, her voice rushed and edgy. She told Kathy she'd just gotten a call from Tony's uncle, James, and something was wrong up at the Dutchers' house. Tony had been there since the day after Christmas and Jenny hadn't heard from him since New Year's Eve. James had called the cops when he got no answer from Carl and JoAnna after three days of constant calls.

Jenny asked Kathy if she could drive her up the mountain from Colorado Springs to the police station in Divide, then called James back and told him they'd pick him up on the way. James was scattered and inconsolable on the other end of the line. Jenny hung up quickly, unable to listen to his fears.

She grabbed her purse and went to the front porch to wait for Kathy. She'd been taking a nap before heading to work at ten that night and was still a bit fuzzy, though creeping terror was quickly sharpening her senses. She'd called Fabulous TNT's, the club where she worked as an exotic dancer, to let them know she wouldn't make it in tonight. She waited, allowing herself finally to think about Tony.

She'd given him a new watch for Christmas and her roommate, Jennifer Pickles, also a dancer at Fabulous TNT's, had given him a nice blue CD player with headphones. But he'd spent most of the school holiday with his dad, Charles Dutcher (with whom Jenny hadn't lived since Tony was a toddler), and a couple of nights with his Uncle James in Colorado Springs, returning to her house Christmas Day to exchange gifts.

Mother and son had endured a rough year; their schedules clashed. It seemed that whenever they saw each other, Tony was mad at her and she was too exhausted to do anything about it. But exchanging Christmas gifts a week ago, they had passed the time affectionately and with ease.

Jenny had been in the stripping business since she was barely nineteen, when Tony was a two-year-old and she'd left Colorado Springs for a career in films on the West Coast. There she'd met Paul Vandresar, a strapping performer with a carefully sculpted and tended physique and a kind personality. Jenny particularly treasured his sweetness toward Tony.

They married and returned to Colorado Springs when Tony was ten, to be near Jenny's family and so that Tony could resume a relationship with his grandparents, Carl and JoAnna. Charles, Tony's dad, had begun to get his life together over the years his boy had been gone and was eager to spend time with him. Paul handled the complicated family dynamics well, and Jenny was glad Tony had more family to love him, especially the elder Dutchers, who gave him a place to run wild and just be a boy.

But around this time last year, the beginning of 2000, Paul had begun to behave strangely—paranoid and irrational. Doctors told him he was bipolar and prescribed different medications to help him, but nothing seemed to work. Finally, he scared Jenny enough that she left the house and took Tony to stay at her sister Kathy's house until things blew over.

Tony didn't want to leave his stepfather alone. A close bond had developed over the years between the two. One afternoon after school he went over to visit Paul and found him crying and miserable, inconsolable, unable to sleep or sit still. Tony couldn't leave him, he told his mother over the phone, and he missed several days of school sitting with Paul. Finally, Kathy and Jenny went to the house and insisted that Tony leave with them. A day later, they sent Kathy's son Justin over to the house to check on Paul. Justin found him hanging from the stair rail, dead.

Nine months of grief and friction between mother and son followed. Jenny grieved for Paul and for her son's loss of innocence. Tonight, she had no idea what she would have to face at the sheriff's office.

As Kathy's car pulled into the driveway, Jenny said a quick prayer for her son's safety. She hugged her sister when she got into the car. There was no way, she told her, she'd have been able to keep her car on the road all the way to the Divide sheriff's office on this dark night.

•◆•

Charles Dutcher worked in the kitchen of the upscale Blue Star Restaurant in Colorado Springs, a job he'd grown to love. When Tony came over now to visit Charles and his new wife, Rhonda, Charles would whip up a chicken dish he'd learned at the restaurant or make his boy home fries or a good burger.

Charles had met Jenny when she was sixteen and he was seventeen. Their high school love was hot and fast, and though they never married, they had lived together and had a child, Tony, when Jenny was barely seventeen and Charles had just finished high school. They were wild about the baby and enjoyed a good year of obsessing over him, barely able to pay the rent on their income from odd jobs. Things began to fall apart, though, when Jenny discovered how much money she could make stripping and Charles was arrested on a drug charge.

A headstrong boy, Charles Harrison Dutcher had grown into a young man who seemed to invite trouble his way. He was thin and small but hard-muscled, strong, and stubborn, too. JoAnna had given him her father's name, Harrison, a fact that made him proud. Grandpa Harrison had lived to be 107 years old. A picture of him with his long beard and stiff overalls, standing next to JoAnna, hung in the Dutcher family living room.

Carl had raised young Charles to be a soldier. When he and his brothers got out of control as children, Carl lined them up and made them stand at attention until their legs gave out. Once, Charles had continued to stand long after Ty and James had fallen to their knees, staring straight ahead until he passed out and collapsed straight backward like a character in a Bugs Bunny cartoon. Charles remembered this incident with pride.

He had signed up for military service the year he and Jenny had Tony but had been arrested before he was to report to duty. He spent enough time in prison to lose his hold on Jenny and to lose his father's love and respect. Carl had never forgiven his son for the stupid thing he did at eighteen and Charles couldn't forgive himself, either, for letting his parents down.

After Jenny left and took Tony to California, Charles was so angry he couldn't love anyone. He got into more scuffles with the law and his parents. But Jenny eventually returned to Colorado Springs and with her came Tony, a reason for Charles to clean up his life.

That boy ran around in circles barking like a dog when they got back from California, Charles said. Tony was out of control at age ten, but time with Carl and JoAnna had helped him. As he saw more of his grandparents, he also saw more of his father, and eventually the two developed a comfortable bond. When Charles talked to him these days, he always asked Tony how he was doing in school, if anybody was bugging him, and if he needed anything.

Tony spent many weekends and much of the summer at the Bear Trap Ranch house, where he was the light of Carl and JoAnna's lives. It gave Charles some consolation to know that Carl Dutcher thought this was a boy who might turn out to be OK, a boy he could teach the military discipline he'd failed to instill in his three sons. If Charles's father couldn't love his old-est son, then at least he could love Tony.

Charles had chopped and prepped vegetables, heated pans, and sautéed dishes for the comfortable, wealthy clientele of the Blue Star, wondering why he hadn't heard from Tony since New Year's Eve and why his parents' answering machine was so full it couldn't accept any new messages. He would drive up to his folks' place tomorrow and see what was going on.

•◆•

"Tell me where to go," Kathy said. The car heater was cranking, and she could make out Jenny's frightened green eyes even in the darkness.

"Divide, the sheriff's office." Jenny's voice cracked on the word *sheriff.* "Damn, I'm so scared."

Kathy took her sister's hand as she backed the car out onto the empty street. Unlike her petite younger sister, Kathy was a tall woman. Jenny had always been so little and pretty, it seemed that Kathy and everyone else who loved her always wanted to protect her. Jenny described James's frantic call and said she hadn't spoken to Tony herself since Saturday.

"You OK?" asked Kathy as the she pulled the car onto Highway 24 West and wove into the open lanes. Few cars were headed west at this time of night.

Jenny shook her head no and looked out the window at the passing lights of the city, hoping for a mistake. Maybe Grandma and Grandpa had taken Tony on a trip somewhere in the mountains, a New Year's surprise. Maybe that's why they hadn't answered when James had called over the past few days.

"I'll bet they just took off somewhere together," said Kathy, echoing Jenny's thoughts.

Jenny tried hard to smile.

When she'd last talked to Tony on New Year's Eve, he'd sounded excited. He said Isaac Grimes, an old friend, was coming up to spend the night and would be coming by her house to pick up a sleeping bag. Isaac hadn't come by, but Jenny didn't think anything of it. The boys hadn't hung out at all this school year. She hadn't seen Isaac in over a year. Still, Tony sounded happy and Jenny was glad of that.

Tony liked the watch his mother had given him for Christmas, black with yellow and orange lightning bolts on the band. He'd stuffed it in the pocket of his green camouflage jacket and had taken it with him up to Grandma's. When JoAnna had picked him up the day after Christmas, Jenny had kissed her boy and told him she loved him.

She was glad of that.

Kathy stopped at a west side apartment complex, where James Dutcher, disheveled and distraught, climbed into the backseat. Jenny offered him a word of assurance that everything would be all right, and the car pulled back onto the highway. James, a balding man with big round eyes and a belly to match, stared disconsolately at the passing streetlights and into the darkness as the car climbed Ute Pass.

Thirty minutes passed and the winding mountain roads grew darker as the car sped through Woodland Park to Divide, little more than a collection of buildings at the intersection of Highways 24 and 67. The sheriff's office, a plain cinder-block building, sat at street level on the left, the driveway plunging down a steep slope to the parking lot in the back.

A silver-haired man with a white cowboy hat and a blue plaid shirt held the door for Kathy, James, and Jenny as they entered the small building. Handcuffs and a leather holster hung from the belt that held up his neatly pressed Levis.

"Mrs. Vandresar?" he said, extending his hand to Jenny.

Jenny nodded yes and pushed her hair back from her face. He led her to a small white room with a clock and a calendar on the wall, a squared-off love seat shoved into a corner. Jenny sat down on the love seat, and the man who'd introduced himself as Park County Detective Bob Horn spoke to her quietly. Beside him, in a chair that looked too small for his body, was Leonard Post, the DA's investigator. Cathy and James stayed behind in a small waiting area outside the room.

Horn explained that James Dutcher had called earlier that day asking the sheriff's office to check on his parents, whom he hadn't heard from for several days. Horn and several other law enforcement officers had gone to the house, where they had found two people, Carl and JoAnna, dead inside.

He paused and lowered his voice. On the hill behind the house, he said, they'd found a boy's body in a sleeping bag.

Jenny stared hard at Horn, her eyes darkening, and a wail arose from her throat. "I want my mother . . . I want my sister!" A woman identified as a victim's advocate emerged and slung a blanket over Jenny's shoulders. Jenny pushed her hands against her face and leaned into the wall.

Horn quietly leaned forward and explained that they couldn't be sure it was Tony they'd found. James had said there was another boy up there spending the night. No one had identified the body yet and there was no ID to be found. Leonard Post, bulky in a heavy jacket, took a seat next to Jenny on the small love seat and softly placed a hand on her shoulder, reminding her they were not sure of the identity of the body they'd found. It could be someone else, he told her, possibly his friend Isaac, who James had said was spending the night with Tony.

An expression of resignation crossed Jenny's face. Her eyes settled straight ahead and her speech flattened. "I doubt Isaac was up there. He and Tony haven't seen each other for a long time."

Post asked if Tony would have been carrying any identification. The boy on the hill had none. "Tony didn't have any ID because he left his wallet at my house. The last time he went up he left it there." She twisted in her seat and pressed her forehead against the wall, letting out a moan.

Post asked her to describe Tony. She did.

Six feet tall. Around 120 pounds. Brown hair with bleached tips, the color of hers. Hair about collar length, shaved on the sides. He'd been wearing a green military-style field jacket. He carried a set of keys on his belt, one to her house and one to a Jeep. He didn't drive yet, but he'd had a car left to him by his stepfather.

Jenny hugged herself tight, arms crossing her chest. Arms. She needed arms. She extended her hands forward, reaching.

"I want my sister!" she cried again, and Horn let Kathy into the room. She knelt in front of Jenny and began pushing the loose hair that had fallen from her ponytail out of her sister's face. Jenny collapsed forward, her face in her hands, and Kathy held her tightly, stroking her hair.

"I have nothing anymore," Jenny cried. "I have nothing anymore. I have no son." Kathy rocked her gently.

Before excusing himself from the room, Post explained that there were details of the investigation, of how the victims were killed, that he wouldn't be sharing at this point, not even with the family.

"As this progresses, there will be things I can't tell you," he said, and Kathy nodded. "Anything I can tell you I will. All the evidence will be sent to Jefferson County, where the medical examiners will examine the remains."

The woman who'd brought Jenny the blanket settled next to her as Kathy stood and followed Post to the corner of the room.

Tentatively, the woman reached for Jenny's hand and stroked it. She handed over a box of tissues, and Jenny grabbed a handful, smashing her face into the soft white cloud.

Post and Kathy talked seriously on the other side of the room. Jenny stood up and the blanket dropped from her shoulders.

"God, I can't listen to them anymore," she said loudly, wiping her mascara-smeared eyes. "Tony will be OK. He'll be OK. Tony will be OK."

The clock on the wall read 10:32 p.m. as Jenny walked out of range of the video camera that had taped the worst moment of her life and was still recording the hushed voices of Investigator Post and her sister Kathy, discussing what would happen next. They looked like reasonable people discussing something that made sense, something within the realm of imagination.

For Jenny, nothing would ever make sense again.

•◆•

Around ten, Charles Dutcher had just stepped outside the kitchen door of the Blue Star for a smoke when he saw his nephew Justin, Kathy Creech's boy, walking toward him across the parking lot. He hadn't seen Justin in a long while, though he'd always liked him. Justin was seven years older than Tony, a big brother of sorts.

"What's up, Justin?" said Charles, extending a hand.

"I don't know, man," said Justin, his face etched with worry.

He told Charles his mother had sent him; he needed to come up to Divide to the sheriff's office where she had taken Jenny and James. Something was wrong up at Carl and JoAnna's house.

Charles freaked. He didn't have a car; he'd gotten a ride to work. He'd have to go by the house and tell Rhonda what was going on. Justin told him not to worry; he'd drive Charles up.

Charles told the other guys in the kitchen that he needed to leave and threw on a coat. As Justin drove toward the trailer park where Charles and Rhonda were living temporarily, Charles said he was supposed to have gone up there on New Year's Eve to camp out with Tony. It was kind of a tradition of theirs, he said.

Last New Year's Eve, Y2K, when everybody thought the world was going to end because all the computers and clocks and satellites in the world would be fucked up by the change from 1999 to 2000, he and Rhonda had camped on the hill with Tony, waiting for the catastrophe. They'd joked that Colorado Springs and Denver could go to hell and they'd be fine up on the mountain with everything they needed to survive. Cut off from the ridiculous grid that ran everything in the city, they could cook venison steaks on an open fire, heat with propane, and draw water from the well.

They had slept beneath the stars through the last night of 1999 and were supposed to have done it again this year, but Charles was scheduled to work. He'd called Tony and told him he was sorry but he couldn't come up. Tony had sounded good and said he was camping out anyway. Charles knew Tony would be fine, but he hung onto the sour taste of regret parents swallow when they've disappointed their children.

He'd make it up to him, Charles told himself. When he saw Tony again, he'd make sure his son knew he wouldn't let him down again.

CHAPTER 3

Thursday, January 4

The day began startlingly clear, brittle, and bright as only a Colorado morning can be. High on the rock cliff above the Dutchers' earth-colored mobile home, the lean-to was stripped of Tony Dutcher's body. A sober entourage of strong men zipped the ruined boy's body into a black plastic body bag and carefully felt their way down the hill with the dark, stiff package propped on their shoulders.

Left behind, yellow plastic crime scene ribbons trembled in the midwinter air around Tony's backpack, his blood-drenched sleeping bag, and a Scrabble board. From the high vantage point of the lean-to, most of Apache Trail and the elder Dutchers' entire driveway were easily visible. Hawks circled overhead against a bluebird sky as deputies combed the rocky hillside for clues.

Inside the house, Charles and James Dutcher tried to help Investigator Post and the sheriff's deputies piece together some evidence. The night before, at the Divide police station, Charles Dutcher had been informed that a body, likely his son's, had been found on the hillside.

Early in the morning, just past dawn, deputies had escorted Charles up the hill to Tony's fort. He'd identified Tony's body, covered except for his face, drained of all color.

Charles had felt the life emptying out of him. After many years of separation and struggle, he and Tony finally had formed a relationship. He was finally ready to show his mother and father that he could be a parent to his own child. Now they were all gone—Tony murdered beneath the first stars of the new year, his parents in their pajamas in the close confines of their home in the woods. Walking down the hill to the house, Charles suddenly felt ancient. If he'd only come up and camped out with Tony, as they had planned, none of this would have happened. His dogs, large mixed breeds, would have gone nuts when the intruders approached; he was sure of that.

The murderers would be the dead ones, not his mother, his father, and his son.

In the kitchen, Charles and James Dutcher located their mother's plastic pill dispenser with individual compartments for each day of the week. No pills had been taken since midday New Year's Eve. JoAnna was rigorous about taking her medication, including Coumadin, a blood thinner she took each night before bed.

Investigator Leonard Post played the answering-machine tape, filled to capacity with three days' worth of inquiries: "Hey JoAnna, where are you? Give me a call"; "Mom, I've been trying to reach you. Call me back"; "Hi, Tony. It's Dad. Call me."

In Carl Dutcher's bedroom, deputies carefully identified, wrapped, and packaged as evidence each of the guns they found, all loaded: a hunting rifle, a 12-gauge shotgun, a Ruger .22 pistol, a Colt ultra 10 pistol, a revolver, a Bulldog pistol, a Mossberg .22 rifle, a .410 shotgun. There were ten guns altogether, lying on every open surface in the room, including the bedside table.

Charles and James speculated that when Carl got up in the middle of the night for a drink of water, or when he arose for his morning coffee, as he always did, at 4 a.m., the killer must have been waiting in the hallway. They figured the killer must have known he couldn't take Carl in the bedroom where all his weapons lay.

Charles and James observed, as Clay Briggs had the day before, that normally a rifle in a soft camouflage case was propped up in the corner of the living room. The case was still there, but the AR-15.223 rifle was missing. Also missing was Carl's prized .454-caliber revolver.

The sons recoiled when they saw the devastation in the bathroom, where their mother's body had been found. The pipes beneath the bathtub had been destroyed in the volley of gunfire, and the toilet was broken into several pieces.

Charles, unable to cry, swore instead.

"Whoever did this is mine," he said. "They better not ever show their faces again, 'cause when they do I'm gonna fuckin' kill 'em."

•◆•

The autopsies conducted during the next week would record the physical devastation suffered by Carl, JoAnna, and Tony Dutcher.

Six bullets had hit JoAnna Dutcher as she cowered in the bathroom, trying to take cover behind the toilet. One entered her cheek and exited her neck. One hit her front right shoulder, fracturing the joint. One flew through her forearm as she held it up to protect herself, fracturing the elbow joint. One bullet barely grazed her right fingertip. The bullet that killed her went through her left breast like an arrow and entered her lower chest area, striking her liver, pancreas, and bowel, ripping through her abdominal aorta and fracturing her lower spine before exiting out her lower back.

The two bullets that entered Carl Dutcher's body, one in the chest and one in the abdomen, shattered four ribs, tore through his bowels, lacerated his aorta, and fractured his upper spine.

Tony Dutcher's autopsy listed only one mortal wound—a large, deep cut to the throat, stretching beneath his chin from jawbone to jawbone. The other small marks on his face and on one fingertip appeared to be postmortem in nature. Tony was dressed in layers—a jacket over a Metallica shirt, thermal pants over jeans, no socks. There was no indication of a struggle in the coroner's reading of the fifteen-year-old's dead body.

As sheriff's deputies closed the house and secured the crime scene the second day of the investigation, the Dutcher sons left for Colorado Springs, preparing to bury their dead. In one afternoon, while Guffey and the rest of Park County were eating the leftovers of the holiday ham and enjoying football on television, their family had been completely and forever dismantled. Jennifer Vandresar had lost her only child. James had lost his parents and a nephew.

Charles, the oldest Dutcher brother, had lost his only son, his mother, and his father. Moreover, he had lost all hope for a future that included love, forgiveness, or kinship with any of them. Rage roared in his ears. The sons of bitches had trapped his mother and gunned her down.

They're mine, he told himself.

They're mine, he told the cops.

Those sons of bitches are mine, he told anybody who would listen.

•◆•

Jim Howell, Leonard Post's fellow investigator at the DA's office, and Colorado Bureau of Investigation Agent Dave Sadar wasted no time moving ahead with the investigation.

A former boyfriend of Jenny Vandresar's, named by both Charles and James as a potential suspect, was found to have a tight alibi for his whereabouts on New Year's Eve.

Down in Colorado Springs, the officers located Tony's friend Nathan Hickman and talked to him at his mother's house. Nathan said he and Tony had been best friends since sixth grade. The last time he had seen him was on the Wednesday or Thursday before school let out for winter break. He'd talked to Tony by phone two days after Christmas.

Nathan had never been to the Dutchers' outpost, he said, but another friend, Isaac Grimes, had visited the house before. Nathan remembered that Tony had got upset with Isaac, maybe about two years ago, because he couldn't keep up with the hard work that building the fort required.

Tony told Nathan that he practiced his martial arts and shooting whenever he visited Carl and JoAnna. And Nathan recalled that Tony had lots of knives and a bayonet. Tony had said that his father, Charles, would be up there with him this New Year's Eve.

The investigators asked Nathan about Tony's hobbies. Nathan said Tony liked to collect military-type equipment and clothing, knives, and memorabilia. Isaac did, too, he said, but Tony and Isaac hadn't been getting along well recently.

Agent Sadar and Investigator Howell thanked Nathan and his mother for letting them visit and wished them well. Nathan's mother, glad to see them go, closed the door.

Sadar called Leonard Post to tell him they had no new leads but would file a report on their visit with Nathan Hickman.

Post said he'd gotten one promising lead. His name had been listed as a contact in the *Gazette*'s front-page story, for anyone who might have information about the murders. He expected he'd be getting a lot of crank calls, but he'd received a call late in the afternoon that sounded legitimate. Robin Grimes from Colorado Springs, Isaac Grimes's father, had called to say he might have some information related to the killings.

Sadar and Post made plans to visit the Grimes family the next day. Isaac's name was the only consistent thread running through their conversations with everyone so far. Tony's former best friend seemed their closest link to the boy on the hillside whose face Post couldn't forget, his frozen eyelashes tangled with sleep.

CHAPTER 4

Friday, January 5—Monday, January 8, 2001

Leonard Post and Dave Sadar arrived at the Grimes house in Colorado Springs at about one in the afternoon on January 5. The house was a low rancher on a quiet street of flat lawns turned brown in the dry, frigid winter air. Two early-model Land Cruisers were parked in the driveway, rusted and in various states of repair.

The officers knocked and Donna Grimes immediately ushered them into a sparsely furnished living room. A piano cluttered with sheet music stood against one wall. Donna introduced the officers to her husband, Robin, a tall bulky man, and her son Isaac, a gangly teenager with short hair and his mother's sharp features. Two little boys who looked to be around six or seven, Isaac's younger brothers, raced in sock feet through the living room from time to time.

Post thanked Rob for calling him the day before and said he knew the news of the Dutchers' deaths must have come as a shock to them.

"We've known Tony since he was twelve," said Rob. "We just can't believe this has happened."

"I know that you and Tony were friends, Isaac," said Post, focusing on the boy, who had the look of someone who was here to learn something. "Did you ever go up to his grandparents' place?"

Isaac explained that he'd been there several times in the past, the last time in November before the Colorado Big Game season, sometime before Thanksgiving, to pick up his rifle, inherited from his grandfather and kept at the Dutchers' place because his parents didn't want a gun in the house.

Carl, said Isaac, had taught him how to shoot; his parents had signed a release for this. But that was a while ago, maybe Labor Day two years ago.

"When did you last see Tony?" asked Post. He wrote as Isaac talked, his left hand curled around his pencil, scribbling in the upside-down fashion of many southpaws.

Isaac said he'd last seen Tony before Christmas break at school, but Tony had called three times over the holiday and Isaac had called Tony as well. Around two in the afternoon on New Year's Eve, Isaac called to wish Tony a happy new year and Tony invited him up, but Isaac said he had other plans.

"Tony's friend Nathan Hickman has told us that you and Tony weren't getting along anymore, Isaac. Is that true?" asked Post.

Isaac said yes, over the last year he and Tony had not been as good of friends as they once had been, and he really didn't know the reason for the change. At one time they had shared hobbies, collecting military paraphernalia and dressing in camouflage, playing soldier, but Isaac wasn't into that so much now and Tony had asked him once, "Where's your patriotism?" They were just on different wavelengths.

"Did you notice any watches of Tony's?" Post asked.

Tony had a broken pocket watch that hung on his belt, said Isaac, and a wristwatch with a leather band decorated with orange flames. He didn't wear it, though, just carried it in his pocket. Post asked if Isaac knew of anyone else who might have been in the mountains with Tony, or of anyone up there he didn't get along with. Isaac mentioned Charles and James, Tony's father and uncle.

Post returned the focus to New Year's Eve. Rob, who had sat quietly up to now, got up and produced the caller ID box that showed three calls received by the Grimeses, made by Tony, at 3:01 p.m., 6:23 p.m., and 7:24 p.m. Isaac's sister Liz had taken the first call and told Tony that Isaac was at work. Rob took the other two and said that Tony had sounded manic. He said, "Isaac's supposed to be up here; he said he was coming and I'm worried about him. It's hard to find this place in the dark." Rob said he'd asked Tony how he thought Isaac was getting there, and Tony said he thought his mom was driving him up. Rob told Tony that wasn't possible because Donna was working, and Tony got upset.

"Did either of you, Mr. or Mrs. Grimes, know of any plans by Isaac to go to the Dutchers' that night?" asked Post, looking from one to the other. They both shook their heads no.

"Isaac, where were you on New Year's Eve and New Year's Day?" asked Post.

Isaac said he and his friend, Jon Matheny, who had picked him up at work, had gone to their friend Glen Urban's house and hung out in his garage for a few hours on New Year's Eve, then spent the night at Jon's house. Isaac said he'd been home by nine the next morning, with Jon, and had spent the rest of the day with his family.

"That's about all we need," said Post, pushing on his thick haunches to stand. He and Sadar shook hands with all three of the Grimeses and gave them business cards in case they remembered anything else.

"Will you be at the funeral?" Post asked.

Isaac dropped his eyes to his feet and mumbled he didn't know but probably, yes. Donna drew a protective arm around her son.

The officers walked out into the bright chilly air and were gone. Inside the Grimes house, a tense silence followed. Donna fixed the younger children a snack and began preparing a dinner they all could eat later while she was at work. Isaac went to his room.

When Rob stuck his head in the door to check on Isaac, the boy made a strange request. He wondered if his dad could fit a pipe in the window next to his bed since the lock was broken. Rob thought there was plenty of reason for Isaac to be anxious and afraid, given what had just happened to Tony Dutcher.

"Sure," he said. "I'll do it tomorrow."

• ◆ •

While they were in Colorado Springs, Post and Sadar paid a follow-up call to Jenny Vandresar, whom Post hadn't seen since the awful night in the Park County Sheriff's office. They called her from the car and said they were coming over just to clarify a few things she'd told them that night. Jenny sounded tired, a little woozy, but said sure, come on over. She was staying at her sister Kathy's house.

When the officers arrived, Jenny stood waiting at the door, dressed in a bathrobe and sipping on a cup of coffee. They told her they'd just visited Isaac Grimes and his family. What were her thoughts about Isaac?

Jenny looked barely awake, her eyes nearly swollen shut. She said she knew Isaac but hadn't spoken to him for over a year, a long time in a child's life and in hers. She repeated what Tony had told her on New Year's Eve: Isaac was coming up and would be dropping by her house to pick up a sleeping bag. He never came by.

"Ms. Vandresar," said Post gently, "can you tell us again what Tony got for Christmas, that last day you saw him?"

He got a blue CD player with earphones from her roommate, a Leatherman tool, and a wristwatch, she said. She gave it to him the day after Christmas; it had orange flames decorating the band.

"Ms. Vandresar," said Sadar, "have you thought of anyone who might have harmed your son?"

"All I know," said Jenny, her heart barely beating in her chest—was it still there?—"is it had to be someone familiar with the property, who knew where Tony's fort was located."

Sadar and Post excused themselves and left Jenny to rest. She looked as though she would like to sleep now, maybe forever.

• ◆ •

On the way back up the mountain, Sadar and Post dropped in on James Dutcher.

"Am I a suspect?" asked James, clutching the door, his eyes darting from one cop to the other. The men crossed the threshold into his apartment.

"Everybody's a suspect at this time," said Sadar.

James said he'd take a polygraph test if that would help.

"Mr. Dutcher, did you kill your parents?" asked Sadar, looking at the nervous man in front of him and wondering how he could hold a gun steadily enough to make a shot.

"No sir," said James.

"Is there anything about your mental condition that would allow you to kill your parents and not remember?" asked Post, glancing at Sadar.

"No way," said James, his eyes wide and scared. "No fuckin' way."

In subsequent days, James would ask Post to come see him again. After thinking hard, he wanted Post to know that he was sure of one thing: The last time he had spoken to his nephew, Tony, on New Year's Eve while JoAnna was making chili in the kitchen, Tony said that Isaac Grimes was there and would be camping out with him overnight. He sounded happy.

"Did Tony *say* Isaac was coming up, did JoAnna *say* Isaac was coming up, or was he there?" asked Post. Had James talked to Isaac? How could he be sure?

"Tony told me he was there," James said, a little sad that no one ever believed him. It was the curse of the mentally ill; nobody ever believed you.

Isaac was there. Tony had said so.

• ◆ •

That same afternoon, January 5, Colorado Bureau of Investigation Agent James Crippin and two Park County sheriff's deputies were processing the thirty- by forty-foot garage and gunsmith shop at the far end of Carl Dutcher's driveway. A neighbor knew where Carl kept the combination to his gun safe, and the officers found it easily.

Crippin wrote in his notes that the "gun room's door had previously been entered by use of force" and inventoried a large number of firearms and accessories and a large volume of ammunition. "Taken into custody" from Carl's safe were two wills, one for JoAnna and one for Carl, dated 1969, leaving all their possessions and property to the American Cancer Society. Also taken and placed with the rest of the evidence gathered in the house was a letter from middle brother Ty Dutcher to JoAnna, written from a jail in Georgia, dated August 2000. In it, Ty said he didn't want anything from his mother other than love.

•◆•

For the next few days, officers followed up on numerous reports as they tried to connect the Dutcher murders with other crimes that had occurred in the area. Someone was doing break-ins in the Stony Creek subdivision; someone had found spent shell casings on his property; someone had seen a car on New Year's Eve and heard some guys yelling and laughing. Gunshot volleys had been heard in every corner of Park County well into the early morning hours of New Year's Day. Deputies dutifully noted all the incidents.

On January 8, Deputy Bob Horn recorded a telephone interview with Ty Dutcher, who had flown in from Atlanta shortly after his parents' deaths but had to return to Georgia to work on January 9. Ty called the sheriff's office to complain and register his voice. He introduced himself as a reformed drug addict. He was not happy with his brother Charles. He was sure Charles had changed the funeral date to January 9 just so that Ty couldn't be there.

"He's the violent one," said Ty, "a bully."

Both Charles and James were manipulators, said Ty, who would go so far as to deny visitation of their children to JoAnna if they didn't get what they wanted from her. Charles, he said, was capable of killing his parents and even his own son.

Horn hung up, unsettled. Was there no respect for the dead? How could families carry on this way?

A few days later, Charles would tell Leonard Post that Ty was a madman and should be considered a suspect. Post had already checked Ty's alibi for New Year's Eve and knew that the middle Dutcher brother had been at work in Georgia that night.

There was no saving grace surrounding a murder, Post knew, and absorbing the murders of three family members at once was unthinkable. But he'd seen families pull together in the past when violent loss shattered their lives. The Dutcher murders seemed to have blown up an already volatile family, scattering its members like buckshot, the reverberations of the shot deafening them to one another. There would be no consolation for the Dutcher brothers until the killer was caught, and maybe not even then.

CHAPTER 5

Tuesday, January 9

Leonard Post drove down the mountain, headed for the Church for All Nations in Colorado Springs, where joint funeral services would be held for the deceased Dutchers. The mere mention of the word *funeral* conjured memories that Post couldn't shake: too warm air, careful manners, hushed voices. He'd been to so many during his career; all the grieving mothers, fathers, sons, and daughters sang a mighty chorus in his head.

Post had first taken a job with the law in 1967 in Jefferson County when he was just twenty years old, investigating a homicide in Wheat Ridge, near Denver. It was exciting work putting together clues and trying to crack the case, and he loved the camaraderie with other cops, but neither he nor his wife particularly liked the traffic and noise of the Denver suburbs. In the mid-1970s, they returned to Salida, where Leonard had been born and raised, where he had been a football star and his wife, Tenny, had been his high school sweetheart.

Post had become sheriff of the quiet town on the Arkansas River, epicenter of the Colorado river rafting community, with a public hot springs pool, spectacular views, easy access to skiing, and hundreds of jeep roads cutting into the surrounding national forest. Some of those roads led to crystal clear alpine lakes where a man could drop a fishing line and sit all day, listening to the forest's breath. It was a good life. Post had handled mostly minor scuffles and answered complaints about vandalized garbage cans, domestic troubles, and loose dogs.

In the 1990s, when he retired to spend part of the year traveling in a big recreational vehicle with Tenny, Post was hired by the district attorney's office of the Eleventh Judicial District to be a part-time investigator, working with police on current cases and specializing in cold cases—unsolved felonies that had left victims' families lost in a fog of uncertainty and the DAs with a less than stellar record.

Now in his mid fifties, Post looked forward to the time a few years from now when he could retire for good, sea kayaking in the bays around Port Aransas, Texas, in the winter and helping out on his father's ranch near Gunnison in the summer.

This case, the Dutcher murders, was taking more of his time than any case in recent years, and he had a feeling it would be a long time before his days would be his own again.

He pulled into a parking lot off Austin Bluffs Parkway, in front of a modern, industrial-looking cement-block building, the Church for All Nations. He needed to get a seat in the back before everyone arrived where he could watch from a distance, observing people while their guards were down. He would grieve in his own professional way for the violence inflicted, for the loss of life, for all the pain and sorrow yet to come. But his appearance at the Dutcher funerals was professional. He was on duty.

This was Kathy Creech's church, a charismatic Christian congregation she'd leaned on heavily over the past two decades. Neither Charles nor Jenny had a church, so Kathy asked her pastor, Dr. Tutter, if he could accommodate the family. He was happy to be of service.

Kathy had been alarmed by confusion and mixed messages from the downtown funeral home where the bodies had been returned from the Jefferson County coroner's office and immediately cremated. In an effort to keep the investigation under wraps, information about the nature of Tony's mortal wound had been withheld from the family. Jenny had not been consulted before her son's body was incinerated, and she disappeared into an even deeper state of grief when she realized she'd never see Tony again, not even in repose. Kathy, Jenny, and their mother, Tony's other grandmother, had felt shunned by the Nolan Funeral Home managers, who had taken their orders from Charles.

The memorial service had fallen into Kathy's hands, though, and she was relieved that Tony would be commemorated in the house of God where she worshipped.

Charles, determined that there would be something of his mother, his father, and his son for mourners to view at the funeral, had brought down an assortment of memorabilia and laid it out on tables. Representing Tony were his military pin collection, some of his knives, and his martial arts sword. Church members cast sideways glances at the unusual tribute. Kathy was mortified.

But her attention was riveted on Jenny, who was eating sleeping pills at a rate that would induce a coma in anyone else. Jenny couldn't face this day sober, and Kathy understood; her little sister required a steady and constant arm.

Charles, in thick-soled black boots, stood at the door greeting guests, looking a little like an Old West undertaker with his handlebar moustache and long ponytail. The Dutchers had always been an unconventional family, and nothing had changed, thought Kathy, except that any light that had ever shone on them was now extinguished.

Leonard Post watched as Donna and Isaac Grimes entered the sanctuary, stopped to give Charles a hug, then shuffled off to seats in the middle of the room. Donna kept a protective arm around Isaac's shoulders as the boy looked at the display on the pulpit.

Three urns, each with a photograph of the person whose remains it contained, stood side by side on the front pew.

An enlarged ninth-grade school portrait of Tony made him look younger than in real life. JoAnna was represented by a studio portrait showing her young and lean, her champagne blond hair swept up and teased into a 1970s-style bouffant, her lips frosted the same color as her hair. Carl, photographed in black and white, in full dress military uniform, was dark and handsome.

Leonard Post watched carefully as Isaac glanced at his friend's face, then dropped his eyes quickly.

An elaborate floral arrangement of bird of paradise, Tony's favorite flower, had been constructed around his cello, the instrument he'd taken up the semester before his death, and stood on a tripod pedestal on the altar.

The service was long and complicated. Neighbors and friends spoke on behalf of the Dutchers and Tony. The pastor delivered a sermon about the Good Shepherd and these, his sheep. A lengthy slide show of family photos projected onto a big screen concluded the service: Carl in his military dress uniform, JoAnna in a 1970s minidress and vinyl boots, Carl holding JoAnna in his arms as if to cross a threshold, both of them laughing.

Then came Tony in a parade of childhood costumes: Teenage Mutant Ninja Turtle, riot police, soldier in full camo. Post watched Isaac and noted again that the boy could not look at the images of his friend but looked at his feet instead. Donna Grimes noticed, too, and gently pulled Isaac's head to her shoulder. How could a fifteen-year-old comprehend this, she wondered, when she couldn't?

Kathy Creech thought the funeral would never end. She regretted the decision to hold all three services jointly, wishing that her family had memorialized Tony privately instead. The enormity of three deaths in one room was just too much. Although the service was meant to celebrate their lives, it was more a reminder of the unlikely and untimely nature of their deaths—violently delivered on the same night, on a remote hillside far away from this comfortable suburban church. She wondered if there would ever be a time when she would be able to remember Tony as she had known him, not as he had died.

Leonard Post filed out of the church amid the mourners, their knees creaky from sitting so long, all cried out, tissues crumbled to bits in their clenched fists. The murder was now nine days old, and investigators and police were nowhere near an arrest. The funeral marked the end of the shock phase and the beginning of another more intense investigatory period. Nothing was simple about this case, and Post expected things would get more complicated from here on.

He drove back to Salida enjoying the silence of this January day, nature sleeping. It would be months before there were any signs of life along Colorado roadways beyond the occasional sight of a fleeting deer, a spark of startling movement in the paralyzed winter landscape.

PART TWO

Out of the Shadows

CHAPTER 6

Below Guffey lies Hartsel, a tiny way station on U.S. Highway 24 buffeted by wind and populated by gas stations. A hand-painted sign on the side of the road advertises four businesses:

- Espresso
- Silversmith
- Real estate
- Native art

Beyond Hartsel, heading east, lies South Park, a flat expanse of rangeland stretching between the front and middle ranges of the Colorado Rockies. Sightseers doing seventy-five miles per hour across South Park often screech to a halt when they catch sight of herds of bison munching hay on the side of the straight, narrow highway, their massive furry humps matted with burrs.

Beyond South Park lies gentle Wilkerson Pass, then Lake George, a settlement named for the body of water created there by the damming of the South Platte River, a trophy trout stream. Along 24 from Hartsel to Lake George in warm weather, motorists might spy a fly fisherman in a white cowboy hat, wading through the tall golden grass to the edge of the South

Platte, preparing to drop a line. In winter, the South Platte becomes a frozen silver ribbon winding through fields of winter stubble.

Down from Lake George lies Florissant and a winding section of highway bordered by rounded gray boulders the size of elephants, stacked precariously by some prehistoric cataclysm. The mountain communities of Divide and Woodland Park prepare travelers for the final descent through Ute Pass and its red rock cliffs to the sprawling city of Colorado Springs, spilling eastward from the Front Range of the Rockies and Pikes Peak. A flat, high desert city of a half million people, Colorado Springs's suburbs extend northward toward Denver and many miles eastward across the sun-baked plains.

Due west of the center of town, Pikes Peak, massive and white-capped, fourteen thousand feet tall, looms above and beyond the city. Affectionately called "America's mountain," this is where, a hundred years before, a traveling East Coast professor, Katharine Lee Bates, jotted down the lyrics to "America the Beautiful," an unforgettable ode to spacious skies, amber waves of grain, and purple mountain's majesty.

Palmer High School, the oldest high school in town, sits smack in the center of Colorado Springs, at the northeast corner of the turn-of-the-century town square. Across the street, Acacia Park, a leafy haven of crisscrossing paths and shuffleboard courts, hosts dozing homeless men, stretched out on the soft grass, and successive generations of drug dealers, peddling the pharmaceutical du jour.

Two thousand students roam the Palmer campus, a cluster of nondescript redbrick buildings. At the entrance to the main building, black-and-white photographs of notable alumni—most of them balding businessmen and bankers—comprise the Wall of Fame. One notable stands out: a buxom brunette with impressive cleavage and a shiny black wig, a late-night television celebrity named Elvira, Mistress of the Dark, formerly a Palmer student.

In the middle of Nevada Avenue, the street that divides the Palmer campus from the rest of downtown, a tall bronze equestrian statue dominates the intersection. Mustachioed General William Jackson Palmer, the city's founder, sits dapper and straight-spined atop his steed, his head inclined toward Pikes Peak.

In the past, Palmer students have been known to paint the testicles of General Palmer's horse red or gold or green as a senior prank.

A Civil War commander in the Union Army, Palmer came west to seek a fortune in gold mining and built a castle for his family nestled among the red sandstone rock formations in the foothills west of the Springs. He laid out the original grid plan for the city's streets, insisting that each street be wide enough for a horse and buggy to comfortably execute a U-turn. He nicknamed his city at the foot of America's mountain "Little London." It would be a place of culture and civilized beauty nestled between the harsh eastern plains and the rugged Rocky Mountain wilderness.

But Colorado Springs's fame and wealth ultimately came from its many military installations, including the U.S. Air Force Academy, Fort Carson Army Base, and NORAD, the North American Aerospace Defense Command buried deep in the side of Cheyenne Mountain at the south end of town.

In the 1990s, Colorado Springs had enjoyed a small economic boom and some national attention surrounding the flood of evangelical Christian organizations that chose to make General Palmer's town their home, including the multimillion-dollar nonprofit ministry Focus on the Family, whose leader regularly consulted with the president of the United States on national policy. Dr. James Dobson had been a popular if controversial child psychologist in his early career, publishing the best-selling child-rearing manual *Dare to Discipline*, urging tough love before it became a catch phrase. His ministry to America's families—a hybrid prayer, publishing, and broadcast enterprise—employed hundreds, reaped millions, and even had its own exit sign on the side of the interstate highway.

On weekdays at noon, the streets of downtown Colorado Springs fill with Palmer High School students. Boyfriends and girlfriends locked in each other's arms, jocks cutting jokes and walking backward across busy crosswalks, packs of gangly freshmen and herds of sophisticated seniors spill out of the school, past Palmer's statue to Acacia Park and into the businesses lining the town square—pizza joints, bagel shops, sandwich stands, and coffee shops.

During the fall of 2000, the trees in Acacia Park shed their leaves and Tony Dutcher and Isaac Grimes began their sophomore year at Palmer High School. The boys had been best friends throughout junior high, but their friendship had ended freshman year when Tony took up with a new best friend and Isaac met a kid who would change his life forever, Simon Sue.

•◆•

Isaac awoke on December 31, 2000, with a familiar start. Christmas was over and with school out for the holidays, he could sleep as late as he wanted. But his internal clock woke him early. Down the hall, his little brothers had just begun to stir in their shared bedroom, babbling in their small, high-pitched voices, happy to face a new day of playing and watching videos and building with the new Lego blocks Santa had brought them for Christmas.

The younger brothers were a source of constant entertainment to Isaac, and he enjoyed the hours he spent babysitting them. He and his sister, Liz, eighteen, used to be tight but had grown apart this year and no longer hung together except when they passed in the kitchen or the hallway, or when they argued over her boyfriend or his friends.

Liz particularly hated Simon Sue, her classmate at Palmer, who had taken Isaac into his fold and held him close since last spring during Isaac's freshman year. Everyone knew Simon was a freak, Liz had told Isaac. Just before school let out for the Christmas holiday, the halls had buzzed briefly with stories about a speech that Simon had given in forensics class. As the story went he had bragged to the class, telling a story about a friend of his father's in Guyana who was a hit man. Simon had bragged, smiling, to the astonished class that the man, his godfather, had taught him how to break and enter and how to be a sniper. Nervous laughs dissipated, and class and teacher alike wrote the speech off as just another instance of Simon's well-known penchant for hyperbole.

Liz believed it was Simon and his creepy friend, Jon Matheny, who had slit her tires back in the fall, one night when she was visiting a friend's house nearby.

She'd confronted Isaac then and they had fought bitterly. He denied knowing who had cut her tires, costing her nearly three hundred dollars, several weeks' worth of paychecks. With their father out of work with a bad back and their mother paying the bills now, both Isaac and Liz had to earn most of their own spending money.

Isaac had once been a kid, goofy and free like his little brothers, but never lucky enough to have a constant companion as they did. The closest he'd come to that was in junior high with his first and only best friend, Tony Dutcher. He and Tony were a pair at Horace Mann Junior High School, compadres dressed in camouflage, playing military games, drawing guns on their notepads in class, and planning their futures as special agents.

Every day at lunch, no matter how bitter the weather, Tony and Isaac hunkered down on benches outside the cafeteria door and ate their sandwiches. The teacher on lunch duty during the winter months tried to entice the boys indoors, but they persisted. Their goal was to eat every meal outside for the entire school year, training themselves to withstand natural forces.

The boys had also shared their collections of military patches and pins. Isaac's grandfather, Clifton McCain, was retired U.S. Air Force, and Tony's grandfather, Carl Dutcher, was retired U.S. Army, a veteran of the Vietnam War.

But Isaac's mother had made him stop wearing camouflage and drawing guns and talking about weapons at school during his eighth-grade year at Horace Mann, when chaos erupted sixty miles up the road at Columbine High School in Littleton, on the southern edge of Denver.

There, on April 20, 1999, a boy named Eric Harris and his best friend, Dylan Klebold, had planted bombs and opened fire on the school, killing twelve students and a teacher, then turned their guns on themselves, ending the massacre with their own suicides. Bombs the boys had built in the Klebold's garage failed to detonate; had they worked instead of being safely dismantled, the attack would certainly have killed more.

Down I-25, in Colorado Springs, all ears were glued to the radio, all eyes to the television as that day's events were patched together. At first, reports said that twenty students had been killed. Everyone watched in terror as a boy trying to escape the school clung by his fingertips to the ledge of a third-story window, then dropped heavily to the ground below, breaking his ankles. For months after the shootings, boys who dressed in dusters—long coats worn by cowboys—were considered suspicious because of rumors that the two boys who had shot up Columbine were part of a group called the Trench Coat Mafia.

That rumor was found to be untrue—Harris and Klebold preferred camouflage to dusters. In fact, Eric Harris wasn't part of any group except his band of two with Dylan Klebold. Harris, described as a good student who was well spoken, wrote in his diaries about all the things and people he hated: country music, the WB cable channel, and most people. He especially hated racists. In his diary, he admitted, "I lie a lot. Almost constantly, and to everybody, just to keep my own ass out of water."

Psychological experts would later weigh in on the personalities of Harris and Klebold, but in April 1999 they were just two scary boys with a mission. At the end of the day they had taken up arms against their classmates and killed themselves as well, leaving everyone to wonder and speculate what it all meant.

In Colorado Springs, for a few months after Columbine, boys like Tony Dutcher and Isaac Grimes who worshipped guns and dressed in military fatigues were viewed as potential terrorists. Eventually things settled down, but school life would never be quite the same. By the time Tony and Isaac entered Palmer High School in the fall of 1999, security had been ramped up and student IDs were required of any teenager walking through a school door. Some schools installed scanners and metal detectors. A student at Palmer's hockey rival, Mitchell High School, was suspended for keeping a pocketknife in the glove compartment of her car on the school parking lot.

The summer between junior high and high school, Isaac and Tony had parted the way friends that age often do, with no discussion and no real reason. Isaac spent the summer babysitting his little brothers, caring for vacationing neighbors' pets, watering their flowers, and mowing their lawns. He helped out at the Ascension Lutheran Church Vacation Bible School.

Tony stopped showing up at the Grimes house. He had taken up karate and was handy with a martial arts sword his father, Charles, had given him. He still dressed in camo and carried an olive drab military-issue backpack.

The idea of high school terrified Isaac. Liz had told him about Palmer's crowded hallways and the long distances between classes. He wished he could somehow manage to learn without going there. And when he finally did go, he found that Tony had a new best friend. Tony and Isaac were in Latin class together, and Isaac felt alone every day, looking across the room at Tony, until Simon Sue, a junior in the same Latin class, asked Isaac if he liked to play chess.

It was a miracle. He loved to play chess! His favorite partner, his sixth-grade teacher, Mr. Lowell, had played with Isaac until his death last year of a heart attack. Mr. Lowell was only thirty-two and his death came on the heels of Isaac's grandfather's, leaving another big hole in the fifteen-year-old's life.

Isaac had begun to think that he'd never find another chess pal, much less that Simon Sue, one of the best chess players in the school, would ask if he'd like to join him at the Hillside Community Center on Wednesday nights for chess tournaments. Isaac was thrilled to get back into the game, especially with an older, respected player.

But the Wednesday chess games, as it turned out, lasted for only about a month.

Shortly after the two boys met, Simon began teaching Isaac about the political situation in Guyana, the small South American country where Simon's extended family lived. Isaac appreciated Simon's knowledge of military and political history and was especially impressed to learn that Simon was an agent in a secret paramilitary organization, Operations and Reconnaissance Agents, the OARA. Simon said the OARA stood ready to serve should a coup arise against the standing Guyanese government, the People's Progressive Party.

Simon showed Isaac and another kid, Jonathan Matheny, photos of himself dressed in military attire, videos of his father's home in Guyana, Guyanese coins, and his father's extensive gun collection, kept at a second Colorado Springs house the family owned. Isaac had a gun of his own, a hunting rifle willed to him by his grandfather, but he had never seen guns like the ones Simon showed him—semiautomatic and automatic weapons, machine guns, SKSs, AK-47s. Simon's father, Keith Sue, used the second home as a workplace, where he repaired cars in the yard.

Isaac pledged his allegiance to the OARA, promising to serve under Simon as the group's intelligence officer, and most Wednesdays were spent either at Mr. Sue's house, learning to assemble and disassemble weapons, or up on Rampart Range Road, between the Springs and Woodland Park, shooting guns at the public range. Jon drove the threesome wherever they went.

It was pretty fun being a soldier in Simon's small army, until one day Simon insisted that Isaac assist Jon in a robbery, a "raid" as Simon called it. The target was the home of Gabe Melchor, another Palmer student who'd been a friend of Simon's until things turned sour between them. The purpose of the raid, as Isaac understood it, was to steal guns that would become part of the stash of artillery ready to be run to Guyana if needed.

Isaac knew that his parents would kill him if he got caught stealing or messing around with guns. He was scared and tried to beg his way out of the raid. He made excuses.

Enraged, Simon told him he was in way too deep, that he didn't get to make decisions about what he would or would not do for the organization. He'd signed an oath to follow orders.

Isaac did what he was told.

By July, the summer between his freshman and sophomore years, Isaac's rank in the OARA was lieutenant colonel. He was required to make reports that he typed into his computer, listing all of his income and expenses broken down to the penny. He babysat for his brothers and worked at Carl's Jr. fast-food restaurant, and all of his checks were turned over to Simon for the

OARA's bank account. On the reports, he noted any distinguishing marks on his body, his height and weight, and any weapons he had received. On a report dated July 20, 2000, Isaac noted he had been issued five weapons, including an assault rifle and three other rifles, plus a bag of pocketknives. The knives, the report noted, had been seized in a raid on the house of another neighbor kid, Darrin Dodge, also a former friend of Simon's.

"I am still in possession," the report continued, "of eight bladed weapons that were taken from Major Matheny due to his state of probation." Jon had been placed on probation by Simon for failing to carry out a mission.

Isaac's parents, meanwhile, were unaware of the stash of weapons he kept hidden in his bedroom. And when Simon returned from a vacation in Guyana on the Fourth of July weekend and came over to Isaac's house with a Guyana flag draped across his shoulders, Isaac's parents didn't see the M-16 concealed beneath the flag. In Simon's absence, Isaac had been a little too free with the group's money, spending it on tropical fish and other items for his bedroom. Now, Simon told Isaac, he owed the OARA two thousand dollars and was officially on probation. Isaac felt the number was far larger than what he actually owed, but he was in no position to question Simon's bookkeeping and fund-raising on behalf of the organization.

Midway through sophomore year, Isaac was still in the OARA but his status had gone steadily downhill. He was still on probation and his weapons had been taken away. Jon, on the other hand, had been promoted to a position of authority over Isaac, while Simon had grown increasingly hostile and angry with Isaac for being such a weak member of the group. Finally, two weeks earlier, in mid-December, Simon had left with his father, Keith, for his uncle's house in Canada, leaving Jon in charge with specific orders that another raid be conducted, this time on Tony Dutcher's grandfather, Carl Dutcher.

Each night since Simon had left town, Isaac had posted a sign in his window, under Jon's order that he let him know his whereabouts at all times, then returned to the living room at midnight to await his mother's arrival home from work. For months now, both Jon and Simon had told Isaac that they knew his mother's route home, and that if he tried anything funny, they knew where to find her.

Now New Year's Eve day, Isaac recalled the plan for the day: He would work as usual until five at Carl's Jr. Jon would drive him to work and pick him up. Isaac would tell his parents he was having New Year's Eve dinner with Simon's uncle, Lennox Sue. After work, he and Jon would call Simon in Toronto for instructions, then load the car and head to the Dutcher house near Guffey if Simon so decreed.

Isaac jumped from his bed and bolted to the bathroom, where he threw up clear bile from his empty stomach.

Two thousand miles away, from Toronto, Simon was checking in with Jon by telephone several times each day. The raid seemed inevitable.

A few nights before, Jon had driven with Isaac to Guffey to case the landscape and plot a route to the Dutchers' trailer home. Isaac had pretended to forget the way. The roads were too dark and confusing, he told Jon. For that misstep, he had received a serious reprimand from Simon over the phone.

Isaac actually did know how to find his way to the Dutchers'. In November, he'd given directions as Keith Sue, Simon's father, drove the long, confusing route to the Dutcher house over a maze of pitted and rutted country roads. Simon and his dad had taken Isaac to pick up his hunting rifle, stored at the Dutchers'. They were planning a big-game hunting trip and hoped to bag an elk or two.

When they arrived at the plain little mobile home off the rutted dirt road, its siding the color of the dust surrounding it, the Sues stayed in the car while Isaac knocked on the door. Carl seemed glad to see him but was curious about the dark-skinned, Asian-looking men in the car.

Isaac took his gun from the man he'd come to know as Grandpa and got back into the car.

Simon interrogated Isaac, his lieutenant, about Carl Dutcher and his views. Isaac told him Carl had bad memories of Vietnam and didn't like "oriental people." Simon took it badly, Isaac recalled, saying he'd heard Tony Dutcher's father and uncle were drug dealers and he wouldn't doubt if Tony had followed in their footsteps. He railed against the Dutchers. Carl had probably raped Vietnamese women when he was in the war, Isaac remembered Simon saying. Simon ordered Isaac to design a raid on the Dutchers.

Isaac presented a plan he knew was botched, hoping Simon would cool down and focus elsewhere. But that strategy failed. When Simon saw the ridiculous plan, he screamed at Isaac and smacked him across the shoulders and head with a stick he sometimes carried.

"You're lucky," Isaac remembered Simon later telling him. "We were going to take you over to Jon's and shoot you."

A second plan, devised in part by Isaac and refined by Simon, was in place now, and tonight Isaac would go to the Dutchers with Jon or risk harm, possibly death, to his family and himself. Simon had shown him the sniper points he'd staked out in the Grimeses' front yard, from where he could shoot Isaac's little brothers, Liz, and his parents. He'd told Isaac he could get him anytime: when he was taking out the trash, or through his bedroom window when he was sleeping. Isaac had recently started sleeping on the floor in front of his bed.

Often when babysitting his brothers, Isaac helped them build forts with their Lego blocks. Both little boys admired their big brother's ability to create helicopters and spaceships, cars, and encampments with the brightly colored plastic pieces. They surveyed his hands with wide eyes and tried hard to remember his every move.

Sometimes Isaac joined his brothers as they watched one of their favorite movies, Disney's *The Little Mermaid*. The little boys loved retreating into the story of Princess Ariel and her escape from the undersea kingdom of her father, King Triton, to a world above water where true love awaited. But on land, Ariel faced obstacles placed in her way by Ursula, the sea witch. Would she be able to save the underwater kingdom and return to her father? Isaac and his brothers knew that she would, but that in doing so, she would sacrifice her voice. Still, every time they watched *The Little Mermaid,* they were caught up momentarily in the drama of young, idealistic Ariel, separated by danger and reckless adventure from her wise, loving father.

At one thirty, the afternoon of New Year's Eve, Isaac's heart sank when he saw Jon Matheny's car pull up in the driveway. It was settled; he was going to work, and following his shift at Carl's Jr., he would go wherever Jon took him. He pulled on a warm jacket and said good-bye to his mother and father and little brothers, not knowing exactly when he'd see them next. Then he took his place in the passenger seat of Jon's red Mercury Topaz and settled in for the silent ride to work and whatever lay beyond.

He knew there would be no turning back.

•◆•

Donna Grimes arrived home from work at midnight on New Year's Eve and discovered that Isaac wasn't there. She roused Rob and asked if he'd heard from Isaac.

"No," Rob said. "But Tony called earlier, wanting to know when Isaac would be coming up to Carl and JoAnna's. He sounded like he'd been waiting."

Donna knew that Tony and Isaac had barely spoken this school year and that there was no way Isaac would have planned to spend the night with Tony after all these months. She knew Isaac had left for work with Jon this afternoon; she had watched him climb into the car. She had seen Jon's dark, raccoon eyes darting toward the front door of the house before pulling off. And since nobody from Carl's Jr. had called to ask his whereabouts, she assumed Isaac must have shown up for work.

Then, though she couldn't say why, she thought of her father's hunting rifle, the one he had left to Isaac in his will, and she rushed to her son's bedroom. She knew Isaac had recently retrieved the gun from the Dutchers for a hunting trip with Simon Sue.

Isaac's room was neat and clean, the bed carefully made. Donna began to search. Her heart lurched, then settled when she saw the wooden stock of the rifle, curved and smooth, neatly tucked into the trunk beneath Isaac's bed. She went to bed but barely slept, not knowing where her son was sleeping on this cold night, hoping that he was sowing some wild teenage oats somewhere with his friends and that he would be safe.

•◆•

The next morning, around nine, when a disheveled and pale Isaac arrived home with Jon Matheny at his heels, Donna lost it.

"Where have you been?" she yelled, her voice breaking, her angry brown eyes filling with hot tears. "I've been worried sick."

Isaac explained that he and Jon had gone over to Glen Urban's house after work at Carl's Jr. and stayed a few hours, then spent the night at Jon's. He was sorry she had worried, Isaac said, his lips blue, his skin pale.

"Why was Tony expecting you?" Donna asked, her heart still coiled with confusion and fear. "He called looking for you."

"I don't know," said Isaac, shrugging off his mother's concerns and retreating into his bedroom.

Donna scuttled around the house, picking up messes here and there. The younger boys begged her to read to them and she did. It was January 1, 2001, she explained to them, the first actual day of the new century, the twenty-first century.

Would the world be different, they asked, now that it was a new century?

Not so different, said Donna, though deep in her heart, in a place she couldn't name, she wished it would be different. In a different world, a new world, maybe Isaac, her oldest son, who looked so miserable all the time, would be happy. Maybe Rob's back would heal and their lives would return to normal. Maybe she wouldn't have to worry and work so much.

Maybe in a new world, a new century, everything would be all right for her family. She silently offered a New Year's wish for this simple thing.

CHAPTER 7

Simon Sue was a petite young man, just a little over five feet tall, weighing barely one hundred pounds at age nineteen. With his high cheekbones, full lips, large almond-shaped brown eyes, shiny black hair, and smooth complexion, he looked like his older brothers, Kevin and Marlon, one now a proud U.S. Marine, the other intent on going to law school.

Simon's father, Keith, had acne-scarred skin, narrow eyes, and coarse dry hair, characteristics eclipsed in Simon by his mother's more refined features. Mother and son were close; Nadia believed her youngest son was someone very special, though he wasn't like her other sons. Simon was funny. He'd never gotten a driver's license but always had a friend, Jon Matheny, drive him wherever he wanted to go. At nineteen, Simon still enjoyed hearing his mother sing the Guyanan folk songs he had fallen asleep to in his childhood. He loved the smell of her curries and joined her cooking in the kitchen on Sundays.

Simon was close to his father, too, but in a different way. Keith didn't show affection; he was quiet and could be harsh. But he was intent on teaching Simon how to make money. A gun collector, Keith had taught Simon the value of investments in firearms and their strong resale value. Slight like Simon, Keith was compact and hard, muscular and slightly hunched from bending over the engines of the cars, mostly Japanese imports, he repaired in the backyard.

Simon had grown up in the Old North End of Colorado Springs in a small pink bungalow among kids who later became Palmer High School's star athletes and student government leaders, like Jesse Luken, captain of the football team, a big, handsome kid who could scoop up Simon with one bulky arm. Simon had grown up jumping on the trampoline and playing chess with Jesse and the Ocasio boys, Mike and Matt, with Pat O'Meallie and Ben Everett, academic stars and popular kids at Palmer.

In third grade, the boys played after school at the Sues' Caramillo Street house, in a tree house fort above the garage.

Simon was a charismatic kid, typically the leader of any childhood game. Pat and Ben remember a day when Simon armed them all with pieces of PVC pipe and sent "his troops" out into the neighborhood to find kids to beat up.

Ben, the sensitive son of a child psychiatrist, begged off, saying he was too scared to do that.

"Fine," said Simon, handing him a broom. "You can stay here and clean."

The marauding warriors, to Simon's disappointment, announced upon their return they couldn't find anyone to fight.

As a young boy, Simon had trouble reading and had a hard time paying attention in class. His mind wandered. One day in kindergarten he was sent home for bringing a real machete to show-and-tell. When the principal talked to his parents about the incident, they explained that the machete was a gift from Guyana and Simon was proud of it. Still, the story became legend at Steele Elementary School in Colorado Springs and followed Simon all the way to junior high.

Another time, Simon reportedly took a classmate to his dad's Caramillo Street house, just around the corner from the elementary school, and showed her his dad's gun collection.

She told her friends years later that Simon had jokingly told her she'd better learn to sleep with her eyes open.

Simon was proud of his machete, his father's guns, and his heritage. His parents had immigrated to the United States from Guyana shortly before he was born. Like many Guyanans, their ancestors came from the Far East—his father's family from China, his mother's from India.

In Colorado Springs, Keith owned three houses: one where Nadia, Simon, and Marlon lived and he sometimes slept; one that was rented to another family; and one that was used as his workplace. Keith sometimes slept at his workhouse though he took his meals at Nadia's. The Sues lived modestly. Their neighbors generally saw them as hardworking immigrants who pursued the American dream with restraint and discipline.

Throughout high school, Simon was an avid coin collector. He kept bags of gold coins beneath his bed, many from Guyana, with little trade value, and a couple thousand dollars' worth of American coins. He attended meetings of the American Numismatic Association in Colorado Springs, where he talked enthusiastically with older collectors. They were impressed with this articulate young man who knew as much about coins as they did, if not more.

And Simon excelled at chess; many peers thought him the best player in the school. He regularly beat Chess Club champions from other schools and taught younger kids at the Hillside Community Center how to play.

But neither his size nor his chess prowess set Simon apart as much as his fascination with violence—random, organized, and otherwise. His friend Cody Pegram, who'd lost more chess matches to Simon than he could count, put it this way: "When you looked into that kid's eyes, you knew he wasn't thinking about what everybody else was thinking about. He had something else on his mind."

A few of the things on Simon's mind, according to his friends, were terrorism and armed revolution, guns, knives, explosives, imperialism, colonialism, Stalinism, leadership, and power.

Cody and others agreed that despite his fragile appearance and his jovial personality, Simon was a badass, a guy people didn't say no to.

"He was a badass like Macbeth was," said Cody. "He seemed OK in normal life, but he knew how far he would go to get what he wanted."

Senior year, Simon spent his afternoons with Isaac Grimes, Jon Matheny, and Glen Urban, three boys he had gotten to know in classes they shared and in the halls of the school, learning their wants and needs, their skills and weaknesses. One by one, Simon had recruited Jon, Isaac, and Glen into the OARA, a secret paramilitary organization that, according to Simon, operated well below the radar of family and friends, though Simon told the boys that his father had formerly been a top agent and was now retired from the organization.

The OARA, Simon told his recruits, was intended to root out drug dealers, do good deeds, and support the People's Progressive Party (PPP) of Guyana. The OARA, Simon said, must be kept secret from parents and anyone else who might impede its progress. According to Simon, the OARA was a cell group of a much larger international organization supporting the PPP. An organizational chart showed many small triangles, all linked together to form a much larger triangle. Simon explained to his troops that this was how terrorist organizations were organized as well, by individual cells in independent locales that, when put together, formed a larger, geographically dispersed group.

In Guyana, Simon explained, his father was a close friend of the president, and his mother was a member of an influential family. In Guyana, Simon said, a coup could occur at any time, destabilizing the country. When that happened, he and the OARA would be called to action. When they left the United States to fight for the liberation of Guyana and the PPP, Simon said, he would find beautiful Guyanan wives for his friends Isaac, Glen, and Jon, heroes of the counterrevolution. Simon was already engaged to a lovely young woman who had pledged her virginity and fidelity to him. They'd become engaged last summer when Simon spent a month in Guyana. He kept a lock of her black hair in a green velvet bag, tucked inside a safe at his dad's house.

And though Simon frequently complained that the blacks were messing up everything in Guyana, he told his troops he hated racists. Growing up, he'd been called chink or gook enough times to sharpen his sense of outrage, and what Simon didn't like he would not tolerate. Racists had picked on him when he was a little kid at Steele Elementary School and had looked down on his father.

During the last six weeks of 2000, Simon kept one dark eye focused on the racist, drug-dealing Dutchers, a family that perfectly encapsulated everything he hated. He'd whipped his troops into shape, even whiny Isaac, who kept trying to get out of assignments but who now owed the organization more money than he could pay and knew Simon would collect what was owed him one way or another. Simon helped his father pack for the family's Christmas trip to Canada and stashed an international telephone calling card in his wallet. Though Toronto was a thousand miles away, Jon and Isaac would be just a phone call's distance from their commander.

•◆•

Jon Matheny was Simon's driver, second in command of the OARA. Jon liked being left in charge of Isaac when Simon was away in Canada, but it wasn't easy keeping constant vigil as Simon had asked him to do. A serious boy with dark-rimmed eyes, a close military haircut, and a lingering layer of baby fat padding his shoulders and cheeks, Jon found it harder and harder to get away from the house without some serious hassle.

His mother, Bonnie, bugged him constantly to spend more time at home. There was something about Simon, the way he looked her in the eye, his ultrapoliteness, that didn't sit right with her. It was as if he were always acting, trying too hard to appear on the up and up, like Eddie Haskell on television's *Leave It to Beaver.*

Besides driving Simon everywhere, Jon also drove Isaac Grimes to work and picked him up at the end of his shift. Between his demands as a chauffeur and his own part-time job, he spent increasingly more time away from home.

Bonnie wanted the Christmas holiday to be the way it had been when Jon was younger, when he was content to spend hours reading or watching movies with his sister, Heidi.

Heidi, sixteen, was autistic and developmentally delayed and attended special education classes at Palmer High School. She was nervous and had an uncanny radar that picked up on friction in the house, causing her to rock and moan and twist her hands. Jon had always been able to calm her better than anyone else, but now he simply didn't have the time to be there for her all the time.

Besides, when he was at home, Jon had to face his father, whose presence enraged him.

Ed Matheny and Jon's mother had divorced the year before, but Ed still lived in the house. Jon disliked his father for being weak and dependent. For years his mother had worked steadily, supporting the family and taking care of Heidi while Ed floundered. The odd domestic arrangement confused Jon and he preferred to avoid it.

Jon had always had a tough time in school, and junior year was no different. In ninth grade, a doctor had tried to put him on antidepressant medication that might help him stick with tasks and concentrate better, but he couldn't focus on anything. He fought with his mother and raged at his father. The psychiatrist said he was depressed. Jon said no way was he going to take drugs that messed him up.

He split up with his best friends from junior high. One of them remembered the day he and Jon were skipping class together outside the Palmer High School gym. "Jon told me, man, we're not going to make it to twenty-three," his friend recalled, adding he didn't think anything of it. Frankly, he said in retrospect, he'd felt the same way.

His sophomore year, Jon met Simon and soon became a regular presence in the Sue household. Mr. Sue helped him work on his car. Mrs. Sue cooked for him, and Simon and Jon did chores around the house. It was a good and orderly place to escape to. And Simon gave him focus and responsibility as an officer in the OARA.

On the afternoon of December 31, 2000, Jon left the house and started his red Mercury Topaz. He drove through the quiet streets of Colorado Springs to Isaac's house and picked him up, then drove south to the shiny shopping area around the Colorado Springs World Arena, to Carl's Jr., where he dropped Isaac off for his afternoon shift scraping the greasy grill, wrapping burgers, and mopping floors.

Around five, Jon called his mother and told her he would be having dinner tonight with Simon's uncle, Lennox Sue. He hung up the phone and waited for Isaac's shift to end. A call to Simon would confirm his actual New Year's Eve plans.

•◆•

By the fall of 2000 the ranks of the OARA had expanded to include Glen Urban, a Palmer senior. He thought Palmer High School and school in general sucked, though he hoped to attend college once he graduated. His classmates thought Glen something of an oddball, a little nervous and goofy, thin and tall with glasses that slipped down his nose, wild hair, and a big Adam's apple bobbing in his neck.

Simon shared physics class with Glen during the first semester of their senior year and told him one day he'd heard Glen could build or fix just about anything. He wondered if Glen would be interested in doing a job for him. Glen said sure. He was a wizard with tools.

Glen lived with his mom and a younger brother in a neighborhood near Palmer, where he spent most of his time in a backyard garage that he'd turned into a workshop. His parents had divorced when he was young, and he saw little of his father. He smoked a cigarette every now and then but wasn't into drugs or alcohol. He and Anthony Jacobs, friends since they were kids, still liked to do the same silly things they'd done together when they were little, like shooting potatoes out of a pipe cannon manufactured in Glen's garage. They'd detonate it on a hillside next to King Sooper's grocery store and watch the spud soar across lanes of traffic into a neighborhood in the far distance.

Chauffeured by Jon Matheny, Simon Sue took Glen riding around town during lunch hour one day and told Glen the same story he'd told Isaac Grimes about the OARA, the PPP, and Guyana. Glen was intrigued. Finally, he thought, he'd actually have something to do besides pass time waiting for high school to end.

Glen had known Jon, a kid he thought directionless, since his sophomore year, when they had woodworking class together, but had only recently come to know Isaac and Simon. Isaac seemed like a nice kid. He was quiet. They'd barely spoken more than a few words and had never been together without Simon or Jon around.

Glen was blown away by Simon's breadth of knowledge and all the things he could discuss with seeming authority—weapons systems, how jet engines worked, geopolitics, terrorism. When Simon befriended Glen in physics class, then explained that he could easily get him power tools to use in his home workshop, Glen thought that was incredibly cool. Within just a few days of signing on with the OARA, he had a set of new titanium drill bits still in their wrapping. Simon said his father collected tools and there were more where the drill bits came from.

Glen's initiation commenced with a few odd jobs for Simon, all relatively easy tasks. In return his workshop was outfitted with a special metal saw and calipers; he didn't think much about how his wares would be used and didn't really care. He liked being given a task and executing it. He liked the rewards.

Simon said Glen didn't need to know everything that was going on in the organization; he simply needed to follow orders. As with U.S. Special Forces military operations, he would be informed on a "need-to-know" basis.

Glen didn't see much of Jon or Isaac over the Christmas holidays while Simon was in Canada. He spent New Year's Eve 2000 with his friend Anthony. Life looked pretty good to him on the verge of 2001. At least it wasn't as boring as it used to be.

•◆•

Simon arrived back in the States just before Tony Dutcher's funeral. Shortly after a lunch meeting with Glen, where he alluded to the events of that fateful night, Simon convened his troops and coached them on the alibi he'd made up for their whereabouts on New Year's Eve. If the cops questioned any of them, the story would go like this: Jon picked up Isaac at Carl's Jr.; then the boys dropped by Glen's place early that evening. Glen had a bottle of rum out in the garage and the boys hung around drinking for a while. Isaac, who wasn't accustomed to drinking, got tipsy, and Jon took him to his house to sleep it off. They spent the night there and returned to Isaac's the next morning. This story would jibe with what Isaac had already told investigators when they came to his house.

Simon thought of every detail. The boys would need to agree on what clothing Jon and Isaac were wearing that night. Glen needed to complete his part of the alibi with what he'd done later that night.

No matter what, the boys were instructed, Simon's name was not to be mentioned.

Jon and Glen, known by investigators to be friends of Isaac Grimes, were questioned at school during the first week after break ended, and each repeated the story they had practiced telling Simon over and over until they had it exactly right, corroborating Isaac's story of his whereabouts on New Year's Eve.

Jon told Simon afterward he was worried that his tire treads could link him with the Dutchers if he'd left treadmarks on the dirt roads around the house. With Glen's help, Simon arranged for Jon to get new tires.

Jess Brooke, an old friend of Jon's, saw him at school that first week back. Jon walked toward her, then straight past her, staring off into space and ignoring her greeting. She remembered that he was white and zombielike, so pale she felt sure he must be sick.

Eventually, Simon was questioned at school as well because his name had come up as a mutual friend of Isaac, Jon, and Glen. His interview with law enforcement officials went well. He was out of the country on New Year's Eve, Simon calmly told the officers.

He looked them directly in the eye and said he had no idea what Jon, Isaac, and Glen had done the night Tony Dutcher and his grandparents were killed. The alibi he had created for his troops was airtight, he believed, and would protect them all.

CHAPTER 8

March 8, 2001

Colorado Bureau of Investigation (CBI) Agent Dave Sadar and DA Investigator Leonard Post stood and fidgeted as they waited for the Grimes family—Rob, Donna, and Isaac—to arrive at the Colorado Springs Police Department interrogation room. Post paced with his bull head down, planning his questioning strategy, while Sadar watched the door.

Weeks of interviews with Tony Dutcher's friends and family members had turned up nothing that implicated anyone in the events of January 1 more than Isaac Grimes, the Palmer High School sophomore who used to be Tony's best friend and whom Tony had called repeatedly over the holiday weekend, asking if Isaac would come up to the Dutchers' to join him for a sleepover.

Briefly, fingers had pointed to the Dutchers' own family members. Isaac Grimes himself had told Post he wouldn't be surprised if one of the Dutcher sons had murdered three of their own. Bob Horn of the sheriff's office continued to insist that Charles was still a suspect despite Post's certainty that Charles was merely a surviving son and father driven wild with grief, desperate to find and kill the creep who'd taken Tony's life and forever ended his own chances of reconciliation with his parents.

Isaac's friends had corroborated his alibi for the night of the killings, but that was easy enough for a bunch of kids to do. And no one except for Jon Matheny could or would account for Isaac's whereabouts from five o'clock in the afternoon New Year's Eve through nine the next morning. Who could confirm that Jon and Isaac were telling the truth about their whereabouts?

One detail had bugged Post since that first day at the Grimes house. Isaac had mentioned a watch he said Tony Dutcher had shown him—a black face with a yellow lightning bolt—but Post knew Jenny Vandresar had given Tony the watch for Christmas, just before he left for his grandparents' house and his final camping trip. If Isaac Grimes had seen the watch, Post figured, it had to have been sometime after Christmas, though Isaac claimed he hadn't been up to the Dutchers' at all during the holiday.

Robin and Donna Grimes entered the interrogation room with Isaac wedged shoulder-to-shoulder between them. Sadar stuck out a hand to shake Rob's.

"Still hobbling around, huh?" he said.

"Yeah," Rob replied, frowning, and placing a hand on the small of his back.

"He's having surgery next week," said Donna.

"Uh-oh," said Sadar, "probably not a good chair for you then?" He pointed to a molded plastic chair pushed up to the long table. "What are they going to do in the surgery?"

Rob pulled the chair out and slowly lowered his body into it. "Replace three disks, L4, L5, and S1. Put titanium cages in there. The low ones down by the tailbone."

"Oh wow," said Sadar, shaking his head and taking a seat across from Rob. Donna sat next to her husband with Isaac on her other side.

Post joined the group at the table.

"Sorry to haul you out of school," he said, leaning forward and soberly focusing his watery eyes on Isaac's. "I appreciate this," he nodded at Rob and Donna.

"We've come to a point in this investigation where we need to talk to you again. We need to rehash some things that we talked to you about before. Some of it's going to seem repetitious, but there's been some new pieces of information that we're gonna talk about, too. All we ask from you is that you relax and be truthful to us, please, 'cause it's an important day for you."

"It's imperative!" blurted out Isaac, glancing at Post, then looking down at the table, embarrassed.

"It's easy stuff, though," said Post. "Either you know or you don't know."

He explained that other people had said things that circled back to Isaac. "To clarify again, Isaac, what was the last time you physically saw Tony? When would that have been?"

Isaac scratched his head, thinking. "At school sometime. Probably like the week before Christmas break."

Post switched to his fatherly tone, as if he were coaxing a kid to eat breakfast cereal he didn't like, or to do his homework.

"OK, so it's before Christmas break. I know it's hard remembering and we know that Tony was not real faithful about coming to school about then. He was starting to miss several days." Post paused for a reaction and got none, then switched directions.

"What'd you do when you spent time up at the Dutchers' with him?" Post asked, trying to warm the boy up.

"Whenever I was up there, we'd play Scrabble. He always lost but he liked to play it," said Isaac. He described sleepovers from junior high days when he and Tony slept down by the pond with a rain poncho on the ground and a sleeping bag on top. He said he'd usually sleep outside for four hours or so, then go inside when he got cold. Sometimes Tony came in, too, and slept on the couch. When he came in from outside, Isaac climbed into JoAnna's antique German bathtub in the living room or slept on a beanbag chair, next to the couch. Sometimes when they slept outside all night, they'd wake up when Grandpa came down to the pond to feed the geese. If they were inside, they usually woke up early, when Carl got up to make his morning coffee.

Isaac mentioned that Tony always slept with his backpack on, with all his clothes on. He'd cover himself up, he said, "with jillions of blankets" inside the sleeping bag.

Rob perked up at this, remembering camping trips with Tony.

"I remember when we went camping at Westcliffe," said Rob, "Tony had knives in his backpack on that camping trip, including one that his grandpa made him for his birthday. Carl bought the blades and then put the handles on them. He let Isaac make one, too. We still have that one. Those were good sharp knives.

"Didn't Tony have a machete, too?" Rob asked Isaac, and his son nodded eagerly.

"Yeah. He had a sword his dad got him at the Renaissance Festival, and a lock-back knife his mom got him."

"Whenever he came over, he'd show off his new knives that he got," said Rob. "And he always wore a military backpack, olive drab. He had camo face paints he kept in a medic bag with waterproof matches and gauze."

Donna, Post, and Sadar watched as Rob and Isaac bonded over their shared memory.

"Did he ever show you any watches?" asked Post, interrupting the reverie.

Isaac said Tony had shown him one before school was out, given to him by his dad, with a big black dial and yellow flames on it, and he also wore a watch on his belt.

Isaac barely stopped for breath, remembering Tony detail by detail, including his plans to build a lean-to on the hill above his grandparents' house. Tony had piled rocks around in a circle the last time Isaac visited, outlining the fort he planned to build.

"He talked about it like it was a big thing, a big secret," said Isaac. "He said he wanted to make a big igloo with rocks. He always had plans, big plans for stuff."

Isaac said he and Tony had talked about his coming up over the holiday, but Isaac had told Tony he had plans already to go to Simon Sue's uncle's house for dinner. Besides, he said, "It'd be crazy to try to find that place at night. You'd get lost."

Seeing an opening, Sadar moved to the alibi.

"We've talked with Jonathan and everything," he said, nodding at Isaac, "so you're saying Jonathan picks you up at . . . "

"Like between five and five-thirty. After work we went to Glen Urban's and sat around his garage and, uh, had a little bit of rum to drink. Glen was working on one of his contraptions. We stayed till about nine. Glen asked if we wanted to go to a party with him but we didn't go. After that, we went to Jon's. He kinda snuck me in through the back door."

Donna Grimes stared at her son, her face turning red at the mention of the word *rum*.

"You were *drinking*?" she asked, incredulous.

"We're sorry, Mrs. Grimes," said Sadar, "we just have to get it straight."

Donna glared at Isaac, then at Rob. She crossed her hands on the table.

"It's OK," she said, visibly shaken. "I understand that this is more important than that, than drinking." A brief, embarrassed silence passed through the room as Donna regained her composure.

"Right, right, and that's just the luck," said Sadar, turning to Isaac. "It will be that way for the rest of your life. The one night anybody really asks about is the night something like that has gone on."

The family shared a weak chuckle.

Isaac continued. "Jon made a little bed for me and we just crashed out. He took me home around nine the next morning."

Sadar shook his head.

"See, and that, when you write it all down and you put that on paper, what that amounts to is from nine to nine, nobody knows where the heck you were. Is there anything else in that time frame? Did your mom see you? Your dad? Did Heidi see you? Did you guys call anybody? Did anybody come over? Did anything happen that helps us out?"

Isaac looked down and shook his head no.

"Donna, had he done this before ever, as far as going out and staying out?"

Donna said no, but she was still reeling from the drinking discovery. She was frustrated by all she didn't know about Isaac. "It had kind of been winding up to that, where he would go out with Jon and then not come home until, like, being out after work. We gave him permission that night to go to the Chinese dinner and then spend the night with either Jon or Simon," she said. "I mean, we were expecting him to call; then he didn't call . . . "

"And that's when Tony called and I started trying to track him down," added Rob.

"And that's when we found out he wasn't at Simon's cousin's house," said Donna.

"We're concerned about those calls from the Dutchers'," Post said to Isaac. "Something led Tony to believe that you were coming up because he not only talked to you about it, he talked to his mother about it."

"Last year, or the year before, I was supposed to go up there," said Isaac, "but I got in trouble and I couldn't, so maybe he took it as I was gonna make it this year or something like that."

Post let Isaac know he wasn't buying it. He shifted his body again, stretched his neck to the side, then shook his head slowly.

"No, I don't think so. It's hard. We're trying to put together the puzzle, and this is a piece that's not fitting. Why was Tony preparing for visitors and for you specifically? Thank God you didn't show up there, but I want to know."

Isaac screwed his eyebrows upward, thinking hard.

"In looking at Tony's camp, he was waiting for somebody to come," Post said. "To be honest with you, he has a Scrabble game up there. He has extra clothing and sleeping bags up there. He's waiting for somebody. Now who could that be?"

All eyes focused on Isaac.

"That could be me," said Isaac, "since he made the calls. He's probably waiting for me."

"Were you going to go up?" Post persisted.

"We, like, we talked about it. I don't know if he wasn't listening or what, but I know I said no, I'm not going to be there cause I had plans."

Post glanced at Sadar and shook his head. Sadar raised his hands to his shoulders as if to say, "Oh well."

"I'm gonna ask you straight up here, son," said Post, his voice growing firm. "Is everything you've said to this point straight up? It's gotta be, because your future relies upon it."

"Yes, it's straight," said Isaac. "And I know this is very important."

"This is kind of like the last swing at the ball," Post persisted. "I want to be able to scratch your name off the list but I can't. We're gonna turn the heat up on Jonathan this afternoon, and if there's anything you're not wanting to say, we've got to know. I don't care how bad it is. And [I need to know] if there's somebody else you're covering for, because when this lab stuff comes back, it's going to tell some stories."

The room had grown tense. Donna and Rob clutched hands and both looked toward Isaac. They were terrified at what he might say but wanted to hear him say it.

"That watch," said Post. "Tony had it in his coat, but the problem is that his mother gave it to him for Christmas, on Christmas Day."

Isaac scrambled, insisting that Tony mentioned the watch on the phone.

Rob, who had remained quiet, slammed a hand down on the table, his face wincing .

"I don't believe anything you're saying about the phone call or the watch. Listen, you need to be honest here, gut-level honest." Isaac's head dropped to his chest, bobbing between his bony shoulders.

"Straight up," added Sadar, taking Rob's cue. "Twenty-eight years of doing this—your alibi's bad. The watch story is bad. Tony expecting you is bad. The Scrabble game is bad. My honest opinion? You know a lot more than you're telling, OK?"

Post stood up and asked to talk to one of the parents outside the room. Rob, moving stiffly, walked out with him. This was an old interrogation technique; release the pressure in the room to make it easier for the person in the hot seat to speak.

Donna turned to Isaac. "Please," she begged. "Please be honest and tell the truth." She stroked his hand and told Isaac that she knew he had lied to her and Rob, but he had to tell everything he knew to Sadar and Post. Isaac glanced at the hand then turned away from it.

"You don't lie to these people," she said. "'Cause then what part of the story do I believe after that?"

Isaac looked at his mother, his eyes registering her presence as if for the first time that day.

Sadar spoke to Isaac in a voice that implied confidentiality.

"You don't want us to paint the picture and tell the story as we see it," he said. "You want that story to be through your eyes. It's also like the first guy around gets the deal, too. 'Cause I know you didn't get up there alone."

Post stuck his head back into the room, asking to speak to "Mom." Donna stood and walked out with Post as Rob returned to the table. He looked at his son sternly.

"If you know anything you haven't said, don't admit anything," said Rob in a steady near-whisper, avoiding Sadar's eyes, focusing exclusively on Isaac's.

Donna returned at that moment.

"Can I talk to Isaac for just a minute?" she asked. She looked like someone with a good idea, eager to put it to work.

"Sure," said Sadar, "in any of the rooms in the hall." Rob grimaced and stiffened, watching tensely as Donna and Isaac walked out of the interrogation room together to talk privately. Post invited Rob out for a cigarette. The two men walked out, one stout and short, the other tall and leaning, leaving Sadar at the table alone. Sadar looked directly into the camera and smiled.

"I think he's our guy, buddy," he said to an invisible presence. From beyond the open door, the distant sounds of keys jingling, doors closing, and voices talking mingled with the fuzzy silence of the interrogation room.

●◆●

Within minutes, Isaac, Donna, Post, and Rob returned to the quiet room, waking it back up with the scrape of chairs, the sound of water pouring into glasses, their bodies settling heavily at their places around the table.

"Is there somebody you're protecting here, Isaac?" Post asked. "I think your folks want to know. They deserve to know. They're good people. No matter how bad it is, they have the right to know what's going on."

Silence followed.

Sadar interjected. "What do you think should happen to whoever was involved in this?"

Isaac didn't flinch. "I think they should be killed," he said in a voice that might have been answering a math question.

Post gathered himself and lowered his voice.

"Look, we've worked for two months, based on your story, and run in a big circle right back to here," he said. "I'm gonna ask you one more time; please if you're covering for somebody, we can take care of that. You'll be safe. Your family will be safe. But you gotta tell us what you know. I think your folks think there's a little more to this story than you're telling us today. Am I right, folks?" He raised his thick gray eyebrows and cocked his head toward Rob and Donna.

Together, they nodded. Donna's brown eyes were wide and wet. If his face said anything, Rob's said he hoped this was coming to an end soon. He stood up and left the room once again with Sadar.

Isaac put his hands over his face and asked for a moment to collect himself, then looked up after a long pause, asking to speak to Post privately. Post refused. Isaac was underage, and the interrogation needed to proceed by the book, with his parents present.

"You're not in custody," Post explained. "You can leave right now. I want you to know that. You don't have to talk to me. You can talk to a lawyer if you want one. If you can't afford to hire one, we'll get you one. At any time throughout this thing, if you get where you feel you should talk to your folks privately, we'll let you. But Isaac, we gotta get our cards on the table. We've played ours to you; we've been honest with you. You gotta be honest with us, son. Now what's the story? Say it in front of your folks, too. They love you."

"Yes," Donna whispered.

"Come on, Isaac. What is it, son?" urged Post.

Isaac turned to Donna, his eyes reflecting, what was it? Terror. "OK," he said in a barely audible voice. "Don't say anything, OK?"

"I won't," said Donna.

"All right. Do you know about a country called Guyana?"

A shiver went through Donna. Simon Sue was involved. She should have known.

Isaac explained that there were two main political parties in Guyana, then added, "Now what I'm about to say, if this gets out of this little circle, I'm gonna die. My whole family line is going to die. I mean every Grimes from here to Illinois. Every McCain from here to who knows where, right?"

Post and Donna sat silently, their eyes fixed on the boy, trying hard not to show their disbelief.

"OK, the PNC (People's National Congress) was the ruling party back when Guyana first started, and it was supported by the FBI and the CIA," Isaac said, his voice low and cautious. "They were an extremely corrupt kind of government. The PPP (People's Progressive Party) has come into power over the past few decades. They're more Marxist types. They're pretty straight up. The thing that they hate, though, is drugs. It's like bad people, right? And they hate racists."

Post asked Isaac to speak up.

"This is hard enough," Isaac shot back, "'cause I have more pressure than you can imagine. So anyway, I'm recruited back in freshman year to the PPP. They have worldwide contacts. They have trained people everywhere, all right? Essentially, Special Forces doesn't stand a chance against these people. These people are the best in the world, the PPP guerrillas."

He looked at his mother, silently begging her to believe him.

"So my particular area is the OARA. Write that down. That's the Organization, wait, no, Operations. Operations and Reconnaissance Agents."

Post scribbled on the notepad in front of him, casting a sidelong glance and raising an eyebrow at Donna who was frozen in place, listening to her son.

"Is this conversation being recorded?" asked Isaac.

Post tried to evade the question, then said no, it wasn't being recorded. Isaac asked if he was absolutely sure, and Post assured him no, it was not being recorded. It was not an easy lie to tell but he felt it was necessary to keep Isaac talking.

"They picked them out as racist, because they are," he said. "The Dutchers."

"You mean Simon and his father?" Donna asked. She wanted to know everything the little bastard had said and done.

"Just Simon. Not his father," Isaac said.

"So Simon Sue is a member of this organization?" asked Post. "High end or low end?"

"He's high end," said Isaac.

"And he met the Dutchers when you all went to pick up your gun . . . " Donna began, but Post interrupted her.

"Hold on, hold on, hold on," he said, trying to rein the conversation back in, but Isaac was off, telling how Jon was in trouble back in March with the organization, and how he had been put on probation over the summer.

"Essentially, I abused funds," he said. "So I'm put under probation for that."

He turned to his mother.

"Remember after the picnic? The King Soopers picnic when we came home and Simon was holding the flag?"

Donna nodded, holding her breath, her eyes quick and bright.

"Simon had an M-16 under that flag."

Donna's eyes dropped to the table and her hand flew up to her throat, her mouth releasing a suppressed breath. She pictured a big black gun, cousin to a machine gun.

"So anyway, I'm under probation. I have to pay dues. I have to pay stuff. I have to pay him all my money," Isaac continued.

"So when you said you were buying bonds, that wasn't true?" asked Donna. Isaac shook his head, pained that his mother had to know another of his lies.

"And what I had to do is I had to gather intelligence on them. On the Dutchers."

"What else?" urged Post.

"Then, after that, I'm free and clear."

"So you gathered intelligence and . . . "

"Jon went up and whacked 'em with an NHMIV stolen from Gabe Melchor's house. It's like an AK-47." Isaac continued, animated, almost manic now, insisting that Jon brought back evidence for him to put prints on, then took it back up to the Dutchers', that Jon made two trips to the mountains that night.

"Where's the AK-47?" asked Post, skeptical, continuing to take notes.

"I don't know, probably at the Caramillo house, Keith Sue's house on Caramillo Street. It's like a storage house for Simon's dad, but we had access to it."

"What was stolen from the Dutchers' that you know about?" asked Post.

"A .454 and an M-16," said Isaac.

"So the guy that shot the Dutchers is Jonathan?" said Post.

Isaac nodded a confident yes.

"OK, did you harm anybody yourself. Tell me now, please."

Isaac hesitated, then said he saw Tony get his throat cut with a Frontiersman knife, that Jon came up behind him and cut his throat. He said he wasn't sure if Tony was awake or asleep, that Jon brought Isaac up the hill and he sat on a rock, right by him.

"So you saw it happen? You saw Tony die?" asked Post.

"We went down the hill and Jon told me to get in the car," he said. "Then I heard five shots. Two first, then three. Then Jon came out with the rifle and the pistol. He yelled, 'Get the fuck in the car,' and on the way back, he told me that I had passed, that I was a loyal member."

Post persisted.

"Isaac, there's a coat inside there with blood on it, by the sofa. You wore the coat, didn't you? Did you participate in killing the Dutchers?"

"No, I watched," said Isaac.

"I'll be asking Jon the same questions tonight," said Post, "so you need to tell the whole story. Were you in the trailer when the Dutchers were killed?"

"Yes. We waited around a bit. Then Jon made me eat food over the sink while he held a gun to my head," Isaac said, his face straining like someone trying hard to remember something correctly. "Then Grandpa came out and he shot him twice. I didn't see him shoot him, but then Grandma came out and she ran into the bathroom. He went to the door and killed her."

Post leaned forward slowly.

"Are you aware, Isaac, that this coat you had on had blood on it? How did it get blood on it? Whoever had that coat on cut Tony, right? Did you do that?"

Isaac dropped his head and nodded yes.

Donna hugged herself and squeezed her eyes shut.

"So you actually killed Tony yourself?"

Isaac nodded yes, then yes again, looking down, defeated, exhausted.

Donna didn't have to open her eyes to know that Isaac had confirmed what he'd done.

"So you were sleeping next to him at one point? Or how, how did you get the jump on Tony?"

"I just came up behind him while he was sitting up," said Isaac, his voice beginning to quiver. He looked at his mother, but she couldn't look at him yet. His head dropped forward, so low it almost touched the table.

"He wasn't asleep?"

Isaac shook his drooping head no.

"So it's you and Jonathan and Simon?" asked Post.

"Simon just orders it. He doesn't do anything. He's too high up," Isaac mumbled, glancing at his mother.

Donna was wiping her eyes now, still avoiding Isaac's.

"So who told you that you, to get off probation, had to do this?" asked Post.

"Simon and Jonathan," said Isaac.

Post stared disbelievingly at Isaac.

"How did you get involved in this?" asked Donna, her voice thick with sorrow.

"I don't know," said Isaac, sniffing.

"Did you want friends so badly?" she asked, her voice more tender.

"Yeah." The quiet air measured the width of that loneliness.

"They're just, they're everywhere. You don't know until you're in it. They're everywhere," Isaac said, shaking his head.

"What would they have done to you if you violated your probation?" asked Post.

"Well," Isaac said, "if I broke my probation . . . twice I've come this far from getting shot." He held up a thumb and forefinger about an inch apart.

"So you have this whole secret life," said Donna, trying to take it in. "God," she moaned. "Why did you kill somebody?" She cried quietly into her hands.

Post turned to Isaac, leaving Donna with her grief.

"Are you under the influence of anyone right now? Do you know what you're doing?"

"I know I'm in the gun site," said Isaac. "*You're* in the gun site."

Post backed off his line of questioning. He tried to convince Isaac that confessing was the right thing to do, telling the boy he'd seen how hard it was for him to keep the truth inside.

"I can give you where all the guns came from and all that," said Isaac.

"Write down where they came from and what you know about them," said Post, handing Isaac a pad of paper and a pen.

Donna began talking, partly to Post, partly to herself.

"The night that Isaac wasn't there and we were getting the calls from Tony, I came home from work that night, and Rob and I both felt extremely agitated. I mean, it's just like something's horribly, horribly wrong and we couldn't put a finger on it. We looked in Isaac's room to make sure his hunting rifle was there, and it was there. And I mean, you know, just that feeling. We looked for his gun and it was there and nothing was amiss."

She looked over at Isaac.

"So you kind of had suspicions that bothered you," said Post.

"Yeah, and part of it was a lot of times Isaac was just trying to be his own man and do stuff, and I just wanted to have a feeling, beyond a shadow of a doubt, that he wasn't into anything. This is beyond anything that I could imagine."

Both adults watched as Isaac scratched his head and wrote down as much as he could recall.

The door opened and Rob hobbled in, knowing the second he saw Donna's face that something terrible had been said. He lowered himself into a chair, grimaced, then reached over to take her hand.

"Isaac has confessed to being a participant in the murders at the Dutcher home," said Post, pausing to let Rob take it in.

"He's in trouble. I told you people I wouldn't lie to you. He actually did kill Tony is what he tells us."

Post turned to Donna and Rob, his eyes sorrowful. "I'm just so sorry, but we had to get this out."

Rob looked at his wife and his child and nodded weakly, biting his lip.

"Yeah, we can't live with this. It's gotta be the truth or nothing," said Donna.

"It looks like Isaac has gotten wrapped up in some pretty heavy stuff, and I'll let you and your wife talk about that," said Post. He told Isaac he would be charged tonight and again tried to assure him that confessing was the right thing.

Post turned away from the family and slowly left the room, closing the door behind him.

The room felt smaller somehow with just the three of them there, as if secrets could be told but there were no secrets left to tell. Donna quietly explained to Rob that Isaac was involved in a secret paramilitary group led by Simon Sue, and the group had ties to Guyana. Rob had seen Isaac's frequent Internet searches of Guyana newspapers and had always felt uneasy about both Simon Sue and Jon Matheny.

Rob dropped his head to the table and began to cry. Donna rubbed his back, and Isaac watched silently as his father's shoulders shook and he wept freely.

"So you've been lying to us," Rob said finally. "I knew it. And you knew I knew it, didn't you?"

Isaac looked down, too ashamed to meet his father's eyes.

"Are you all hard inside?" Donna asked, afraid to hear what he might say.

"They trained me not to think about it," said Isaac.

"Why did you let them train you? As soon as you saw it was strange, why did you let them train you?" his mother urged.

"I don't know," said Isaac.

"But you were making other friends—from church, too."

"Who killed the grandparents?" Rob asked, raising his head, anger beginning to rise.

"Jon."

"You didn't love the Dutchers enough to stop him?" asked Donna.

"I don't know."

Leonard Post came in through the door, opening the room again to police procedure and cop talk and a solemn announcement that Isaac would be arrested and put in jail as soon as they were finished here.

"We're not going to mistreat the boy. I can tell you that," he said to Rob and Donna.

"Are your folks safe here, son?" he asked, hoping to calm Isaac's anxiety.

"No," said Isaac, emphatically.

"No? Then what do they need to do?"

"I don't know," said Isaac. "They're not safe."

Post was losing his patience.

"Well," he said, "these people can't kill the world."

"Yeah, they can," said Isaac. "You think this police department is anything? Once you see these people . . . This police department is nothing."

"We'll bring the SWAT team," said Post.

"He loads all his guns with cop killers," said Isaac.

Exasperated, Post asked Donna to join him in the hallway for a minute. He took her by the elbow trying to move things along.

Rob, exhausted, turned to his son.

"Was I that bad, Isaac? You couldn't talk to me about all this stuff?"

"Yeah, it was that bad."

"No, was *I* that bad?"

Isaac looked at his father, the man he loved more than any other man in the world.

"No," he said softly.

"How come you couldn't talk to me?" Rob pleaded, reaching for him across the table.

"'Cause they made me not. They trained it out of me."

"I just don't know how you could have given in to this."

"You don't know till it happens."

Post and Donna came back in, Donna with her shoulders set, trying to look strong for Rob and Isaac. Her black eyes darted from man to boy, boy to man, leaning across the table toward each other.

"OK," said Post, looming over the table, "we're going to have to process Tony here—I mean, Isaac." The hours of digging had taken a toll. It was true, the thought breezed through his mind. This kid was dead, as surely as Tony was.

"Do you have anything in your pockets that you want to leave with your folks here? Oh, and the clothes you were wearing that night, what happened to them?"

"We burned them," said Isaac.

Post turned quietly and left the room once more. Donna, Rob, and Isaac sat at the table together.

"I'm sorry," said Isaac, screwing up the courage to look at his parents, his voice breaking.

"Isaac, you're our child," said Donna. "And we love you. And you became such a stranger."

"They're in the CBI too," said Isaac.

"This organization you're in, they're in the CBI?" said Rob, struggling to understand.

Isaac nodded.

"Is that why you didn't want Agent Sadar here?" said Rob.

Another weak nod from Isaac.

"Do you feel like you've been brainwashed?" asked Donna.

Isaac nodded his head, then shook it from side to side. "Yeah," he said, "you know?"

"Yeah," said Donna. "Isaac, God forgives even this." She dropped her face to her hands and let the tears flow. "My heart is broken," she finally said in a wet voice.

"So is mine," said Rob.

"They used you. How could you let them use you?" said Donna, her voice rising, then softening. "I still love you, you know."

Post slipped quietly back into the room.

"Is Jon here?" Isaac asked. "Is Jonathan here right now?"

"No, we gotta get some paperwork before we go grab him," said Post.

Isaac began to sob, the bravado of his confession fading, his words barely distinguishable. He sputtered the word *please.*

"What's that?" said Post.

"Can you make sure he doesn't contact me?"

"Sure," said Post. "Are you scared of him, or what? Are you scared of him or Simon the most?"

"Him the most because I come into contact with him more."

"OK. We'll deal with this guy."

"So they'd never, they would not be locked up together?" said Donna.

"No. No, I'll guarantee it," said Post. "I've got to go check on the car."

Donna tried to comfort Isaac. "I just wish you had told somebody before this happened," she said.

Isaac said nothing, crying, snuffling now.

"Did you ever think about killing us?" she asked.

"No," he said, letting out a big sigh. "I thought of killing myself."

"You know if you can help stop these people and do some good, then they can't hurt anybody else," she said. "So you were nervous when you were sleeping with your door open and having Dad put a pipe in your window and stuff. You were really afraid."

"Yes," said Isaac, taking her hand. "Gotta go to work?"

Donna shook her head no.

"Don't talk about it a lot. Especially not the organization," he said.

"No, no, I'm not gonna explain," she said. "I'll just say you were involved in the murders." Her voice choked on the word.

Post returned and asked Isaac to recount again where the order for the hit on the Dutchers' had come from, how the plans had been made. Isaac explained that Simon had ordered him and that the plan had initially been drawn up in early December, but it had been bad and Simon had rejected it.

"He tore it up and I was beaten for it," Isaac said.

"You were beaten?" said Donna, as if this were the most surprising information she'd heard up to now.

Isaac nodded.

Post double-checked the addresses of the two Sue family homes.

"Who beat you?" said Donna, her fingers brushing the stuck hair away from Isaac's wet face.

"Simon," he said.

Donna drew Isaac deep into her arms and rocked him softly as he continued to cry.

"It's OK," she said. "It's all going to be OK."

•◆•

Leonard Post put Donna, Rob, and Isaac into an unmarked car and drove out of the police lot into the streets of Colorado Springs. The clock tower of the old courthouse on Nevada Avenue glowed golden and constant. Isaac got a last glimpse of Acacia Park and Palmer High School as the car slid past the redbrick auditorium, the statue of General Palmer and his horse.

Post drove Rob and Donna home. They assured Isaac they'd see him first thing tomorrow, then walked inside, where they knew they'd have to put their two little boys to bed before they could cry again. Isaac gave Post directions to the Sues' houses on Caramillo and Columbia Streets, pointing them out as they drove by, then settled down low in his seat for the ride to the Spring Creek Juvenile Detention Center in the middle of downtown. His mind was completely empty, but fear still radiated throughout his body.

That night, after the little ones were tucked in, Donna Grimes answered the telephone four times. Each time it was Simon Sue, asking for Isaac, his best manners on display.

"He's not here," Donna said and hung up angrily. When the phone rang again, the masquerade was replayed. With each ring, her heart grew smaller and harder, until finally it was a rock in her aching chest. Terror followed her to bed and inhabited the small house, which suddenly felt flimsy to Donna, as if the smallest gust of wind could blow it down, leaving her, Rob, and their children exposed to the dark night, birds flung from their nests.

CHAPTER 9

In the Old North End of Colorado Springs, where the core of Palmer High School students live, screened sunporches on second floors of turn-of-the-century houses close their doors and windows for the winter. Elms, maples, and oaks lining the wide avenues and grassy medians of the original part of the city are skeletal and bare. On north- and south-running streets, sturdy, multistoried houses stand, well-tended witnesses to the city's relatively short history, dating back to 1871.

Intersecting the main avenues is a grid of east-west streets flanked by multi-colored bungalows and Victorian cottages, many of them added onto with new porches and patios, a patchwork of middle-class creativity and enterprise.

It was to one of these east-west streets and a salmon-colored 1920s bungalow that the Colorado Springs Police Department (CSPD) was called to assist the Park County Sheriff's Office on the evening of March 8, to conduct a search of two houses barely two blocks apart—one on East Columbia Street and the other on East Caramillo Street. A quick title search showed the owner of both to be Keith Sue. Isaac Grimes's description earlier in the day of OARA activities at the Sue houses had prompted Leonard Post to secure search warrants.

Officers searched the Columbia Street house first, the Sue family's official residence. The house was modest and neat. Several portraits of Simon and his brothers lined the walls, the boys posing tallest to shortest like stair steps, Simon tiny and gleeful at the bottom of the steps. Outside, several cars were parked closely together in the narrow driveway. Inside, Nadia Sue, dark-eyed and attractive, sat nervously on the living room sofa as police officers searched Simon's bedroom.

Simon was there, too, huddled close to his mother, hoping the officers wouldn't tear up his room too much.

When the officers emerged, they had a box of gold Guyana coins and an academic planner from Palmer High School with blank pages in the back where Simon had noted payments made to him from Isaac Grimes. The page was marked "probation to the OARA." The police confiscated two of Simon's knives and, from a trunk at the foot of his bed, a loaded assault rifle.

Officers found thirty-six guns, most of them military assault rifles, wedged into a closet in the small pink house. They tagged Uzis, SKSs, and AK-47s, one by one, preparing to take them away.

Simon was advised that he needed to get ready to go downtown with one of the officers, Delmar Wedge, for some questions. He cheerfully agreed, saying he wouldn't mind taking a ride in a police car.

Meanwhile, the search shifted to the Camarillo Street house where Keith Sue frequently worked and stored various merchandise. Keith greeted the officers at the door and ushered them inside. Outside in the driveway and backyard sat between fifteen and twenty cars.

Inside, the house was dark and musty, with no feeling of domesticity. From the front door, through the corridors and up the stairs, against every wall were boxes upon boxes of stereo equipment, computer printers and cartridges, hand tools, clothing, DVD equipment, beauty supplies, stereo speakers, and car speakers, most still in their original wrapping.

A gun safe was opened, revealing more guns, most of them handguns, and a box of ammunition.

Keith explained to the police that he was a collector. Still, because Mr. Sue and his son had been implicated by Isaac Grimes in his confession, and the gun stash had been mentioned in Isaac's account of the OARA's activities and training, all of the weapons would be confiscated and checked for registration and legal ownership.

Among the items found in the Sue homes, several were of particular interest to the police. One was a shiny .454-caliber revolver, like the one reported stolen from the home of Carl Dutcher. Also found among the house's trove of unexpected treasures was a swath of cloth ribbons bearing the inscription "OARA."

•◆•

When Dave Sadar began questioning Simon Sue at the Colorado Springs Police Department Operations Center on the evening of March 8, Simon was animated and visibly excited. Because he was nineteen, it wasn't necessary under Colorado law for his parents to be present when he was questioned.

Sadar and Investigator Leonard Post had spent several hours earlier trying to break Isaac Grimes and Jon Matheny, with mixed results. Matheny, accompanied by his mother, was stone-faced and silent and refused to answer any questions, denying any affiliation with the OARA or Simon Sue, as well as any knowledge of the Dutcher murders.

Isaac Grimes, however, had given Post the information he'd been seeking since early January when he first discovered the bodies of Carl and JoAnna inside their trailer and Tony Dutcher on the rocky hillside above it. Isaac admitted cutting Tony Dutcher's throat and accused Jon Matheny of shooting the elder Dutchers. He said that Simon Sue had ordered and orchestrated the murders, supervising by telephone from Canada.

Grimes had been placed in immediate custody in the city's juvenile detention facility, pending transfer to the Park County Jail once formal charges were filed. Despite admitting nothing and against his mother's protests, Jon was arrested, too, and was now in detention, awaiting formal charges.

On the ride to the station, Simon had chatted excitedly with Detective Wedge, telling him he'd once played chess with Wedge's boss, Police Chief Lorne Kramer. Simon thanked Wedge for getting him out of the house and strode through the police department halls looking curiously from side to side. Wedge got him settled in an interrogation room, then disappeared.

Now Sadar sat across the table from Simon, who looked like a kid at a birthday party, glancing around excitedly. He wore a long-sleeved black shirt with white buttons down the front, silky like a pajama top, and a pair of jeans.

Down the hall, CSPD officers were questioning Glen Urban, named by Isaac Grimes as an accomplice in the case and a fellow member of the OARA.

Sadar wore a blue knit shirt with thin white stripes and a powder blue windbreaker. His glasses were propped atop his head; his brown hair was carefully combed over in front and balding at the crown. He rubbed his forehead; it was ten o'clock and he'd been at it since midafternoon.

"You guys didn't tear up my room, did you? You didn't take my guns, did you? Will they do ballistics testing? On all my guns? Will I get them back?" Simon chattered, glancing around the room, then staring directly into the camera.

"I have nothing to fear." His eyes switched to Sadar. "Do I incriminate myself in any way by saying anything?"

Sadar explained that the guns were being checked to see if they were stolen, and that there were search warrants on his father's two houses because of things Jon and Isaac had said today.

"I can't promise anything," Sadar advised Simon. "I can't say whether you need a lawyer. I don't know what you're going to say. If you took part in any crime—well, I don't want to give you any guarantees."

"Detective Wedge gave me some guarantees on the way over here," Simon said, extending his arms forward across the table and locking eyes with Sadar. "He said I could talk to you guys, go home, go to school tomorrow, and have my life go back to normal if I tell you what I know."

Sadar explained that Simon was not under arrest and that he had not been accused of a crime, that technically he didn't need any guarantees at this point, and if he did, Detective Wedge couldn't provide them.

"Look," said Sadar, "Isaac Grimes has named you as the mastermind behind the Guffey murders and several other crimes, including robberies, committed by the OARA."

"I'm not God," scoffed Simon. "I have no control over other people's
minds."

Sadar scribbled on a yellow legal pad and asked Simon what exactly he
did know about the Dutcher murders or the crimes Isaac had confessed to
this afternoon.

"Isaac and Jon told me to hide some stuff, a .454 revolver, I think. I don't
know where it is now."

"Do you know where the gun came from?" Sadar continued.

"I assumed [the gun] came through Carl," Simon said. "I told [Isaac and
Jon], 'Carl's a crazy radical—a racist—it's going to be another Ruby Ridge.'"

Sadar probed: How did Simon know Carl Dutcher was a racist?

"Me and my dad went up to his house to get Isaac's hunting rifle last fall.
I met Carl then," Simon said. "Dutcher looked like this burly old dude."

He laughed.

Sadar took note, then led Simon back to the guns, back to Isaac and Jon.

"They brought me three guns," Simon said. "One rifle is locked up with
my dad's stuff. Glen destroyed another."

"Were you the leader of an organization, the OARA, that Isaac Grimes,
Jon Matheny, and Glen Urban pledge allegiance to?" Sadar pressed Simon.
He explained that Isaac had said he had to turn his paychecks over to Simon,
and so did Glen and Jon.

"No," said Simon. "That's retarded."

Then he looked down and continued. "We did have a little group but it was
nothing like that. The purpose was to do good and to report drug dealers."

Grimes, said Sadar, had said that the OARA stole guns from families in
the neighborhood, and that the money Simon saved went for an automatic
weapon, purchased at a gun show, the one confiscated from the trunk in his
room earlier tonight.

"My guns are for investment value," Simon said, one hand on the table, his head propped on the other. He pointed two fingers toward Sadar. "I really enjoy marksmanship. My father taught me that guns are a good investment. I'm big in weapons. I don't want that to incriminate me. A lot of Republicans around here don't trust the government."

Sadar paused, not knowing quite how to respond. His mind silently formed the words Simon had spoken a minute ago—Ruby Ridge, the 1992 standoff between white separatist Randy Weaver and the FBI that had ended in a melee including a barrage of gunfire.

"Did you ever threaten Isaac Grimes at gunpoint?"

"I never forced them to do anything," said Simon, explaining that he had taken Isaac in as a benevolent gesture.

"His parents were kind of cheap, you know? They were going through a hard time. If he needed shoes, we bought him shoes. Any buying and selling of guns we did was legal. We were just a good citizens' group."

Simon was having a hard time sitting still and leaned farther across the table toward Sadar with every question, opening his hands in expressive gestures. Now he leaned back and smiled again and tried to change the tone of the conversation.

"You guys are all right," he said. "I'd like to hang out with you sometime."

Sadar shook his head, then settled his chin in his open palm and leaned on the table.

"Did you ask them to do the Dutchers?"

"No, that's retarded," said Simon. "I have nothing to gain from that."

"And why didn't you tell us what you knew when we came to talk to you at Palmer?" Sadar didn't move.

"I was stuck in a hard position," Simon said. "If they were capable of killing the Dutchers, how did I know they wouldn't come after me?"

Sadar got up and stretched, then left the room as Detective Wedge came in and took his seat. Simon leaned eagerly across the table, as if toward a long lost friend.

"All right! Officer Wedge!" Simon beamed.

Wedge wasted no time. "Don't play games with them," he said. "Tell them the truth. What you're doing is playing games now. Stop lying to them."

"I won't play games," said Simon, subdued, his mouth taking on a near pout. "My mind's hurting these days."

"Your mind's fine," said Wedge. "You're smarter than any of these guys."

Simon nodded and smiled, then snapped back to attention, his eyes wide. "He's for real," he said, referring to Sadar. "He's the CBI man. He's like the FBI of the state."

Wedge nodded.

"When he comes back in, I'll tell him the AK-47 was chopped up." Simon leaned toward Wedge in a friendly gesture, extending a hand. "I thank you very many thanks for enlightening my mind."

Sadar came back into the room and Simon addressed him immediately.

"I'll tell you the story now because this guy's given me some peace of mind."

Then Simon confessed, but not with complete contrition, to destroying the murder weapons used on the Dutchers, with the help of Glen Urban.

"The guy [Carl] was a known drug dealer," he said, his eyes cast downward. "They're [the Dutchers] good for nothing. Their family are drug dealers. Tony does drugs. Isaac turned against Tony because he bullied him. Tony was into all this patrol shit."

What about the OARA? Wedge persisted. What had Simon done besides help destroy the murder weapons?

"Jon wanted his tires changed [after returning from Guffey]. I think my dad changed them," he said, then added, "No, I don't know if he did or not." Sadar noted the need to question Keith Sue about this later.

Simon admitted that he'd returned to the States on January 3 and Isaac and Jon had told him then what they'd done. He told Sadar it was his understanding that Jon took out the grandparents and Isaac killed Tony. He apologized for keeping this information from officers when they talked to him before. He admitted helping make up the alibi that all the boys shared, indicating he merely wanted to protect his friends.

He explained which guns were stored at his father's house and which had been destroyed.

"Am I in trouble?" Simon asked Wedge, his eyes beseeching his new friend. "I look up to you guys. You inspire me." Simon waited for a response but got none. The two men shared a brief, bemused glance, then turned back to Simon.

Wedge told Simon that Glen Urban, down the hall, had just confessed to helping destroy the murder weapons.

"I hope he isn't still going with his rehearsed alibi," Simon said. "If he is, can I correct him and save his ass? 'Cause I'm going to save him."

Simon said he'd take an oath and swear that anything he said now was the truth. This was a historic moment in his life, he said, and he wanted to make the most of it. Wedge and Sadar left Simon alone briefly. He glanced at the door once, then sat quietly. A box of tissues and a Styrofoam cup sat atop the vinyl table. When the men returned, the boy looked excited to see them.

"Listen," he said, "I gave you the evidence you needed. You're honorable men. I really mean it. You guys inspire me. I was just a dumb kid."

"Oh, this will mature you, it surely will," said Sadar.

Sadar told Simon that Detective Wedge would take him home now, but not to leave town, that he would be in touch.

"You think I could hang out with you guys sometime?" Simon said and then beseeched them one more time as he headed toward the door: "My mom and dad are going to bitch me out. What will I tell my parents?"

CHAPTER 10

The arrests of Isaac Grimes and Jon Matheny set a new flurry of press and police activity in motion, and the Dutcher murders reclaimed headlines after two months of waning interest. Denver newspapers quickly picked up the story when rumors of a secret paramilitary organization grabbed the interest of reporters. While Columbine remained in the news as civil suits were filed or settled, this story represented a new wave of boys-gone-bad violence, just down the road.

At fifteen, if Isaac Grimes was prosecuted and convicted as an adult, as Colorado law required for murder charges, he could become the youngest inmate in the adult prison system.

Colorado Springs newspaper reporters scrambled around the front doors of Palmer High School, seeking friends who would talk about either of the accused boys, with little luck. Two named suspects, Simon Sue and Glen Urban, remained at large and were not saying anything.

Palmer High School officials promptly expelled both Sue and Urban from the school. If they were to graduate or get a GED, they'd have to do it elsewhere. Both boys enrolled in New Directions, an alternative school where many local youths went when they got in trouble with the law. Police had easily secured Glen Urban's cooperation the first time they questioned him, but they hadn't arrested him because they wanted to use him in their continuing investigation.

In fact, they had wired Glen with a microphone so that they could monitor a telephone conversation between him and Simon. The result was less than helpful. Simon was meticulous in his refusal to say anything to his friend that might connect him with Jon or Isaac or to implicate himself in any way. Glen was disappointed; all along he'd hoped to be the one who exposed Simon's tyrannical reign to the cops and the rest of the world.

On March 13, a major break in the case came from someone previously unknown to investigators, a Coronado High School junior named Anthony Jacobs, Glen Urban's best friend. Park County Detective Bob Horn first received a call from Brent Urban—no relation to Glen—a Coronado guidance counselor whose student had come to him saying he knew the boys arrested for the Dutcher murders. The counselor said that Anthony was visibly frightened and seemed to know a lot about the so-called organization associated with the killings.

Horn immediately called Anthony Jacobs's home phone number, provided by Urban, and got Anthony's mother on the phone. She said her son had awakened her at two in the morning the night before and told her all he knew about the murders. He'd been a good friend of Glen Urban for most of his life, she said. She'd been considering whom to call with the information but was frightened for Anthony's safety.

The next day, March 14, Detective Richard Gysin of the Colorado Springs Police Department, assisting the Park County Sheriff's Office, arrived at Coronado High School to interview Anthony Jacobs. Anthony asked if they could talk in Gysin's unmarked car rather than inside the school.

"I've been wanting to talk to the police for a while," said a shaken Jacobs, "but I was afraid."

Gysin assured him that he was not a suspect in the case, that he was not in custody and was being interviewed as a witness. Jacobs said he understood and had nothing to hide.

Glen Urban had been his friend since he was two years old, back when his parents and Glen's parents were friends, when both couples, now divorced, were still married. They were like brothers, Anthony said. He'd met Isaac Grimes, Jon Matheny, and Simon Sue through Glen over the last few months—Jon first, in December when Anthony was hanging out at Glen's garage and Jon showed up.

That was when he first heard of the OARA.

"I didn't know what it stood for," Anthony told Gysin, "but Glen told me he was a member. He kept me guessing about it so I would be kept out of the loop."

But as weeks passed and Anthony saw more of Jon and Glen's other new friends, he asked more questions, and Glen told him more about the organization. As he understood it, there was a link with Guyana, a country whose people were very poor and whose government officials were very rich, according to Glen. Simon had told Glen there might be a revolution there, and Simon was organizing a militia to fight if needed. Simon had originally been part of a different militia but had broken off to form a new one. Once, in Glen's bedroom, Anthony had seen a paper marked with the initials *OARA* and what looked like a hand-drawn rank outline of the organization.

Glen was happy to be in the group, said Anthony, at least the "mechanized corps," of which he was a part. New tools started showing up in his garage workshop, including a 15-amp chop saw, something Glen could never have afforded himself.

Anthony had met Isaac Grimes briefly in December, just long enough to say hi. Afterward, Glen told him that Isaac had embezzled OARA funds and was in trouble, that Jon and Simon were ready to kill Isaac for his theft and had, in fact, threatened him with a gun. Once, Glen said, Simon had told him if he wanted to watch Isaac eat shit off the floor, Simon would make Isaac do it.

"Did Glen ever tell you if Isaac was given any particular mission to get back into good graces with the group?" Gysin asked.

"I haven't heard of anything like that," said Anthony, "but Glen had to do missions to show his loyalty to the group."

His first job was to "build a new handle for Simon's Uzi," Anthony said, and one time Glen was asked to melt down a bunch of lead to see if they could contrive a way to get weapons through metal detectors. The thinking was that lead wasn't detectable, and that if you could wrap a gun completely in lead foil, perhaps the gun wouldn't be detectable either.

Jon seemed like a nice guy, Anthony said, though he was "pretty much glued" to Simon.

Gysin, aware that Anthony might be telling this story in collusion with Glen, changed directions, asking him where he'd been on New Year's Eve. Anthony confirmed that he'd hung out with Glen, they'd shot the potato cannon, and later that night they'd gone to a party. Glen was the designated driver since he didn't drink. They shot off fireworks at midnight, hung out in Glen's room for a while; then Anthony went home. He didn't see Isaac or Jon at all that day.

A few days later, when he heard about the triple murder in Guffey on television, Anthony "got a weird feeling," especially when he heard one of the victims was a Palmer kid.

"Had you ever heard the name Dutcher mentioned before by any of the kids?" asked Gysin.

"No," said Anthony, "but I had a weird feeling Simon might be involved."

"Why Simon?"

"Because he was kind of demonic," said Anthony.

Again Gysin thought this could be Glen talking through his friend. He asked Anthony to explain why he believed that about Simon.

Anthony remembered a conversation with Simon in which Simon had said he wanted to blow up Balanced Rock in the Garden of the Gods because it was cemented in place and he thought that was "just horrible."

Balanced Rock was a popular tourist destination in the Springs where tourists could stand next to a twelve-foot-tall, precariously balanced red rock boulder and have their photos taken looking as if they were holding it up with one arm.

"Was there anything else?" Gysin asked. What boy hadn't had fantasies of blowing up Balanced Rock?

"Well, once I told Simon about a kid who beat me up all the time when I was younger," Anthony said. "Simon told me he could kill that kid for me if I wanted."

"And how would he do that?"

"He said he'd hang him upside down from a tree and punch him and beat him until he eventually died. He said he'd do something to his mouth where he couldn't speak."

A brief silence followed. It was midday, and it was growing warmer in the car the longer the two talked. Anthony looked settled in, as if he wouldn't mind staying longer.

"What did you do when you heard about the Dutcher murders on television?" Gysin asked.

Anthony said he'd called Glen and asked if Simon was involved. Glen had said he knew nothing at the time, then a couple weeks later told Anthony that he'd been taken on a ride in Jon's car with the three other members of the OARA and had been told that they were responsible for the murders. They hadn't said how or why they did it other than to mention, "Tony's dad did bad things."

Anthony added his own personal opinion about the motive: "They killed the kid because he knew about the OARA."

Soon after the ride Simon had asked Glen to destroy several things, Anthony recalled. One night Anthony had walked into the garage and seen Glen with Simon and Jon, burning a knife handle on the workbench. Glen later told Anthony that Simon had had him cut up a knife and put the pieces in a jar. He thought Jon and Simon had thrown it in a Dumpster behind a church.

A couple days ago, Anthony said, Glen had told him about destroying an AK-47 under Simon's orders. Simon had said the gun had a "bad history." Glen had cut it up with his metal saw and put the pieces into a paint can.

Anthony had been at Glen's on March 7, the night before Isaac Grimes's confession, he told Gysin. Glen had told him he had to leave as Jon was coming by to drop something off. At around 9 p.m., as Anthony was leaving, he had seen Jon pull into the alley. When Anthony called Glen later, Glen told him that Jon had dropped off the AK-47 and some other things. Anthony thought that Glen had given the police the other things, but he wasn't sure.

Anthony told Gysin that Glen had said he wanted out of the organization but was waiting to get some information on Simon that would get him arrested for the murders. Isaac had confessed to the police before Glen could do that, and now Glen was left out in the world with Simon.

Glen told Anthony he had signed a four-year commitment to the organization and couldn't get out. He was angry that Simon had plotted to kill people in the United States when he'd told Glen that any killing that took place was to be in Guyana, that no one in the United States was supposed to be hurt. Glen had started to see what kind of organization it was, he told Anthony, that Simon was an idiot and the whole organization was "unprofessional and disorganized."

As Glen had described it to Anthony, at first he believed the group had a serious purpose, but the more he was around Simon, the more he realized Simon just talked about blowing things up and killing people. Glen had said Simon didn't really like white people and would have preferred to have minorities in his organization, but whites were all he could get.

"Did Simon have a conscience?" asked Gysin, fascinated.

"He had a conscience about drugs and crime," said Anthony, "but he thought it was OK to take life away. Glen said he got the impression that Simon felt that if no one else would take care of these people [drug dealers] that they [the OARA] should."

Once Anthony had talked to Simon about his own use of marijuana. Simon had told him to quit, that drugs could ruin his life. Then Simon had asked where to find drugs, where to find drug dealers, and how the system worked.

Later, Glen called Anthony and told him that Simon had flipped out on hearing that Anthony used pot and ordered that no drugs were to be allowed anywhere around the organization members or the garage. Anthony said he'd watched once when Simon, Jon, and Isaac drove up to Glen's house, then drove away, Simon fuming, because they'd come to inspect Glen's room but couldn't because Anthony was there. Simon liked his men to keep their quarters neat and inspected them on the tenth of every month.

"Did Simon ever talk to you about joining the organization?" Gysin asked.

"No," Anthony said. But eventually, he added, he felt they might have asked him to join since he was around so much.

"Glen did a good job of making them believe I was stupid," Anthony said, half laughing. "He didn't want me involved."

"Were you aware of any other individuals who may have been killed by this group?" Gysin asked.

Anthony said he'd asked Glen how many others had been killed, but Glen had said he didn't know and if he did, he wouldn't tell Anthony anyway. Glen had confessed that he believed more than these three had been killed by the group.

"Are you telling me the truth?" asked Gysin, skeptically. He felt sure that the OARA was nothing more than just a few punks out of control.

"Look," said Anthony, "I'm here to help my friend, but I'm not lying about anything. I've thought about it, and if I tell the truth, even about Glen's involvement, it'll help him. It's a relief to get this stuff out."

"OK," said Gysin. "What did you hear about the people murdered up in Guffey?"

Anthony repeated the story the police had heard from Isaac Grimes: Simon had ordered the hit, Jon and Isaac had carried it out, and if anyone talked about it, they'd be killed. Simon had talked about killing the whole family of anyone who ratted, Glen had told Anthony.

Fear of Simon had kept him from coming forward earlier, Anthony said. If word got out that he had provided information to the police about Simon or the organization, he believed Simon would come after him. Anthony said he was still scared that his family might be in danger from Simon or Simon's associates. Gysin, handing him a business card, tried to reassure him that he could contact police immediately if he suspected anything threatening.

"Anything else?" asked Gysin.

"Well, Glen is pretty paranoid," said Anthony. He explained that Glen had returned from school yesterday afternoon to find two identical telephone numbers on his caller ID. When he called the number, he discovered it was the inmates' phone at the El Paso County Jail in downtown Colorado Springs.

Gysin wrote this tidbit down and assured Anthony that neither Isaac, Jon, nor Simon was at the jail, so it couldn't have been one of the OARA members who called.

This was little consolation to Anthony, who, like Glen, believed the OARA extended beyond Simon's intimate cell. He shook the detective's hand and climbed out of the hot car into the afternoon light. School was out by now, and the parking lot was filling with loitering teenagers, warming themselves against their parked cars, blinking like moles, their faces lifted toward the afternoon sun.

Anthony joined the crowd, hoping to blend in anonymously. He didn't want anyone to know he'd spoken to the police, least of all anyone who could pass that information on to Simon Sue.

CHAPTER 11

The small town of Fairplay sits at the northern edge of South Park in central Colorado, a massive, flat grassland basin surrounded by distant mountain ranges rising like jagged teeth on the horizon. Ute Indians made South Park their summer camp in centuries past, and herds of game as well as colonies of beaver, muskrat, otter, and bobcat provided abundant food and fur. French and Spanish explorers traded with the Indians of South Park until the land became part of the Louisiana Purchase in 1803, word of its wealth of wild game spread, and a land grab erupted by midcentury. Fur traders moved into the area, then cattle and sheep ranchers, then treasure seekers who'd heard of gold veins discovered at nearby Tarryall Creek.

Surrounding South Park, camps arose where prospectors set up business. Fairplay was one such camp, which eventually evolved into a hard-rock-mining center. Rolling piles of rock tailings, great hills of gravel left behind after the mining process, still greet travelers entering the town from the south.

In the twenty-first century, Fairplay is known principally as the quaint town one passes through on the way to the Breckenridge ski area and as headquarters to South Park City, a tourist-oriented reconstruction of an 1850s mining camp celebrating that bygone lifestyle and era. Few outside Colorado realize that Fairplay is also the inspiration for the remote fictional locale inhabited by squat, foul-mouthed cartoon characters in the wildly successful and gleefully irreverent television series *South Park*.

As county seat of Park County, Fairplay—sitting at an altitude of nearly ten thousand feet, population less than one thousand—also hosts the county courthouse, a branch of the Eleventh Judicial District Attorney's Offices, the county sheriff's department, and the county jail. Contrasting with the typical leaning and windblown wood-frame structures that characterize Fairplay, the buildings housing law enforcement agencies are modern and made of brick, stalwarts against mountain weather and lawlessness.

Following their arrests in Colorado Springs on March 8, Isaac Grimes, fifteen, and Jonathan Matheny, seventeen, were transported to the Park County Jail and placed in solitary confinement, the only accommodations the jail could provide that would ensure that the boys would be segregated from adult inmates and separated from each other. Ownership and management of the jail had been transferred from the private corporation that built it to the sheriff's office in 2000 in response to long-standing complaints that the modern facility stood largely unused. At that time, twelve inmates occupied a building boasting 150 beds.

"Overcrowding a problem? House your prisoners in our park," read a flyer that jail director and undersheriff Monte Gore sent out to agencies seeking temporary housing for their inmates. Gore recruited potential clients from the Colorado Department of Corrections, plagued by a constant waiting list of newly convicted prisoners awaiting cells. The U.S. Immigration, Customs, and Enforcement (ICE) agency and its captive illegal immigrants awaiting transport back to their homelands proved another good source of regular occupants for the jail. At forty-five bucks per head per day, the jail could quickly make up for its former deficit, filling idle beds and county coffers at the same time. The Park County Jail was quickly becoming the biggest business in Fairplay.

As the boys settled into what would become their longtime home, judges, investigators, and prosecutors roared into motion, building cases against the first two suspects in the New Year's murder of Carl, JoAnna, and Tony Dutcher on the far side of sprawling South Park.

So that Jon and Isaac could be removed from Spring Creek Juvenile Detention Center in Colorado Springs and placed within the jurisdiction of the Park County district court, DAs petitioned Eleventh Judicial District Judge Stanley Mayhew for what is called *direct file,* a measure routinely requested by district attorneys' offices in felony cases involving juveniles in Colorado. Where in most states, and in Colorado until the 1970s, juveniles generally went before a juvenile court judge for evaluation before being assigned to adult court, direct file allows prosecutors, rather than judges, to make the assignment without considering any criteria such as prior crimes or psychological fitness.

It was a critical juncture in the case for Isaac and Jon. Direct file paved the way for their transfer to Park County jurisdiction, to adult court, and to the Park County Jail, an adult facility. Inevitably they would face stiffer penalties for whatever charges were filed against them, and active rehabilitation would not become a focus in their incarceration. They would not receive counseling or education within the adult system. Additionally, they would be required to navigate the judicial system and its myriad complications as adults who understood criminal proceedings.

On March 10, two days after their arrest, the Colorado Springs *Gazette* filled two full pages with ruminations about the local boys accused of murder. Interviewing students on the Palmer High School campus, a reporter observed, "Many expressed shock but more were bewildered as to whom Matheny and Grimes are. . . . The pair seemed to be virtually invisible within the 1,800 students at Palmer High School in downtown Colorado Springs."

Grimes was described as a smart kid from a loving family, on one hand, and as a loner obsessed with weapons and war games, on the other. A man answering the door at the Matheny family's Uintah Street home declined to comment, but upon answering the phone later that day, he said, "He's never gotten in any trouble in his life. That's all I can tell you." Coworkers of the boys at Carl's Jr. were described as "scared and teary-eyed." Both Jon and Isaac had worked there.

In a related story the same day, another *Gazette* reporter talked to neighbors of the Dutchers in rural Park County, looking for reactions to the arrests. Following the discovery of the Dutchers' bodies, "some people loaded their guns and locked their doors. One woman let her Great Pyrenees dog patrol her property all night."

Adding to anxiety over the Dutcher murders and time passing with no arrests was the bizarre revelation in mid-January that the notorious Texas Seven, a group of convicts who had escaped Texas prison with a cache of weapons and who were suspected of killing a policeman outside a sporting goods store on Christmas Eve, had been living for a month in a Teller County trailer park, just down the road from Guffey, South Park, and the Park County line.

While a federal manhunt had failed to turn up even a scent of the men, they had settled comfortably into a motor home in the Coachlight Motel and RV Park outside Woodland Park. The convicts, posing as Christian missionaries, had attended Bible study group and were welcomed as nice neighbors, but they were eventually recognized by one of the owners of the Coachlight from photos posted on the Web site of TV's *America's Most Wanted* and were turned in to police.

Four of the inmates surrendered peacefully, a fifth committed suicide as officers closed in on the mobile home, and two others fled to nearby Colorado Springs, where they checked in at the Holiday Inn and demanded airtime on a local television broadcast before giving themselves up. Patrick Murphy, thirty-nine, and Donald Newbury, thirty-eight, were granted five-minute telephone interviews with local TV anchorman Eric Singer. Newbury, who was serving a ninety-nine-year term for armed robbery, said the prison breakout was a reaction to the Texas judicial system, a system "as corrupt as we are. You going to do something about us, well, do something about that system, too."

Down in Colorado Springs, following the televised apprehension of the last of the Texas Seven, the same week as the Dutcher funerals, Jenny Vandresar and Kathy Creech speculated whether the escapees might have been the invaders who had killed Tony and his grandparents. Like the residents of Bear Trap Ranch, they had barely been able to sleep since Tony's murder, vaguely afraid that the murderer would come after them next.

The arrests of Grimes and Matheny brought relief to Bear Trap Ranch residents, who had worried for two months that the killers were still lurking in their neighborhood, and sickening shock to Jenny Vandresar, who'd imagined the killer to be a hardened adult criminal, not a kid, and certainly not Tony's former best friend, Isaac Grimes.

On March 13, the bizarre story of Grimes's and Matheny's arrests was beginning to unravel as the boys made their first appearances in the Park County Courthouse, hands cuffed to chains at the waists of their navy prison-issue sweat suits. Both teenagers looked like swimmers in life jackets, their backs and chests unnaturally bulky due to bulletproof vests worn over their uniforms. Deputies with drawn weapons escorted the shuffling boys into the courtroom, a plain 250-foot-square cubicle with industrial carpeting, no windows, a high-raised judge's stand, and several rows of wooden benches. Sheriff Fred Wegener explained to the press that extra security precautions were in place because one of the teenagers had been threatened, though he refused to say which one.

Judge Kenneth Plotz presided over the first of what would turn out to be two years of hearings. A petite, wiry man with a mussed shock of reddish hair, bushy eyebrows, and a ruddy asymmetrical face, Plotz informed the boys that they were in court to hear the charges against them. Matheny, head shaved and eyes ringed with dark circles, looked warily around the courtroom. His public defender, Nick Lusero, had not arrived and, according to Plotz, would be attending the hearing by teleconference since he had been confused about the scheduling. (Years later, Matheny would recall this breech in an appeal, arguing that his sentence should be declared illegal because of irregularities in representation.)

Isaac Grimes, thin and fragile-looking, glanced around the room; his eyes sparked with fear as his attorney, Shaun Kaufman of Colorado Springs, stood next to him. Grimes had originally been assigned an attorney from the public defender's office, but a call to his parents from a friend resulted in the hiring of Kaufman, a well-known criminal defense attorney with extensive courtroom experience.

Grimes and Kaufman had only barely met before the court appearance, long enough for Kaufman to ask a shaken Grimes what band he listened to.

"Rage Against the Machine," said Isaac.

Kaufman asked if they were right-wing or leftist.

"Left," said Isaac.

Judge Plotz looked grim as he read the long list of charges: Based on Isaac's confession and Glen Urban's corroboration—Matheny had admitted nothing—each boy faced six counts of first-degree murder, including three counts of murder after deliberation and three counts of felony murder, a first-degree charge lodged against participants in murders who might not actually have committed the crime but were directly involved, or who had killed without prior intent. Each also was charged with child abuse resulting in death, two counts of first-degree burglary and theft, and four counts of violent crime with a deadly weapon.

Park County Deputy DAs David Thorson and Sean Paris watched— Thorson, white-haired and middle-aged, his skin as rough as the leather of his worn cowboy boots; Paris, the picture of youthful ambition, dressed in a tidy suit, his dark hair neatly trimmed.

Solemn and silent, the boys were returned one by one to the jail, where each met briefly with his mother. For the first time, Bonnie Matheny and Donna Grimes drove the long road home to Colorado Springs after visiting their boys in cramped holding cells in a faraway jail.

When the short hearings concluded, Paris and Thorson informed reporters that the investigation continued to focus on two possible accomplices to the murders, friends of Grimes and Matheny who'd recently been suspended from Palmer High School.

Isaac Grimes's defense attorney, Shaun Kaufman, meanwhile, stunned reporters by telling them to expect a defense that would cite rock music as a significant influence—specifically, the music of Rage Against the Machine, "left-wing, progressive, Marxist music." In a case of "screaming importance," Kaufman would tell the judge and jury "an incredible story about youths and how they can be easily manipulated by popular music." A *Gazette* story posted the next day was headlined "Lawyer: Band Inspired Killings" and ran a sidebar outlining the history of Rage, including comments by a *Rolling Stone* contributor on the band's "intensely political" music.

Back home in Colorado Springs that night, Bonnie Matheny began crying and could not stop. Her daughter, Heidi, looked on, wanting to know when Jon was coming home. Jon had confessed nothing, had only said to his mother at the police station before he was taken away, "Do what you have to do to get a good lawyer, Mom. I don't want to go to prison for something I didn't do."

Glen Urban and Simon Sue watched and waited as charges against their friends became public and news of two possible accomplices, still in the Springs, fueled the gossip mill.

Donna Grimes was puzzled over the Rage Against the Machine revelation but assumed Kaufman knew what he was doing. She was busy nursing Rob, who'd just had back surgery; arranging for someone to help care for the two youngest Grimes boys; and working. When the house was finally quiet, she, too, cried and could not stop. In a week that had seemed unbearably dark, the one spark of light was Attorney Shaun Kaufman's telephone call saying he really wanted the case and would defend Isaac pro bono. Her son a lost mystery to her, Donna believed she'd found someone who could help her get him back.

Meanwhile, the long road to Fairplay stretched cold and dark, connecting Isaac's and Jon's empty bedrooms to faraway jail cells surrounded by a vast, open landscape and strange men both in and out of uniform.

CHAPTER 12

Glen Urban cleared his throat and struggled to clear his mind. His mother, Cathie Cumming, sat beside him. Glen had the sweet-faced looks and gangliness of a young adolescent and the folksy mannerisms of a young Walter Brennan, awkward and homespun. His mother's round face, smooth and softened by a halo of fluffy auburn hair, reflected little of the worry that had kept her awake for weeks. Cathie was determined to appear confident and strong for Glen. She knew that he had difficulty putting his thoughts together aloud, and that she would have to curb her need to butt in and help him.

They sat at a conference table in the office of Glen's defense attorney, Ed Farry, in downtown Colorado Springs. Also at the table were DA's Investigator Leonard Post, Deputy DAs Dave Thorson and Kathy Eberling, Farry, CBI Agent Dave Sadar, and Park County Sheriff's Deputy Bob Horn. It was April 6, and the prosecutors were trying to solidify the cases against Glen as an accomplice and Simon Sue as the kingpin who had planned the murders of the Dutcher family on New Year's Eve. In exchange for his full confession, Glen Urban would be offered a plea bargain, but the terms remained to be seen.

A month had passed since Isaac's and Jon's arrests, and Glen was counting the days until he, too, would publicly go down. He'd been up-front with investigators since his first interrogation on March 8, and he was cooperating with them now while trying to keep his cooperation off Simon Sue's radar. It wasn't easy. Simon and Glen had both been expelled from Palmer High School as soon as it was learned that they were under suspicion as accomplices in the Dutcher murder case. Now they were attending the same alternative school in hopes of rescuing at least one vestige of normality, a high school diploma.

Glen watched his dreams of college slip down the drain and had a hard time containing his anger about that. He'd made solid A's during his years at Palmer and had never made trouble for anyone until November 2000, when Simon came into his life. Now, poor judgment had bought him a final senior semester of trying to save his sorry ass from years in prison.

"One day I followed Simon out of math class to lunch," said Glen, opening the day's informal testimony, "and he said, 'Follow me.'"

As Glen remembered and recounted it to those gathered around the table, Jon Matheny had tagged along behind as he and Simon walked a few blocks north of the school to Jon's red Mercury. Jon started driving, and Simon started talking, telling Glen he'd heard he was very good at building things and wondered if he could build a few things for him. Simon said he dealt a lot with weaponry, and Glen remembered his adding quickly, "But nothing illegal."

That first day, Simon had also tutored Glen in the history of his homeland, Guyana, and had told him there were organizations in America linked to Guyana though he mustn't speak about them to anyone outside this small circle of friends. Simon said he and Jon were members of one of those organizations and that he'd like to recruit Glen for the mechanized division of his unit.

"We talked the next day, too, and the day after that, and he just told me more and more."

The purpose of the OARA, as Glen understood it, was to be a military reserve unit that would "just sit and wait until someone said come down [to Guyana]" to fight for the People's Progressive Party should there be a political uprising, as there had been in the past. In between car rides with Jon and Simon, Glen had been taken over to Simon's house, where, in his bedroom, there was a Guyana map on the wall and a poster chart of the current government with President Janet Jagan at the top. Glen recollected that, according to Simon, Jagan was "one of the people that knew about these secret organization things; not everyone in the government knew."

Simon said he knew the president personally and that one day he and the other members of the OARA would go to Guyana, walk into her office, and visit her face-to-face.

"At the time I, of course, thought he was nuts and making all this up," said Glen.

Simon had urged Glen to notice how neat and tidy he kept his bedroom, adding that this was a requirement of the organization. Then he pulled a mini-Uzi out from underneath the mattress on his bed.

"He was like, 'This is why you're here,'" said Glen. "[He told me,] 'This is the handle I need you to build, a handle that mounts on the barrel of this gun.'"

Glen's skepticism over Simon's claims had been overshadowed by his fascination with Simon's wealth of hardware and softened by several things Simon had said during those first few days. One was a compelling description of the OARA's existence and purpose, comparing what it was doing in America to the Bay of Pigs attack on Cuba in the 1960s, when Cuban exiles living in southern Florida were trained by the CIA to be guerrilla fighters in a planned attack on Cuba designed to overthrown the Castro regime. Simon's knowledge of the operation impressed Glen.

Another plus had been Simon's assurance that the overall goal of the organization was to improve the quality of life for its members. Glen had worried a lot about whether he would be able to afford college—his divorced mother could barely pay the bills and his father had never delivered on a promised college fund—and Simon, he told the group around the table, had assured him the organization would make sure he got a good education and would always have a place to live.

"He told me if I needed anything, they could get it for me," said Glen. Then Simon had taken Glen over to Keith Sue's house on Caramillo Street and found him a caliper to measure the dimensions of the barrel of the mini-Uzi. That tool and many others became part of the collection of expensive items added to Glen's backyard workshop in the weeks to come.

Beyond offering promises of tools and an enhanced quality of life, including what Glen took to mean financial support for college tuition, Simon had appealed to a part of Glen that was always with him, just not on the surface—his bitter disappointment in his father for not supporting the family better after his parents' divorce.

"Simon said he found Isaac a year ago, and at the time he was sleeping on the floor," said Glen. "[Simon said,] 'We bought him a bed.' This was his little inspirational speech. 'And the shoes he's wearing,' Simon said, 'we bought him those shoes.'" Isaac's father, as everyone around the table knew, had broken his back in the past year, lived in chronic pain, and had to quit work, causing the family considerable economic stress.

"I remember we were standing under an awning behind the Caramillo Street house," said Glen. "Simon said, 'I have become a father to these boys.'"

Simon, said Glen, had taken credit for keeping Jon (also on the outs with his dad) from flunking out of school, for turning him around. Alone with Jon for a brief moment, Glen had asked him what this OARA thing was all about. As Glen remembered it, Jon had said, "Well, it's this simple, Glen. You get trained at whatever you're going to do. You be willing to go to Guyana if they tell you to, and they help you out."

Simon had given Glen a week to think about it, and after that week he'd either be in or out. In the meantime, Glen had told Simon what parts he'd need to build the handle. A week passed and Glen agreed to join the group.

Upon joining, he learned more about the rules of the OARA: no alcohol, no illegal drugs, no tobacco; regular inspections of bedrooms on the tenth of each month to ensure they were neatly kept.

Farry interrupted Glen's recollection briefly.

"Simon's doing the talking, right?"

"Simon does all the talking," said Glen.

"Oh, and another thing," Glen remembered. "The major reason you wouldn't want to join the organization is because if you're responsible for anyone finding out about it, that's punishable by the wiping out of you and your family. Simon told me that."

Glen's mother flinched, though she had heard this chilling claim before. Glen had told her the whole story shortly after Isaac's and Jon's arrests. She'd paced the floors and cried and yelled and oh, how she had ached, her multiple sclerosis flared by the new complications of her family's life. She slept uneasily knowing Simon Sue was still out there and that he'd explained to Glen how he would pump the house full of poisonous gas through the heating vents if and when the time came that the family had to be sacrificed.

Every time Cathie had heard Glen's story, it sounded more fantastic on one level. But on another, the level through which, as a psychologist, she perceived human behavior, she recognized the emerging portrait of a cult leader. This perfectly delightful little boy, Simon Sue, had turned into Jim Jones and enlisted her son as a follower while her head was turned.

Leonard Post listened carefully and jotted notes. Embedded in Glen's story was nearly verbatim corroboration of what Isaac Grimes had told him about Simon and the OARA back in March, when he first confessed. But where Isaac still believed that the reaches of the OARA extended far beyond Colorado Springs, possibly into the FBI or the CIA, Glen ruefully admitted that while he had assumed there were many more people in the group, throughout his experiences there had been only four members.

"In December, Simon told me the list of all the things I should start working on," said Glen. "He wanted me to build two or three large metal armory boxes. I finished the gun handle. I was supposed to build a safe in the garage, and Simon had heard from somebody that if you wrap a piece of metal in lead foil you could go through a metal detector. He wanted to test this theory and asked me to make some lead foil. I fixed a lock for him, too, around mid-December."

While lavishing Glen and his garage with gifts, Simon explained to Glen "his superiors had cut funding, because he had too many weapons and was not recruiting people fast enough."

Where this was leading, Glen explained, was down the same path Jon and Isaac had already been led down. Money had to be raised. Simon said his officials had given him the word. Seven thousand dollars was the amount Glen remembered, enough to pay for Jon and Simon's planned trip to Guyana. Part of Glen's paycheck would have to be turned over to the organization. Glen's paycheck as a shelfer at the public library after school was small, and the amount turned over to Simon would be insignificant, but it was understood that this was a contractual agreement, one that Glen had no say about. Simon said he planned to get a job himself, and to sell some things. And as he had explained to Glen before, it was policy in the OARA that if money was needed, items could be "seized" to be resold, so long as those items were taken from known bad guys. Simon's logic, while odd, was unyielding.

Assistant District Attorney Kathy Eberling was growing impatient with OARA lore that, while fascinating, had little to do with the Dutcher murders or the prosecution's case.

"When did you first know about the plan to kill the Dutchers?" she interjected.

"Five, maybe eight days after New Year's," said Glen.

"Are you sure, Glen, you didn't know prior to the killing?"

The room went silent.

"No," said Glen. "That is a definite no."

The way the group worked was that everyone had to check in with Simon once a day, whether at school, or by phone if school was out of session. And if Simon had information someone needed to know, he would call. Sometime in late December, Glen had called Simon to check in.

"What's up?" Glen had asked his superior and, as he recalled, Simon had told him an important mission was going down in the next couple days. Glen couldn't recall the exact date, nor could he remember whether Simon had been in Canada or in the United States when he talked to him.

"Simon's exact words were: Jon and Isaac are not to be bothered. I thought, OK, they were gonna do a raid and seize something. So I didn't call for a couple of days."

The table's occupants had grown restless by this point, and a conversation ensued among the various law enforcement agents over whether it was actually confirmed that Sue had been in Canada over the Christmas holiday. Talk of subpoenaing airline records and border-crossing records flew around the table until, quietly, Glen interrupted.

"Um, he wasn't using airlines. He was driving. Because I remember his father [brought] some engines across the border in his van. Because I helped load the engines out of the truck when they got back."

"OK," said a weary Leonard Post, swiping his big head with a rough hand. Both Isaac Grimes's and Glen Urban's recollections of Keith Sue's regular presence among the group was disconcerting, but he needed to keep the focus on the boys, the murders, and the cover-up. He'd check into Keith Sue later.

"What happened next, Glen?"

Back in school, the holiday over, Glen had given Simon a ride home for lunch one day. Jon's car was on the blink.

"Simon said, 'You know that important mission that went down around New Year's?' And I said, 'Yeah, I remember.' And he says, 'Well, some people went down.' He said their name was Dutcher. This is how he broke it to me."

Glen said that even though he knew he was not supposed to ask why—that was an OARA rule—he had anyway. Simon had told him the murdered family were crooked people. He told him they were bad people because they were racists and drug dealers and they were threatening people with guns. Glen remembered Simon saying, "That's why I ordered them to go down."

Glen hadn't made the connection immediately with the family whose bodies had been found on a rocky hill near Guffey just a few days earlier, as reported in the local newspapers. Later that day, though, he had asked someone the names of the victims in the Guffey murders and when he heard the name, he knew exactly who Simon was talking about—the fifteen-year-old Palmer sophomore and his grandparents.

Once Glen knew about the mission, he said, Simon had jumped into action, informing all the OARA members that the CBI would be investigating them, that he was going to tell them what to say, and that they were going to go over it until everyone got it right.

"He said, 'You're gonna have to say that Isaac and Jon were at your house from five till nine.' He basically constructed everything. He told me what they were wearing, what we did while we were there, where they parked, that they drove Jon's car. He gave me a bunch of details to say, first in the car one day, then every other time I saw him after that."

The CBI had shown up and interviewed Glen at lunch at school one day, and he had repeated the alibi Simon had concocted, sticking carefully to the script. Around that same time, he said, Simon and Jon dropped off a knife for him to cut up in his workshop. Simon told him to cut it up into tiny pieces and said he'd come back for it in fifteen minutes. Glen cut it up with the metal saw Simon had provided. Then, when Simon returned, they burned the wooden handle with a propane torch.

Glen remembered, "While we were watching it burn, Jon was looking a little depressed to me. He was even quieter than usual. Simon tried to cheer him up, saying, 'The Dutchers went down, didn't they?' There he is just saying it, like yeah, we did something good. And Jon says, 'Yeah, we took 'em down.' He was trying to sound happy about it, I guess, but I think he was saying it with bitter regret."

Eberling asked Glen, "Did you know that this knife you're destroying was the murder weapon?" Glen said he really hadn't known, that there had been so many knives and weapons around, it could have been one that was stolen in a raid, perhaps one that had been stolen from the Dutchers, and Simon had decided he didn't want to be caught with it. Glen described the knife in precise detail: six or seven inches long; a black, rubberized handle with an etched finish; double-edged a third of the way down the blade. He drew a picture of it for the table's attendants.

They took a break.

When they returned to the table, Post summarized: Glen had talked to the CBI in January, cut up the knife, then talked with him at the Colorado Springs Police Department in March on the night of Isaac's and Jon's arrests.

"Were there any other conversations you had with Jonathan, Isaac, or Simon about the murder during that time?" he asked.

"Things were quiet," said Glen. "I took a walk with Simon one time at lunch. He was kind of happy that we hadn't heard from anyone in a long time, that he, he said he beat the system. He told me he was having trouble with Jon's mother because she wouldn't allow Jon to get the passport he needed for a trip to Guyana. He asked me if I wanted to go.

"He coached me on talking to the police. He said I shouldn't move my eyes off or look away when I'm saying something important, that I should just stay loose and try to look people in the eye." This remark evoked a chuckle from the sober group sitting around the table. Glen Urban could hardly be described as loose under the most relaxing circumstances, much less under the official scrutiny of the law. Aggressive eye contact was not his strong point.

"Is the next incident when they bring the firearm?" asked Kathy Eberling, referring to a gun Glen had already admitted cutting up at Simon's request.

"Well, that was at the end [before the arrests of Jon and Isaac]. Simon told me at lunch that we had to go get something, and Jon took us over to the warehouse-type place [the Caramillo Street house].

"All three of us go inside. We go upstairs and then to the farthest north bedroom. Behind the dresser, next to the window, Simon pulls out a white trash bag full of stuff, including the main part of an AK-47. Then he says, 'You need to cut this up.' Simon started taking apart the gun on the bed, but he needed to go home and get something for his Spanish homework, so he just left the bag of stuff and the partially disassembled gun on the bed."

This information didn't escape Cathie Cumming's growing curiosity about Keith Sue, who reportedly spent a good deal of time at the Caramillo Street house. What could a father be thinking, to find a disassembled automatic weapon lying on the bed, out in the open, in his house? How could Mr. Sue not have known about the boys' unusual activities involving dangerous weapons? She had certainly made it clear to her sons that no weapons were allowed in her home. Never in a million years would she have guessed that a gun slept quietly in Glen's hand-built safe in the garage, until this past, strange month.

Glen continued. "Simon asked me what time I'd be free, so that he could drop the stuff off and I could cut up the gun. I told him nine o'clock."

That night, Glen had opened the garage door and found Jon Matheny standing there with the white trash bag. Jon had walked in and dumped the contents of the bag on the floor. Glen remembered seeing the disassembled AK-47, a small bayonet that could be mounted on a gun, leather holsters, and a handle.

"I cut up the gun and put it in an empty can," he said, explaining that he had used a large metal chop saw with a twelve-inch blade, given to him by Simon. "I put the lid on the can and set it, with everything else, in front of the safe in my garage, which was open, and that's the last that I saw of it. In the morning I went to school, and when I came back home, well, everything in front of the safe was gone and the safe was closed."

"Did you believe the weapon was associated with the murders at the time you cut it up?" asked Kathy Eberling, careful to continue to calculate Glen's culpability since the DAs would be offering a plea bargain in exchange for his cooperation.

"No," said Glen. "I thought it may have been stolen. Maybe from the Dutchers."

"Glen, would you be willing to turn over the safe and its contents to us?" asked Leonard Post, gathering evidence in his head.

Ed Farry, irritated at this ill-advised and likely incriminating request of his client, laughed and leaned forward. "Oh, I'm sorry. What am I, a potted plant?"

"It's what you get paid for," quipped Post.

Glen didn't miss a beat. "I cut up the gun. The next day I told Simon I needed to go take a makeup test at school. I did; then I came back to my house and worked with my friend Anthony on his car, and then the police showed up."

Cathie Cumming's knees and hips ached from sitting for so long, and her heart ached when she thought of that night, when two big men had shown up at her door, asking to see Glen. She had freaked and had left them standing on the porch behind the closed door as she looked out the window. A Park County squad car, her mind registered slowly, hesitantly, regretfully. Park County, where those people were murdered. Some odd moments with Glen in the past week began to come into focus. His anger at being asked to speak to police at school. Cathie had told him that probably all the kids were being asked if they knew anything about Tony Dutcher; she had told him it was all right, just to tell them you didn't know the kid. She remembered the look of terror on his face when he saw a newspaper story about the murders. She had called upstairs for Glen, frantic about the cops on the porch.

"What the hell is going on?" she had demanded.

"Don't worry," he said. "I'll tell you when they're gone." Then he had walked out the door to where the officers stood and led them around the house to the backyard, to the detached garage on the alley, his workshop, where he spent most of his time, his sanctuary, the place where Cathie knew Glen was always happy. Her boy the mechanic: his first words had been *mama, daddy, cat,* and *tool.* She had paced and paced, waiting for him to come back into the house. It felt as though days passed until she finally saw her goofy boy's face again, ashen and frightened.

He told her he was going to the police station. Her nightmares had just begun. When Glen finally arrived back home, late on the evening of March 8, he told his mother everything he knew.

The officers around the table asked Glen to corroborate some other procedures of the OARA that Isaac Grimes had reported, like filing reports. He said he'd filed only one when he was ordered to make some lead foil. Had Glen been issued a weapon? Yes, that was standard. The mini-14 was stored in the safe he'd built in his garage but had been removed at some point. Did Simon's father know about the OARA? Glen recalled one day, walking to the Caramillo Street house with Simon, when Simon said he got "a lot of respect" at that house. He was proud of that, said Glen. He said his dad had been in one of the organizations like the OARA, that he used to have a high position but was now retired.

"OK, Glen, big question," said Kathy Eberling. "Why didn't you report this homicide to the authorities?"

Glen gathered his thoughts and swallowed. He knew it would be hard to make them understand.

"We were in the car one time with Jon, and Simon said, 'If these boys go to prison, there's going to be some cleaning up to do, Glen. You know what I mean by that?' And I said yes. He meant by cleaning up that he was going to have to kill me and anyone else that knew me, I guess."

The adults persisted: How could he have known that's what Simon meant?

"He reiterated it many times. I don't remember his exact words and all the times; it was probably different every time, but he kept saying if these boys [Isaac and Jon] go to prison, 'it's bad for the organization and it's really bad for you.'

"I didn't report it because I thought the worst possible scenario that could've happened to me was that I'd say something to the police and Simon would have covered up all the evidence. Simon was a very smart person; he told me he had taken care of everything. There were no loose ends anywhere. I could have told the authorities, and the authorities would arrest him but then have nothing to hold him with. And they'd end up killing me and leaving the country or taking me with them. Who knows? I wanted to stay on the good side of them."

Glen recalled Simon bragging about holding a gun to Isaac Grimes's head but "with all his infinite mercy" giving Isaac a second chance. He said he believed Isaac was "this close" to getting killed.

Cathie Cumming held her tongue. Why was it so difficult for these reasonable adults to understand that Glen genuinely feared for his life and for his family? After all, the person he feared was someone who had reportedly ordered the execution of a family and all of them were dead now. She believed that real evil was at work here, not evil inspired by the devil or Rage

Against the Machine, but evil that used other people for personal gain, evil that didn't blink.

The afternoon wrapped up with a couple of questions about evidence collected at the Urban home, including a uniform Simon had given Glen that was to be worn if he had to go to Guyana—jungle camouflage pants and shirt. Post asked if Glen knew anything about a box of insignia patches that had been found at the Sue house, tags that read, "C55511SS." Glen said sure, he knew about them. They were to go over the pockets of the OARA members' uniforms. They identified the unit.

The *SS* stood for Simon Sue.

The DAs told Farry they would work on the terms of the plea bargain so long as Glen continued to cooperate. Glen and Cathie returned home and tried to maintain as much normality as possible for Glen's little brother and for themselves as they awaited Glen's ultimate arrest.

On April 26, energized by a long interrogation with Isaac Grimes, also entered into as part of a possible plea bargain agreement, the Eleventh Judicial District Attorney's Office, via Leonard Post, issued warrants for the arrests of Glen Urban and Simon Sue. Initial charges against the two were first-degree murder for Sue and accessory to first-degree murder for Urban, charges that would be added to and refined in the weeks to come. Urban was released to his mother on a one-thousand-dollar bond.

Simon joined Jon and Isaac at the Park County Jail in Fairplay, though the boys were carefully separated so that there would be no contact among them. The epicenter of the OARA had shifted not to the jungles of Guyana as the boys might once have expected, but to rural central Colorado—two hours, a mountain pass, and a network of scenic winding highways from their Colorado Springs homes.

CHAPTER 13

In the months since the beginning of 2001, Palmer High School students and teachers had struggled with one drama after another: first the news of Tony Dutcher's murder, then the arrests of Isaac Grimes and Jonathan Matheny, and, finally, the arrests of Simon Sue and Glen Urban on April 26.

Senior Anna Nussbaum, commentary editor of the student newspaper, *The Lever,* tried to find meaningful ways to cover the lurid story of the Guffey murders and the students involved, but she felt stymied in her efforts.

Nussbaum came from a respected Old North End family, residents of a big white house on Nevada Avenue with ample porches and airy bedrooms. Her father, Martin, was a respected attorney; her mother a lay minister in the Catholic Church and a theological writer. Anna was next to youngest of five Nussbaum children, all high academic achievers and school leaders.

Her plans on leaving Palmer High School were to study journalism at a good university. But first, Anna would write her swan song, a long reflection on the strange events of spring semester, 2001, published in the May *Lever*:

> This spring I will graduate from Palmer High School. While on Palmer
> High School's newspaper, we covered lots of stories to the best of our
> abilities, . . . the irony being that the "bigger" the story, the worse the

tragedy. From the typical teen pregnancy to terrorism, we told our truths. But there is one story that was never told, not right.

On New Year's Eve 2000, as I watched fireworks explode in the Denver sky, one of my classmates, fifteen-year-old Tony Dutcher, slept as killers slit his throat and shot his grandparents Carl and JoAnna Dutcher.

When I returned to school that Monday my classmates and I heard about Tony's death from an announcement over the public address system. No one knew how to respond. At the student newspaper we decided not to write a full-length feature about the investigation, but to write obituaries for Tony and an eleventh-grade girl who had committed suicide within weeks of Tony's death. We wanted to gather people together in a room—friends, coaches, and teachers—and have them share their favorite memories. We wanted the obituaries to celebrate the lives of the dead students.

But Tony had been a shy freshman, and we couldn't find anyone who knew him. So we ran the obituaries with words from the students' parents. . . . Tony's read: "It's a great loss for all of us," says his father. "We miss him very much."

. . . That was it, no memorials, no ribbons or prayer services, and the next morning the voice over the p.a. system reassuringly announced sporting events and club meetings: Life went on. We were in the midst of first semester finals.

Ten weeks later, on the day I was preparing to go to regional science fair . . . , Palmer High School was in the headlines again.

Two students were arrested and charged with three counts of first degree murder. Isaac Grimes, who had been at school with us for the weeks after the murder, admitted slitting Tony's throat and watching as another student, Jonathan Matheny, shot Tony's grandparents with an AK-47.

At the newspaper we were overwhelmed. We had planned to cover Valentine's Day and make lists of the best date spots in Colorado Springs. Now, we had to cover "this," and we couldn't agree on how.

We set out to interview the friends of the accused killers, but we couldn't find anyone who had known them well. Two Palmer students had been charged with brutally murdering another student and his grandparents, for no apparent reason, and we needed to acknowledge it, but it was as if it had happened at another school. To other students. To strangers. We watched the evening news to find out about the case. We read about ourselves in the morning papers.

The city press descended on the school, questioning students as they left the building for lunch. But the reporters faced the same problem we had faced; they had trouble finding any students who knew Tony or his alleged killers, Isaac and Jonathan. . . . No one wanted to be associated with them. "It's not like we knew these kids," we thought. "How can they reflect us?"

The principal sternly admonished the press to leave students alone so they could get back to learning. . . . To protect the average students, a panel of the school's best was chosen for a press conference. They were the picture of health: a group of highly motivated, racially diverse kids from every grade. They were the clean cut, student council, lets-not-make-this-thing-any-worse-than-it-is, scholar-athlete crowd. None of them knew the victim, and none of them knew the accused killers, but their fresh faces assured the city that everything was going to be okay. This wasn't Columbine.

And the student newspaper did run a story. We devoted the front page and all of page four to the crisis. The story read, "Suddenly Palmer has joined the ranks of schools directly connected to gruesome acts of teen violence." The writer continued, "While these murders did not happen on our campus, Grimes was in Keith Ferguson's fourth hour Chemistry class, and Jesse Luken often greeted Matheny in the hallway."

If you went to Palmer, you'd know these names: Keith Ferguson was the student body president that year and Jesse Luken was a football star. Both were popular senior classmen. They exist in the history of

Palmer. They exist because they are likable and successful. They made the honor roll and were always standing up to be recognized in assemblies. They have been written into the history books of the school. Tony Dutcher was never written in, and neither were his alleged murderers Isaac Grimes and Jonathan Matheny.

So what happened? . . . The article angered me. Instead of writing, "This terrible thing happened and we can't find a soul who knew these guys," the paper turned to brand name people to tell us who Tony, Isaac and Jonathan were. The accused existed only because popular boys had seen them in the hallway or in class. The fact was, these boys were dead to us long before they were locked away, and most of us met them for the first time on the cover of the morning paper.

. . . But the story wasn't over. Later, things got worse. Two more Palmer students were arrested in connection with the murders: seniors Simon Sue and Glen Urban. Sue is the alleged leader of the group which Urban, Grimes and Matheny belonged to. Phone records suggest that after the murders Grimes and Matheny called Sue to report completion. Twenty telephone calls to the home of Sue's uncle in Toronto were made. Forty guns including two of the Dutchers' guns were found at Sue's house. Urban allegedly destroyed guns and other murder weapons. Sue allegedly threatened to kill Isaac and Jonathan's families if they hadn't committed the crime by January eighth. Sue is nineteen, and with Grimes' testimony he is eligible for the death penalty.

Most of us on the newspaper staff had heard more about these boys, the leaders, the powerful ones, because even among the unknown there is a hierarchy.

On May 28, Anna Nussbaum and her classmates celebrated their graduation from Palmer High School at the Colorado Springs World Arena, just a block away from the Carl's Jr. where Isaac and Jon once flipped burgers and less than a mile away from the spot where the boys had dumped the destroyed murder weapons into muddy Fountain Creek. Nearby, in a concrete culvert, a blackened spot on the ground marked the place where bloody clothes and backpacks had been destroyed in a late night bonfire.

Anna would soon leave Colorado Springs for the University of Notre Dame. Isaac, Jon, Glen, and Simon would spend most of the next two years in the Park County Jail, awaiting the court's determination of how and where they would spend the rest of their lives.

PART THREE

Rough Justice

CHAPTER 14

Though the Eleventh Judicial District Attorney's Office had geared up for four trials, pulling in three Assistant DAs—Dave Thorson, Sean Paris, and Kathy Eberling—and planning to pull out their big gun, Elected DA Ed Rodgers, when the time came, their strategy shifted as the weeks passed.

Isaac Grimes had already confessed to killing Tony Dutcher and would certainly prefer a plea bargain agreement to a sentence of life in prison without parole, the required sentence under Colorado law for first-degree murder, in exchange for his full cooperation in the investigation. Glen Urban, the kid who seemed to be the least involved in the actual killings, had been a cooperative witness up to now and would make a star witness against the others when their cases came to court.

Simon Sue, meanwhile, had confessed to nothing beyond his initial admission of forming a "little do-gooder group," the OARA, of which he was in command, and helping to destroy evidence. And Sue had been out of the country when the murders occurred, so first-degree murder charges against him would be tough to justify, though prosecutors thought he was complicit.

Jon Matheny had admitted nothing, though it was clear to everyone involved that he had at the very least transported Isaac Grimes to the Dutcher home on New Year's Eve and had later brought Isaac down from the mountain. Investigator Leonard Post was as sure that Jon was the gunman who took out Carl and JoAnna Dutcher as he had been about any perpetrator in any case he'd ever investigated. He thought the kid's manner and looks screamed guilt, and he was determined to bring him down despite Jon's determination not to crack.

The chief problem of District Attorney Ed Rodgers was evidence. Beyond nearly matching accounts by Grimes and Urban regarding the OARA, how it worked, and activities surrounding the Christmas holiday, including the alibi all four boys had shared under Simon's tutelage, there was no physical evidence linking any of them to the scene except Grimes. Tony Dutcher's bloodied jacket had been found where Isaac Grimes had left it, neatly folded beside the Dutchers' couch, drenched with blood that turned out to be Tony's. A single fingerprint of Isaac's on a water glass placed him inside the trailer home. But hundreds of pieces of evidence collected three days after the murders had turned up hair and blood and fingerprints belonging to the deceased grandmother, grandfather, and grandson, and nothing to place Jon Matheny at the scene of the crime, even though all three other teens had fingered Jon as the gunman who shot Carl and JoAnna.

Rather than go to trial, the prosecution team would seek guilty pleas from all four boys, applying the toughest charges admissible by law and depending upon the confessions of Grimes and Urban and the threat of their testimony against the others to buoy the cases against Sue and Matheny. Whether Sue and Matheny would accept guilty pleas remained to be seen, so the team would continue to prepare for trials should it come to that.

A few key interviews and some evidence seized at the boys' homes had recently given the prosecutors added ammunition, particularly against Sue.

One piece of evidence, gathered from Sue's home, was a hand-written oath scribbled in unruly handwriting on a regular piece of notebook paper, presumably the oath administered to new members of the OARA. Reading it sent shivers through some of the investigators, hardened veterans of homicide cases, and made some of them giggle. Riddled with grammatical and spelling errors, it read:

I _____ take this oath to serve my superiors to my fullest and utmost potential. I honor the laws and freedoms which have been given to me by the representatives which now direct and govern my actions in this world. I swear that upon my flesh and bone to protect my family as well as serve the Guyanese people of which I stand for. Shall I challenge my authorities of the Guyanese people I swear to accept punishment given to me from my representatives. In the case of treson [*sic*] I allow thru my body and by consent of god that I be executed by my authority which governs me. Within this oath, I uphold honor and truth. I swear to the condition of my honor which involves the prohibition of drugs, alcohol, abuse of power, treson [*sic*], disobedience. I serve these authorities of which have been imposed on to me until death or dismissal. I _____ say and speak that all information I deliver is true and valid and therefore swear to its secrecy and to its laws.

That the OARA existed and that one of its principal tenets was execution as punishment for treason, as Urban and Grimes had claimed, appeared to be true. Whether the group's reach extended beyond the Palmer High School neighborhood of Colorado Springs was still not clear, but investigators were taking it seriously. Post would soon be dispatched to Guyana to seek international links.

Meanwhile, an eight-hour interview with Isaac Grimes in early April, his attorney Shaun Kaufman present, the first step forward in his plea bargain agreement, turned up new details that buzzed in the prosecutors' ears and strengthened the case against Simon Sue.

Grimes's long story painted Simon as a kingpin: a stickler for order and cleanliness, a commander with an unwavering eye, a leader whose orders came from a faraway place where history and politics demanded military readiness and a stealthy guerilla presence.

Simon, said Grimes, had issued weapons and military equipment to his youngest officer in the OARA, including frag vests, ammo pouches, Kevlar helmets, an AP-9 assault pistol, and "thirty-six rounds of full metal jacket," copper-encased bullets. When the boys had gone shooting on Rampart Range as part of their training, Simon had counted the ammunition issued beforehand and afterward.

Grimes said he had been trained how to strip and assemble a variety of weapons as well as how to shoot them.

"He taught me on SKS, on HK91 [a semiautomatic military assault rifle] later. On pump shotguns. On a Glock. And [I learned] to clean them. I spent many hours just sitting and cleaning."

Simon Sue's OARA, Grimes believed, had originated in Guyana, where Simon had undergone intensive training that, eventually, his minions in the States would also endure. Simon wanted to drop Isaac and Jon off in the middle of the jungle and have them find their way out over two weeks, just as he had, said Isaac. At times, Simon talked about the training he'd gone through and how "in that training his mind was warped and all he wanted to do is see little girls dead. He told me that," said Isaac. "He said that I'd go through that kind of training in Guyana . . . in the summer of 2001."

According to Grimes, Simon said he'd been promoted within the larger organization in Guyana over the summer and had gotten permission to create his own corps, the OARA. To lend credibility to his claim, Simon had shown Isaac a gun he said had been issued to him by his superiors, a rare Norinco Uzi, manufactured in China. When Guyana and Suriname began having border disputes in September 2000, Simon had his troops, Isaac and Jon, start running every day in case they were sent down to fight. They would be flown in by private plane, Simon said.

Isaac said that Keith Sue, according to Simon, was one of the founders of the organization back in the 1960s and had been retired the summer Simon was promoted.

Isaac further described his training in "entering a room," recounting how Simon had put him through the paces, practicing sliding through a basement window in anticipation of the raid on Gabe Melchor's house. He described both robberies of the Melchor home, conducted by Jon and himself, in which the boys had stolen, among other things, the NHM90 reportedly used to gun down Carl and JoAnna Dutcher.

Following the Dutcher mission, in February 2001 when Simon was confident his group had successfully eluded the eye of the law, Simon had emphasized to Glen, Isaac, and Jon that they would need to concentrate on finding new recruits for the group. The perfect candidate, Isaac recalled, "would have to be pretty smart, be able to do exercise, be well disciplined, someone who could take orders, a male either of Hindu or Islamic faith," per Simon's specifications. During that month, Isaac had kept up with the situation in Guyana by reading the *Guyana Chronicle* and *Stabroek News,* Guyanese newspapers, online.

Investigators probed one puzzling aspect of Isaac's story: He had mentioned that as part of his training in Guyana, he would be expected to kill a number of black soldiers of the PNC party, the PPP's opposition. If the OARA was supposed to be antiracist, as investigators had heard over and over again from Grimes, Urban, and Sue, why were they planning to go down to Guyana to kill black people?

"I'm not exactly sure," said Isaac. "Simon would use racial words; he'd use anti-Jew words, he'd tell racist jokes and still maintain he's not a racist." Isaac explained that there had always been a conflict between blacks and Asians in Guyana and that Simon had said Isaac and Jon could only marry Indian women. He had often shown them Indian movies and shared Indian music with them.

"What about Rage Against the Machine?" asked one of the assistant prosecutors. "Did that have anything to do with it?"

"No, Simon didn't like them," said Isaac.

Shaun Kaufman laughed. "I really threw the press a good hard left-hit fake, didn't I?"

Isaac shook his head. "I did a double take when I saw that on the news."

Prosecutors quietly took note of Kaufman's glib comment, then moved on to the night of the Dutcher murders. Isaac Grimes once again recounted his experience: how he'd killed his former best friend, Tony; how he'd been ordered by Simon to devise a plan to kill Carl and JoAnna Dutcher; how his life had been threatened repeatedly during the weeks between Thanksgiving and New Year's Eve while the plan was taking shape.

Around mid-December, on an evening when Isaac had joined Simon and Jon at the Columbia Street house, Isaac turned in the plan he'd been ordered to write. Jon, said Isaac, was helping Simon's mom with dinner. The following day, Thursday, during lunch hour, Simon and Jon took Isaac over to Keith Sue's Caramillo Street house and came down hard on him. The plan, Simon said, was crap.

"He said I was conspiring against them, that the report wasn't written well enough, that I didn't do anything right," said Isaac. "He said he'd have to call the people in Guyana to have them analyze the plan. He just yelled in my face and slapped me around.

"He asked me how I'd like to die. He talked about how he hopes I'm conspiring so he can kill me and my family. He hopes that I mess up and kill Jon on the mission so he can kill my family in front of me or take me out to the forest and dismember me."

"What's Jon doing?" asked Post, noticing the urgent shift in Isaac's account from past tense to present. The boy seemed to be reliving the experience.

"Jon's sitting in a chair near me," said Isaac. "He has like a riot baton, this big, long, yellow baton. He's basically just watching. Sometimes he joins in; sometimes he doesn't. Simon gives me, I believe it's two weeks, to live, two weeks that this mission has to be carried out in, or else I'll die and my family. He gives me an early date in January to complete the mission."

Eager to get on with it, Isaac raced through his account of the night he and Jon finally made it to Bear Trap Ranch and the Dutchers' home.

Again, he told the story in present tense:

> Jon picks him up at work. They drive up the Canon City route and over-shoot the cutoff to Guffey, going all the way to Hartsel by mistake. Jon drives furiously, spinning out as he turns around.

Jon instructs Isaac not to touch anything in the house. Don't leave any evidence behind. If Tony's sleeping on the couch, you'll have to kill him there, but wait until two in the morning or so, when Jon will leave Colorado Springs to come back and pick up Isaac.

They arrive. Jon is introduced to Carl and JoAnna as a cousin of Isaac's. Jon leaves Isaac with a backpack, the Frontiersman knife stuffed inside. Isaac screws up and eats in the kitchen. Goulash. Tony announces they'll be sleeping up on the mountain in the lean-to. They climb up together and visit for a while. Isaac borrows Tony's green coat. Tony zips himself up, still clothed, in his sleeping bag and sits half up, resting against a low wall. At around eleven, too early, Isaac scoots around behind Tony as if to retrieve something on the other side of him. He takes him from behind—four strokes across his neck with the knife, maybe, he can't remember. He lays his bleeding former friend down and turns him over, face down in the sleeping bag.

Did Tony see the knife? Post asked. Yes, said Isaac.

Then he runs. He sits in the woods and cries. Thirty minutes maybe. He has fucked up and killed Tony too early. The coat is covered in Tony's blood. Inside the pocket, he fingers a watch, black with a lightning bolt design, a Christmas present. He wanders back down the hill, wondering what he'll do until Jon returns around 4 a.m. He hides the bloody knife and his backpack beneath some bushes and goes back inside Carl and JoAnna's.

He lies on the couch, the bloodied jacket folded and laid in the corner beyond the couch. JoAnna comes out at midnight and wishes him a Happy New Year. Later, he's not sure when, Carl comes out to read for a while. Isaac lies quiet and still. Carl goes back to bed. Isaac has left the door ajar for Jon.

Finally, Jon comes through the door, pointing a gun at the couch, at Isaac, since he doesn't see Tony there. Isaac explains what he's done and that he did it on the hill. They go out and retrieve the backpack and the knife. They wash Tony's frozen blood off the knife in the kitchen sink. Jon hands Isaac a mag light and tells him to lead the charge into Carl and JoAnna's bedroom. Jon's holding a loaded NHM90. Isaac can't budge. He's frozen.

This was what Isaac told the spellbound officers of the law surrounding him.

I just stand still and we stand there for a while. But Mr. Dutcher, he finally goes to the bathroom. Then he comes out. Jon has the gun. He shoots him twice. Then Mrs. Dutcher, like, runs past from the bedroom into the bathroom. And he shoots and misses. She screams and shuts the bathroom door. So he turns to me and he yells, "Cut her fucking throat." He yells at me and I start moving; then he says, "Get out of my fucking way." Then he shoots and I don't know how many times he did. Then he grabbed me by the arm and made me look at her and asked if she was dead. She wasn't. She was just hanging on. He didn't shoot again.

Five shells, Isaac said: He and Jon agreed later that they retrieved five shells from the floor of the hallway and the living room. They ran into the bedroom, across Mr. Dutcher's body in the hallway, and opened the closet. Jon grabbed Mr. Dutcher's AR-15 and threw it on the bed. A revolver, too, and a gun case. Isaac checked on JoAnna one more time, and this time she was gone. The boys rushed out the front door, and the gun case slipped from Isaac's hand to the floor next to the television. Isaac was told to lock the door but his hands were too full, so Jon ran back and locked it. This is what Isaac told the officers and attorneys. They ran to the car, their arms filled with the guns and the backpack, the knife, the mag light. Jon ran fast, but Isaac felt as though his feet were stuck to the ground. He had a hard time moving forward.

The car was parked on the main road beyond the pond, up the long driveway. Jon had the trunk open to dump everything in. Isaac opened the passenger door and banged his head on the door frame. Jon stuffed everything into what looked like an onion bag, woven plastic, and slammed the trunk shut.

There was no mention of the coat, still folded, drenched with Tony's blood, sitting in the corner of the living room next to the couch. Isaac didn't mention JoAnna's little dog, the only living family member left behind in the shot-up trailer home.

Isaac finished his story.

"Jon spins the car around, you know, does a U-ie, and says, 'Good job soldier,'" Isaac said. "And I feel myself believing him." Jon, said Isaac, told him the conspiracy charges against him were now cleared. He gave him a piece of gum. The boys drove home at dawn, down the mountain and through the silent streets of Colorado Springs, early on the first day of 2001. According to Isaac, they arrived back in the Springs around 7 a.m., dropped off the weapons taken from the Dutchers at the Sues' Caramillo Street house, went to Jon's house, and called Simon.

"Jon's talking to Simon and I'm not sure what they're talking about, but Simon wants to talk to me," Isaac recalled. "I get on the phone and he says he trusts me. He trusts me with weapons. He trusts me to do anything now. He says, 'Now you have respect in Guyana.'

"Simon says, 'I'm proud of you, my son.'"

The marathon interrogation ended with weary stretching of dulled limbs and late-night drives home. Leonard Post had heard the story of the night of the murders multiple times now and still couldn't quite believe it. He worried that Grimes, a kid really, wasn't the most reliable storyteller, though it was hard to doubt someone who took complete responsibility for his own murderous behavior.

An exhausted Isaac, his mind flooded once again with the gruesome details of what might have been the last free New Year's Eve of his life—certainly

Tony's last—returned to his cell. He would not sleep for fear of the night-mares he knew would come. He had testified for more than eight hours.

•◆•

A few days after Isaac Grimes had helped prosecutors shore up their charges against Simon Sue, Odeen Ishmael, Guyana's ambassador to the United States, issued an official statement regarding claims that the OARA had ties to the People's Progressive Party of Guyana. "The PPP has made a state-ment that it doesn't know anything about this organization," said Ishmael. Sharief Khan, editor of the *Guardian* newspaper of Guyana, called the exis-tence of such a group "far-fetched." Prosecutors still planned to dispatch Post to Guyana, but any possibility that the OARA extended beyond Simon Sue's expansive imagination seemed more and more remote.

On the first of May, the Colorado Springs daily newspaper reported that fifteen-year-old Isaac Grimes had accepted a plea offer and would plead guilty to reduced charges, according to his defense attorney, Shaun Kaufman. DAs confirmed that they were working on an agreement but pointed out that a plea agreement is not complete until a judge accepts it. Grimes's preliminary hearing was set for May 21, when Judge Kenneth Plotz would hear the details.

Donna Grimes, reading the *Gazette* that morning, was startled to see the announcement before the deal was presented in court. Neither she nor her husband nor Isaac had ever had any experience with criminal lawyers or criminal proceedings, and though she had been available by phone the day of Isaac's marathon testimony, she was not aware that this was the deal maker in a guaranteed guilty plea.

Kaufman had seemed gung ho on proving the Guyana connection when he was first hired, a direction that Robin and Donna believed might turn up evidence that would mitigate Isaac's guilt, proving his claims that he was part of something much bigger than himself, something international in scope and genuinely dangerous. But when Kaufman's investigator an-nounced she wanted to investigate the Sues and the Guyana connection,

Kaufman called her off. Around that same time, he indicated he thought someone might be following him.

Kaufman explained to Donna and Rob that he had told Isaac that the first one to talk to investigators gets the best deal. Regarding a plea agreement that might send their son to prison for as long as seventy years, Kaufman told the Grimes parents, "We are cutting off his arm to save his life."

•◆•

In anticipation of Isaac Grimes's May 21 hearing, the *Gazette* ran a long front-page story in the Sunday edition, pointing out that once he entered a guilty plea, Isaac would become "one of the youngest of the more than 12,000 men incarcerated in the Colorado Department of Corrections prisons." A state spokesperson indicated there were thirteen inmates under the age of eighteen in the adult prison system.

The *Gazette* story set the scene Isaac Grimes faced, a world "where the average age is thirty-four, and only 1.6 percent of the men are less than twenty years old. . . . He'll go to a place where 10.2 percent of the men are serving sentences for homicide, 8.5 percent for assault, 5.8 percent for sexual assault and 6.9 percent for sexual assault on a child."

No place for a child, said a public defender interviewed for the story.

May 21 arrived and, with it, Tony Dutcher's sixteenth birthday. Jennifer Vandresar released balloons in Portal Park, a small oasis in the middle of a central Colorado Springs neighborhood where Tony had played as a young boy.

That same day in Fairplay, Shaun Kaufman arrived in court late, ruffled and visibly agitated. He requested that the court appoint a guardian ad litem, an officer of the court whose job would be to advise Isaac Grimes on legal matters and make sure he was properly treated both in the courts and in jail. Plotz refused Kaufman's request, pointing out that, after all, Isaac had Kaufman to explain the proceedings to him and to protect his interests. Kaufman, unprepared to enter the plea agreement, asked for a continuance, and Plotz reluctantly reset Grimes's preliminary hearing for May 29.

Simon Sue's first appearance before Judge Plotz, to hear which charges he faced, had come and gone. Sheriff's deputies searched the courtroom and scanned visitors with hand-held metal detectors before Sue was brought in. Outside, armed guards stood alert, their guns raised to the sky. Simon Sue appeared in a black-and-white-striped jail uniform, his hands and feet shackled. Plotz set his preliminary hearing for May 30. Jenny Vandresar, in tears, told the press after seeing Simon for the first time, "Everybody's lives are touched or ruined by this. My son won't go to the prom. He won't get married."

May 29 arrived and, with it, news that Isaac Grimes's preliminary hearing wouldn't be taking place. Reporters circled the just-greening lawn of the Park County Courthouse, inhaling charred fumes and dodging soggy piles of refuse. In the predawn hours, a fire had gutted the half of the Park County Courthouse that housed the county clerk's office. Investigators said the fire appeared to be the result of arson. Smoke had spread throughout the building, making the courtrooms uninhabitable until they could be cleaned and ventilated. A sheriff's office representative declined to say whether the fire might be linked to the high-profile murder case in which a plea was expected to be heard that day.

The courthouse would be closed indefinitely. Simon Sue's May 30 hearing was also aborted because of the courthouse fire,

Isaac Grimes passed his sixteenth birthday in the Park County Jail. Security was high, the jailers hypervigilant, wondering if the fire at the courthouse might be related to the constant rumor of threats that circled the jail.

For his birthday, Isaac received a letter from his parents with drawings from his little brothers. The boy who'd grown up helping his father fix vintage Land Cruisers in the driveway of his Colorado Springs home passed his day reading John Grisham's *Pelican Brief* and starting Dickens's *A Tale of Two Cities*, instead of getting a driver's license, the rite of passage that defined freedom in the West, where the road from the city to the mountains led to adventure and autonomy, a sure pathway to manhood.

CHAPTER 15

With the greening of Colorado in late May comes euphoria, preceded by eight months of drab brown foliage, indoor isolation, and volatile weather. In the Old North End of Colorado Springs, high school and college girls sunbathe on rooftops, and Frisbees fly across lawns as the veil of winter is lifted.

In the mountains, frozen riverbanks crumble and caddis flies hover over the rippling surfaces of clear, flowing waters. Meadows surrounding South Park are speckled with early-summer wildflowers, and buffalo grass prairies turn silvery sage.

As Palmer High School's senior class planned graduation festivities without their classmates Glen Urban and Simon Sue, buzz around the school turned to Simon's senior statement, published in the yearbook released during the last week of school, now rotating through the hallways collecting autographs declaring eternal love and admiration.

Back in November, seniors had been asked to submit their statements. Most had posted sentimental song lyrics, love poems, or clever quotes by famous authors. Simon Sue, however, had composed his own and casually submitted it to the yearbook office. The published statement read:

> To annihilate you is of no gain, but to keep you is of no profit.
>
> —Simonus Sueus

Principal Jackie Provenzano was shocked to find Simon's nasty jab in the yearbook just a month after his arrest. "It is not a prank," Provenzano told reporters. "It really is chilling in the context of everything else that happened. It certainly is."

The same day that Simon Sue's biting senior statement was published in the local daily newspaper, a front-page photo showed a fourteen-year-old girl, eyes closed, fervently praying into a microphone across from Palmer High School at Acacia Park. The annual Soldiers for Jesus March filled downtown streets with praying and singing evangelicals, united for a day of support for single-parent families. A Springs woman, single mother of five children, won a new car in a drawing at the end of the day.

•◆•

As Isaac Grimes awaited his arraignment before Judge Plotz in Fairplay, when he would presumably plead guilty according to the agreement hacked out by Shaun Kaufman and the prosecutors, his parents decided that Isaac's defense attorney was too unpredictable and too eager to plea-bargain. The Grimeses fired Kaufman in a letter: "We feel that a more communicative type of representation is needed in order to seek what's in the best interest for Isaac. Not only for now but also for the future. We have chosen to take a different path. Your services are no longer needed on Isaac's behalf or ours, effective immediately."

Kaufman expressed public dismay at the decision, saying he didn't know why he had been dismissed and hadn't had a chance to speak to Isaac about it. He hoped the change in counsel wouldn't affect the plea agreement. "When you're looking at three consecutive life sentences you get very few choices," he said, referring to the penalties Isaac would face if found guilty of murder by a jury.

The message was clear: Donna and Robin Grimes wanted to save more than their son's arm. They wanted him intact. They wanted a new and active defense for their son, who they believed had already lost enough of himself through the manipulation, coercion, and threats of Simon Sue over the past year.

Public Defender J. B. Katz of Breckenridge was reappointed as Isaac's attorney. Katz was a young woman with the muscular calves, casual gait, and practical wardrobe of an outdoor enthusiast. She immediately told Judge Plotz she would need to delay Isaac's arraignment in order to familiarize herself with the plea deal.

The "different path" Robin and Donna Grimes had decided to take on Isaac's behalf also involved the support of a Colorado Springs minister, Promise Lee, a charismatic former convict, an African American who'd turned his life around and dedicated it to bettering a working-class neighborhood in the city. The Grimeses had heard about Lee's Relevant Word Ministries and felt that because Pastor Lee had also been convicted of murder at the tender age of fifteen (Lee and two other teens had been convicted in 1974 in the death of a Fort Carson soldier) and had spent time in prison as a youth, he might be able to counsel Isaac in ways that they could not.

Never one to shy away from press coverage, Lee immediately let reporters know that he was involved in the Grimes case and believed Isaac was involved in a satanic cult. The handsome, sharply dressed minister identified himself as Isaac's spiritual adviser and told reporters he didn't want to jeopardize Isaac's case by revealing too much, but he warned them of surprises to come.

In a *Denver Post* interview, Lee announced, "There was some brainwashing and mind-control techniques being used over the past year within the group. Isaac, as the youngest in the group and the newest recruit, found himself being the victim." Lee urged the public to understand that there was potential for rehabilitation here, that Isaac was not "a throwaway kid."

Holding himself up as an example of someone who'd been rehabilitated and had returned to society as a valuable contributing member, Lee said that during his trial psychologists had recommended he be committed to the state mental hospital and treated with Thorazine. "The psychologist said I would never be a productive member of society," he urged. "Thank God for my attorney, who fought to make sure that didn't happen."

Lee was careful not to diminish the seriousness of Isaac's crime and to be sensitive to the victims' family members, but he urged those involved to understand that Isaac was a child "in every sense of the word," a child who had got caught up in a bad group of kids.

"We've got to look at each case individually," said Pastor Lee, who was known to have confronted drug dealers and crack house operators on his neighborhood's streets. "We can't just say that every kid who commits a certain level of crime should be tried as an adult. This is a wake-up call for all parents and for schoolteachers, counselors, staff, and other kids. This could very easily be your own kids. Never say this can't happen to your family because that's the exact same thing the Grimeses once said."

The Grimeses and advocates for Isaac could not change the jurisdiction of his case nor his being tried as an adult, but they could urge the judge, through public pressure, to consider his youth as a mitigating factor in his crime, and to have mercy when he laid down a sentence for the boy, sending him to adult prison.

Letters of support for Isaac Grimes began to flow to the district attorney's office and to Judge Plotz from friends of the family, church members, and neighbors. The family's minister, Dr. Keith Hedstrom of Ascension Lutheran Church in Colorado Springs, someone who'd known Isaac since the boy was three, and someone who had worked in juvenile corrections in the past, appealed to Plotz.

"I have some issues with the process of determining whether or not a juvenile is adjudicated as an adult," said Hedstrom. "At present, it's up to one individual, the prosecutor. I have a problem with the person doing the investigating making that kind of decision. Isaac is stuck in a county jail with no access to education, to counseling or any of the things that would be available to him if he were incarcerated as a juvenile." Hedstrom argued that age and cognitive ability should be considered in the evaluation of all crimes.

In a letter to DA Ed Rodgers, Hedstrom called Grimes "intelligent, compassionate and [possessing] a willing nature to do good. . . . Unfortunately these are the very traits in an adolescent child that can be manipulated and twisted for evil intent. Isaac is a kid who got caught up in something evil and sinister and did not have the maturity or wisdom to find a way out."

•◆•

The long summer days passed, and river rafting and mountain biking replaced skiing as the recreation du jour. Travelers passing through Fairplay sported kayaks and canoes mounted atop their recreational vehicles. Jon Matheny passed his eighteenth birthday in the Park County Jail, dawdling through the long days, illustrating letters to his mom and Heidi with elaborate cartoon figure drawings.

Simon Sue's attorney announced that Simon would petition the court to be moved to another jail because he couldn't practice his religion, presumably Hindu, at Park County. Jailers remained hyperalert to potential security breaches at the jail and kept the boys inside for fear, whether real or imagined, of sniper attacks on the outside yard. Sue said he needed to see the sun to pray.

Isaac Grimes wrote letters to his family asking for a pirate ship model to help him pass the hours of isolation and inactivity. In one letter, Isaac wrote, "I hate this place. I wish I'd get shot. Then I'd be out of this shitty mess. If I do, don't be sad."

Isaac went on to outline in detail how he'd like to be buried—in a plain particleboard box, with warm socks on, no shoes. He'd like his favorite Bible verse recited, from the Book of Job: "The Lord hath given, the Lord hath taken away. Blessed be the name of the Lord."

Isaac told his mother not to worry about him talking "about all this morbid shit" but said he needed to let someone know his wishes, "or else if I die you might give them shoes to put on me or something like that. Hey, I'm trying to lighten the mood."

•◆•

Investigators, meanwhile, continued to interview potential witnesses and former friends who could help them learn more about Sue.

A nineteen-year-old Springs man named John called D. J. Hannigan of the DA's investigators' office in late June, saying he had seen the newspaper account of Simon's arrest and "it blew me away."

John admitted he'd had his own brushes with the law for computer hacking as a juvenile, and Hannigan noted he might not be a reliable witness. John had done two months in the Pueblo Youth Corrections Center and was sentenced to a year's probation and one thousand hours in community service. He had known Simon since the boys went to North Middle School together.

John was known to deal in surplus military goods, and Simon, a frequent customer, had bought mostly backpacks and flak jackets. Once, however, Simon had asked to buy a book he saw on John's bookshelf, Ragnar Benson's *Big Book of Homemade Weapons*.

"He had been asking me information on how to build a machine gun or how to build an explosive device like a Claymore mine or, basically, just how to build military-grade weapons from scratch," said John.

Though Simon hadn't said why he needed the information, he had been asking John about a mutual friend, "if he would be a good warrior and stuff like that." Simon, said John, really had his eye on that book. During an afternoon visit, John had walked out of his bedroom while Simon was there and had come back to find the book gone. John claimed that was the end of his friendship with Simon.

Isaac Grimes, yearbook photo, 2000.

Jon Matheny, yearbook photo, 2000.

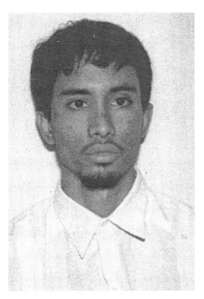

Simon Sue, yearbook photo, 2000.

Tony Dutcher standing on the
hillside near his grandparents'
home at Bear Trap Ranch.

(Courtesy of Charles Dutcher)

Students entering Palmer High School on March 9, the day after schoolmates Isaac Grimes and Jon Matheny were arrested and charged. *(Photo by Kent Trepton. Courtesy of the Colorado Springs Gazette)*

Carl Dutcher in full dress uniform, U.S. Army

(Courtesy of Charles Dutcher)

Carl and Joanna Dutcher, circa 1980s
(Courtesy of Charles Dutcher)

The trailer home of Carl and JoAnna Dutcher near Guffey. Tony Dutcher was slain at his campsite on a rocky ledge high above the house. *(Courtesy of the Colorado Springs Gazette)*

Isaac Grimes, in a bulletproof vest at his first court appearance, March 2001. To his left is Park County Sheriff Fred Wegener.

(Photo by Joseph Kotlowski. Courtesy of the Colorado Springs Gazette)

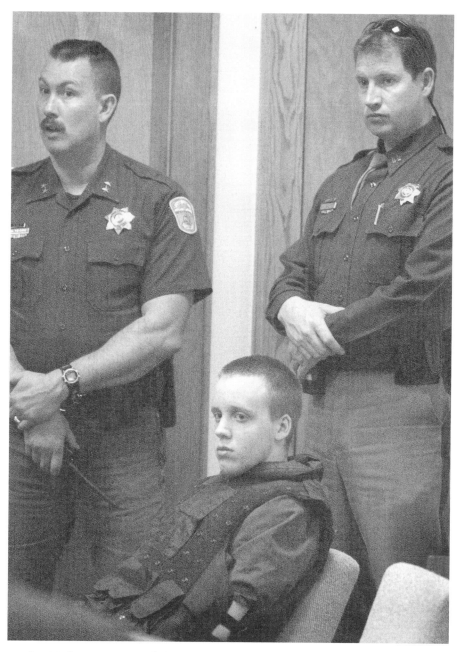

Jon Matheny's attorney failed to appear at the 17-year-old's first court hearing. Matheny faced multiple criminal charges in the Dutcher killings.

(Photo by Joseph Kotlowski. Courtesy of the Colorado Springs Gazette)

The temporary gravestone of the Dutchers, erected by
Charles Dutcher near the Dutcher trailer

(Photo by Kathryn Eastburn)

Hannigan asked if John was aware of the gun stash at the Sues' Caramillo Street house, and John said he'd been shown the weapons collection. He described a room where some fifteen broken-down, pump-action shotguns were lying around, and another room where Simon showed him a Tec-DC9, a semiautomatic handgun like the one used in the Columbine shootings, a cabinet full of Black Talon ammunition, and three "Kalashnikov-style" rifles. John claimed Simon had offered to rent the weapons if anyone John knew was interested.

Beyond purchasing surplus military goods, Simon had wanted to mine his computer expertise as well, said John.

"Simon was interested in different ways to make phone calls," he said, "you know, the extralegal ways. He had asked for some direction, and I gave him some URLs, which are just web directives where he can find that stuff. That's as far as I was willing to go 'cause that's the kind of stuff the Secret Service comes after you for." Simon, he said, had wanted to learn how to make long-distance telephone calls for free, and he had wanted to know how to beat an automatic number identification, the system 911 and the police use to trace a call.

"Toward the end of our relationship, I had been starting to get sort of weirded out about some of the things he was asking for," said John. "It's one thing to ask for, you know, a backpack, but it's another thing to ask for a list of places where you can get 34-0-0 fertilizer—imodium nitrate fertilizer, the kind of stuff they used in the Oklahoma City bombing. He was asking for suppliers' names. I didn't give it to him, but those were in the book I had, the one he stole. It had a list in the back of suppliers for that sort of thing."

Hannigan recorded the telephone conversation and patiently jotted notes. Had Simon ever mentioned his participation in military or police organizations? Had he ever become violent?

John described an incident during high school when Simon had been enraged by a "flamboyantly homosexual" Palmer student. According to John, Simon had organized a posse to go after the kid and a bunch of "drug-dealing types" in Acacia Park. In the end, only Simon and John had marched into the park, Simon armed with a can of pepper spray, a knife, and a bulletproof jacket. The fight had never happened.

John said Simon had been known for his big mouth and was always talking about how "the black people in Guyana were big problems for everybody." John said Simon had shared an interest in *The Turner Diaries,* the fictional manifesto of a white supremacist takeover of the world said to have inspired Oklahoma City bomber Timothy McVeigh, and he had enjoyed discussing military tactics.

"He [talked about] how one would go about getting people to, you know, as he put it, wake up and join with whatever cause you were trying to promote," said John. They had talked about deployment tactics, "like how to deploy a unit here and a unit there, basically just standard military talk."

"Did you ever know Simon to have power over other people?" asked Hannigan.

"Yeah," said John, "it seems like he was pretty good at bullshitting with a lot of people and telling them what they want to hear to get them to do what he wanted."

Investigators filed the taped interview away in the growing mountain of documents related to the Dutcher case.

• ◆ •

On July 23, Jonathan Matheny appeared before Judge Plotz, his new attorney, Elvin Gentry of Colorado Springs, at his side, and pleaded innocent to twenty-seven felony charges ranging from burglary to first-degree murder. Jon had been in the Park County Jail for nearly five months and still had not confessed to any crime or cooperated with officials in the prosecutions of any of his codefendants.

Investigators, placed on the stand by the prosecution, revealed more information about the OARA than had previously been leaked to the press, including damning evidence against Matheny linking him directly to Sue around the time of the murders. Phone records showed that in the days before and after the Dutchers' slaying, including the early morning of January 1, twenty-one phone calls had passed between Matheny's house and the house in Toronto where Simon Sue was visiting relatives.

Plotz set a trial date of December 3 and ordered that Jon Matheny continue to be held in the Park County Jail with no bond.

•◆•

Five days later, in the steamy early-morning hours of July 28, the Colorado Springs community was shocked by news that a woman driving in the wrong lane on I-25, whose car hit another head-on, killing its passenger, was Jennifer Vandresar, mother of Tony Dutcher, the fifteen-year-old boy murdered last New Year's Eve.

The news represented tragedy heaped on tragedy: another mother's son's life suddenly and violently eradicated by the distraught mother of a murdered son.

The police affidavit told the story: Vandresar said she drank three shots of peach schnapps before going to work at Déjà Vu Showgirls, a men's club on the city's south side, on Friday evening. Jenny got off work in the early morning hours and downed more liquor, in addition to popping a couple of pills she claimed one of the other girls had given her. She left the club and turned onto I-25 at South Academy Boulevard, driving north. She didn't realize she was on the wrong side of the freeway.

Two men in another car heading north in the correct lane saw Jenny's yellow Mustang, weaving from lane to lane as oncoming cars swerved to avoid it, and called 911 on a cell phone. The men continued to follow the Mustang for some five miles until it smashed head-on into an oncoming car. They pulled into the left median, hopped the concrete barrier, and stayed at the scene until police arrived.

Dead at the scene was Stuart Edwards, forty-two, driver of a silver Plymouth Colt, returning home from his night job as a press operator at Intermountain Color, a local print shop.

Vandresar was taken to Memorial Hospital and blood-tested for alcohol. The results showed that her blood alcohol content was over twice the legal limit. Officers noted that her speech was slurred and her gait was wobbly. An officer took her to the El Paso County Jail, where she waited until Monday morning before appearing before a judge in a video advisement from the jail. Judge Geoffrey DeWolfe set bail at ten thousand dollars. Jenny requested a public defender and the judge said one would be appointed.

She had one more request of the judge.

"Please," she said, "Send me to the state [mental] hospital."

"You'll have to take that up with your attorney," said Judge DeWolfe.

Before an emotional Jennifer Vandresar had been brought to the jail, she'd said something to one of the police officers at the scene that he would never forget.

"'I'm as bad as they are,'" Jenny said to Officer Robert Patterson.

"I assumed she meant she was as bad as the ones who took her son's life," he said.

Summer nights stretched ahead for another month. While Colorado Springs residents celebrated their respite from winter, inhaling the scents of blooming gardens and enjoying long moonlit nights, Jennifer Vandresar entered the darkest hours of her life beyond the night she had first learned she'd lost Tony.

• ◆ •

Up the mountain in the Park County Jail, secluded behind brick and concrete walls, the four members of the OARA could barely distinguish the change of seasons.

CHAPTER 16

The summer of 2001 was marked by stories of kids with guns.

In Colorado Springs, the trials of fifteen-year-old Andrew Medina, fifteen-year-old Derrick Miller, and seventeen-year-old Michael Brown for the killing of seventeen-year-old Kristopher Lohrmeyer outside a west side ice cream shop dominated the news. Two handguns stolen from homes in the neighborhood had been used in the crime, an attempted carjacking that turned into a fatal shooting. Miller and Brown pled guilty to second-degree murder and received sentences of seventy and seventy-five years. Medina, who claimed he'd only provided the guns to the real killers, was sentenced to life without parole in adult prison.

In Grand Junction, the newspaper reported that a thirteen-year-old boy had taken a .38-caliber handgun from atop his parents' dresser and shot his sister in the collarbone, allegedly because she wouldn't stop vacuuming while he was watching a movie.

Tom Mauser of Denver, father of Daniel, one of twelve students killed by gunmen Eric Harris and Dylan Klebold in the 1999 Columbine school shootings, traveled to Fairfax, Virginia, home of the National Rifle Association's headquarters, and got himself arrested for staging a sit-in on the organization's driveway and refusing to leave.

At issue was an unanswered letter Mauser had sent to the NRA's president, former movie star Charlton Heston, asking why the NRA had fought efforts to ban several assault weapons, including the TEC-DC9 that had been used to kill his son. Mauser had sent the letter to Heston three weeks after burying his son in 1999 and had never received a response. In Fairfax, he was sent to jail and held on a misdemeanor charge for an hour.

Mauser told the Colorado Springs *Gazette* in a telephone interview, "I think the questions are too hard for them. I think they don't like to face people who were victims of gun violence. I felt I had to make a statement."

In Fairplay, on the courthouse door a handwritten sign read, "Pardon our dust but we had a fire." A trailer parked on the courthouse lawn now housed the county clerk's office. Months after the fire, bricks lay strewn around blown-out windows at the south end of the building, the windowsills blackened. Men in cowboy hats, smoking cigarettes and kicking at gravel, lingered outside in the parking lot. Inside, visitors to the courtroom dabbed at their smoke-stung eyes. Well-dressed, suntanned attorneys with shiny bald spots, good shoes, and expensive glasses traded stories about their summer vacations.

Isaac Grimes's attorney J. B. Katz, now joined by Defense Attorney Kent Gray, filed again for more time to consider their client's plea bargain. Isaac Grimes entered the courtroom, his hair grown long and greasy, notably taller and skinnier than he'd been just three months prior. An armed sheriff's deputy accompanied him, while two others, also armed, stood guard at the room's two doors. As he crossed the courtroom to the defense attorneys' table, Isaac nodded soberly to his parents, seated in the gallery. His mother's face went slack, her eyes flashing helplessness, her hands clutched in her lap. Judge Plotz entered the courtroom, a white mustache and beard softening his ruddy face.

"We are not ready to enter a plea," announced Gray, citing the need for expert testing of his client, indicating that he and Katz would have more knowledge of what plea to enter after getting a psychologist's evaluation of

Isaac. Hushed whispers about a possible insanity plea filtered through the quiet, smoke-scented courtroom air.

Prosecutor David Thorson rose languidly, an ironic smile twisting his weathered face. He leaned heavily on the table and referred obliquely to Grimes's prosecution as "the case that won't go away," then told Plotz, "We're not happy, your honor, but we'll take no position." Thorson seemed always to be suppressing a smoker's cough.

Plotz asked Grimes and his attorneys if this meant they were waiving the right to speedy prosecution, and they agreed. He asked if a plea of not guilty by reason of insanity was inevitable if he granted the delay. Gray said there was no way to know. Plotz granted the continuance.

●◆●

September came and with it clear, cool nights anticipating the return of winter. Tall grasses along the South Platte turned golden, the river now barely a ditch, in need of snowmelt to replenish its flow. Elegant curved rows of mowed hay traversed the fields bordering Highway 24 on the perfect autumn day that marked the beginning of Simon Sue's preliminary hearing. Attorneys would argue whether there was sufficient evidence to hold Sue over for trial in a marathon session that, ultimately, would extend over seven months.

Nadia and Keith Sue sat surrounded by family members and neighbors. Kelly Ocasio, whose sons had bounced on a backyard trampoline with Simon countless times, had driven up from Colorado Springs to offer her support. Simon appeared thin, emaciated, and drawn, his black hair combed over. One aspect of his comportment set him apart from his three fellow defendants: He looked all the adults squarely in the eye.

His defense attorney, Ann Kaufman of Colorado Springs, came with a sterling pedigree as a courtroom lawyer. Formerly a public defender known for aggressively pursuing high-profile cases, Kaufman had built her private practice with the same intensity. Her strategy became apparent immediately: She would attempt to paint Isaac Grimes as an unreliable witness, and she would seek to discredit the investigation of the Dutcher murders, especially any part of it linking Simon with them.

But first, Kaufman needed to eradicate any evidence that supported the existence of the OARA with Simon at the helm. She requested that Exhibits 14 and 15, an organizational chart drawn by Grimes and the oath taken from Simon's bedroom, be removed. Plotz said he would rule on that issue later.

Leonard Post took the stand and was led by Kaufman through every inconsistency between Isaac Grimes's first confession on March 8 and his later confession to prosecutors on April 23. Where Isaac had said once that Jon forced him to eat at the Dutcher home, he denied that accusation later. Isaac had said once that Jon had killed Tony, and that had proved not to be true. Where Isaac had said he'd paid the OARA three thousand dollars, that was a likely exaggeration. Where Isaac had said his probation forbade him to possess weapons, he in fact had a hunting rifle in his bedroom and apparently had been in possession of the knife with which he confessed to killing Tony Dutcher.

Post lowered his bull head and quietly affirmed the inconsistencies Kaufman cited. She was efficient, articulate, aggressive, tenacious, and vaguely unpleasant. It felt as if a chainsaw had been unleashed in the normally placid courtroom.

Kaufman tried to implicate Donna Grimes, suggesting that she might have planted the idea of a fundamentalist terrorist organization in Isaac's head during the time she'd been left alone with him at the March 8 interrogation. She suggested that prosecutors had maintained a more than friendly relationship with the Grimes family for months after the initial arrests. Post looked flummoxed.

Isaac Grimes had told investigators that the punishment for violating probation was death, Kaufman pointed out. Yet he had reportedly violated probation before the Dutcher murders by failing to carry out orders for a raid.

"Was anyone in the Grimes or McCain (Donna's) family ever killed or threatened?" she asked Post.

"No," he grumbled.

Lunch break was called, and spectators and attorneys dispersed to various Fairplay burger stands and espresso joints for a quick bite. At a barbecue diner around the corner from the courthouse, hungry patrons sat at the window counter munching chopped-beef sandwiches, perusing old copies of *Gun Dog* magazine.

In the emptied courtroom, Simon chatted amiably with his courthouse guard throughout the break, talking about cars. He wanted to know when the sheriff's office auctioned off their old squad cars; he'd be interested in one.

The courtroom refilled, Plotz returned, and Ann Kaufman resumed. Shaun Kaufman (no relation), Isaac Grimes's former defense attorney, had turned out to be lying when he suggested that Rage Against the Machine was influential in the case, yes? Post nodded. She raised another suggestion that Shaun Kaufman had made during discovery, that the guns stolen from the Dutchers were being collected for a gunrunning organization with ties to Guyana's People's Progressive Party. Assistant DA Thorson himself had said the gun theory "didn't seem to amount to anything that seems to be truthful." Another nod from Post. Agent Rich Marianos of the Bureau of Alcohol, Tobacco, and Firearms (ATF), consulted by investigators in the case, had said "it was a ridiculous claim." Post nodded wearily.

He had recently visited Guyana on an investigative trip, arriving in the capital city of Georgetown. He'd visited Simon Sue's fiancée at her parents' home, a modern house in a relatively prosperous part of town. He'd visited Simon Sue Boulevard, a quiet, leafy street named after Simon's grandfather, an honored native philanthropist, an Indian of Brahmin caste. Post had been warned by local cops not to hang out on the waterfront at night. "You're a white American," he had been told. "They'll kill you for your money."

Post had talked with local police and military officials, looking for a link between Keith Sue, Simon's father, and any kind of organized crime ring or paramilitary group associated with the People's Progressive Party, and he had come up empty. Meanwhile, in the States, the DA's team, with assistance from the ATF, had also come up empty-handed in their quest for evidence linking Keith Sue to the OARA, gunrunning, or any criminal activity. Sue's extensive collection of guns appeared to have been legally purchased and registered. More and more Simon Sue's OARA appeared to Post and the others to be an elaborate hoax, regardless of what it might have seemed to Isaac Grimes, Glen Urban, and Jon Matheny.

Ann Kaufman shifted to the crime scene and enumerated a list of guns left behind in Carl Dutcher's bedroom following the murders: a Ruger 10/22 rifle, a 12-gauge shotgun, a Ruger .22 pistol, a Bulldog pistol, a revolver, a .22 rifle, a .410 shotgun, and others, ten weapons in the bedroom altogether. If this was a gunrunning ring, why had they not been stolen?

Kaufman persisted throughout the afternoon, questioning the veracity of various aspects of the investigation, pointing out missing information, diminishing the notion that the Sues' Caramillo Street house was the headquarters of a secret organization, describing how cluttered it was, and characterizing it as "a tough house to search but an easy house to hide things."

She called CBI Agent Dave Sadar to the stand and similarly picked apart his participation in the investigation. Sheriff's Detective Sergeant Bob Horn took the stand to face intense scrutiny of the gun and shell fragments considered evidence in the case, and the suggestion that they could have come from as many as six different weapons owned by Keith Sue. Horn admitted that the NHM90 that Grimes had claimed was the murder weapon, reportedly stolen from Gabe Melchor's house, had never been reported stolen by the Melchor family.

Kaufman shifted to the knife, continuing to raise questions about Isaac Grimes's credibility and culpability.

"Did investigators ask the Blade Shoppe owners in Colorado Springs, where the murder weapon was purchased, if Grimes collected knives or whether Robin Grimes, who had told Mr. Post he was a collector, collected knives? Could the Frontiersman knife have come from the Grimes home?" Horn said he couldn't answer that question.

Prosecutors countered with two presentations of evidence: first, a chart drawn by Investigator James Howell showing the flow of money from Isaac Grimes and Jon Matheny to Simon Sue's bank accounts.

Kaufman crossed: "Were any of those checks notated with the initials OARA?" The answer, of course, was no.

Phone records showing numerous calls between Matheny's house and a house in Toronto where Simon had presumably been staying over the Christmas holiday were presented again, as they had been at Jon Matheny's preliminary hearing. Plotz looked pained as he endured the tedious presentation again.

Then the prosecutors presented their strongest evidence: the videotaped interview of a nervous, shifty Simon Sue on March 8 at the Colorado Springs Police Department, denying any involvement with Isaac and Jon initially, then confessing to orchestrating the destruction of the murder weapons. The tape showed a kid eager to ingratiate himself with law enforcement officers, a kid who clearly knew more than he was saying. Plotz watched with intense interest.

Kaufman wrapped up by expressing extreme concern about Grimes's reliability as a witness. She wanted to put both him and Glen Urban on the stand to reinforce her claim that their stories didn't hold up, but, she told Plotz, she wouldn't be able to do that until after Urban's sentencing and Grimes's arraignment, when he would presumably enter a guilty plea. She requested that Simon's preliminary hearing be continued until after both boys' cases had been dispensed with. Plotz granted the motion.

•◆•

A week later, while Simon Sue was safely tucked back into the Park County Jail, his defense attorney having raised some serious questions about the case against him, the word *terrorist* suddenly and violently entered the American vocabulary and dominated the country's collective imagination.

On September 11, planes hijacked by terrorists slammed into the twin towers of the World Trade Center in New York City, fell to the ground in rural Pennsylvania, and crashed into the Pentagon in Washington, D.C. Nearly three thousand people were killed. Horrified commuters in the Mountain Time Zone stopped sipping their morning coffee and watched televised images on the morning news broadcasts of commercial jetliners flying into the twin towers, then, minutes later, the giant skyscrapers imploding and crumbling to the ground.

Glen Urban remembered Simon explaining to him how terrorist organizations worked, how cells were planted in geographically diverse locations, each with its own structure, hierarchy, and purpose. When Glen heard later about Al Qaeda's dispersed network across Pakistan, Afghanistan, Europe, and the Middle East—reportedly many cells but with no central hierarchy—he thought of Simon calmly explaining to him how such groups thrived and survived.

In Colorado Springs, U.S. Air Force fighter jets circled the skies around Cheyenne Mountain and the city's many military installations. Across America, parents pulled their children out of school and held them close. Grieving quickly became the national pastime.

Editorials exploring the minds of terrorists appeared, some of them thoughtful, many of them flashy diatribes designed to help readers feel they could better understand violent acts that defied rational thinking. Palestinian suicide bombers, one *Christian Science Monitor* writer observed, "are usually young men and women, carefully picked, brainwashed by handlers, and then watched each step of the way until they carry out the mission." The September 11 Islamic fundamentalists, on the other hand, who turned flying airplanes into bombs, were older, better educated, more established adults mesmerized and driven to action by extreme religious beliefs.

London clinical psychiatrist Raj Persaud, consulting with the BBC, drew criticism for writing about "the ease with which ordinary people can be recruited to engage in harmful acts against others." As an example, Persaud looked to Jim Jones, "reverend of San Francisco's People's Temple, [who] was able to 'program' his followers to commit suicide, or to kill one another on his command. More than 900 American citizens did so in the jungles of Guyana," Persaud noted.

Instead of demonizing all the individuals who carry out terrorist acts, or dropping bombs on them, Persaud suggested, we might be better advised to "focus on a better understanding of the mind-control tactics and strategies that might make even good people engage in evil deeds."

•◆•

As America absorbed the shock of the violent, unexpected attack, in September and October Isaac Grimes met for more than six hours in the Park County Jail with Dr. Frank Barron of Colorado Springs. He would determine Isaac's psychological status and functioning as a prisoner facing a long-term sentence, as an OARA recruit, and as Tony Dutcher's killer on New Year's Eve. A well-known forensic psychology expert in the Colorado district courts, Barron had previously been called to interview suspects in murder cases some eighty to one hundred times.

Separately from Isaac, Barron also interviewed Robin and Donna Grimes and Isaac's older sister.

Barron observed that the OARA, an organization presented to Isaac as opposed to drugs, alcohol, and premarital sex, affirmed his personally held values, "ones that tended to separate him somewhat from the mainstream of his peers and contributed to a social isolation in which he had school acquaintances, none of who represented after school or weekend friends." This isolated social condition dated back to elementary school. Isaac, said Barron, had looked forward to "spending more time away from home after school and on weekends with his new friend [Simon]."

When Isaac was first informed of the political, revolutionary goals of the OARA, he hadn't taken it seriously. Despite the constant display of weapons, he admitted, he had a hard time believing that something serious would come of his affiliation. But "military training intensified," Barron reported, "with shooting lessons, instructions on how to kill with a knife, repetitive weapons maintenance, monthly inspections and repetitive viewing of a particularly gruesome videotape, *Faces of Death*, apparently intended to desensitize Isaac to death."

As the training intensified, and as Isaac was placed on probation for failing to carry out missions ordered by Simon, threats of death as punishment for treason had become more frequent and more believable. During the time when Isaac was on probation, Barron observed, he "appears to have been subjected to various forms of psychological and physical abuse." Specifically, attempts had been made to alienate him from his religion and his church youth group—a group with which he had just begun to socialize—and he had been urged to separate from his family. This had taken the form of talking badly about them, engaging in "intentional disobedience," and "committing acts of theft and vandalism directly against his family." Isaac had confessed to slashing his sister's tires and stealing credit cards from the family, under orders from Simon.

"Threats against his life and that of his family became increasingly frequent and their description more graphic," reported Barron, "such as their being dismembered in front of him. His family would be killed were he to tell anyone, attempt to run away, commit suicide, or fail to provide the money ordered by Simon. Isaac reports feeling that there was no way out of this situation and no one to whom he could go for help."

Isaac had described being randomly kicked and punched, when he didn't expect it, and he had described one particularly bizarre incident to Barron, in which he had been forced to eat sugary snack cakes, energy drinks, and soda syrup until he vomited, then was forced to eat the vomit and continue eating those foods.

Isaac had recounted to Barron the months leading up to the murders, the botched plan, the failed attempts at finding the Dutcher home, and Simon's wrath at the inadequacy of his plan. He had told Barron the now familiar story of how the murders had occurred, the alibi had been set, the weapons destroyed, and, finally, how he had confessed.

Barron offered some clinical observations about his client, noting "his replies were most succinct when topics were being addressed that were potentially emotionally upsetting. At such times he became noticeably more tense and increasingly intellectualized and abstract in his response, in apparent defense against emotion, with which he is obviously uncomfortable." Barron had tested this observation during the second interview by using graphic terms to describe what had occurred during the course of the murders, requiring Isaac to do the same. "At that point, his intellectualized distance from the experience rapidly evaporated and he dissolved into tears, sobbing his regret for what had happened to Tony Dutcher and his grandparents."

Isaac was a kid, Barron observed, who had maintained psychological and interpersonal distance from everyone except his family throughout childhood, a circumstance rendering him devoid of the social skills appropriate to his age "at virtually all phases of his development."

Barron noted significant evidence of frequent experiences of mild to moderate depression throughout Isaac's childhood and into the present, enough to justify a diagnosis of dysthymic disorder or chronic low-level depression. "Since the Dutchers' deaths, according to Isaac, he did not like himself, what he did, or the world in general," wrote Barron. "As a result he has episodically entertained suicidal ideation."

Barron went on to observe significant symptomatology of post-traumatic stress disorder (PTSD) in his client: repetitive nightmares about the Dutchers' deaths and of his family being killed, intrusive daytime thoughts, visual images of the murders, diminished ability to concentrate, and excessive startle response. "Given his long-term psychological vulnerability and limited emotional development," Barron concluded, "it is likely that the ultimate impact of this trauma will be to adversely effect [Isaac's] mental health and increase the risk of psychotic decompensation."

"Psychologically, [Isaac] appears to have been 'made to order' for his role in the offense . . . ," wrote Barron. At the same time, he observed, the evaluation was notable for what it did not find: no indication of a major mental disorder; no evidence of suppressed hostility and rage with a potential for acting out in aggressive behavior; no indication of psychopathy or absence of empathy toward others—in other words, no finding suggesting that Isaac would have been a danger to society and a risk to harm others.

"Obviously, his psychological characteristics would not have predicted that he would kill, but circumstances that apparently overwhelmed him and limitations in his adaptive coping abilities combined to produce just such a result," said Barron. "Given the fact that three people have been murdered, it is likely to seem odd that this examiner currently finds no basis to conclude that Isaac represents a threat to the community or is at risk to harm others in the future. However, this statement does represent the opinion of this examiner based upon a consideration of all available data."

Barron emphasized the significant severity of Isaac's apparent PTSD, which, without treatment, could become chronic, with a potentially debilitating impact on his mental health. "It is of concern that, given the limited mental health resources with the Colorado Department of Corrections, these needs may go unaddressed within that setting," he concluded.

•◆•

It was October now, not quite full-fledged winter, the rocky hillsides just beginning to frost over with snow. Clear skies gave way to thick plumes of moisture-laden clouds building to the west.

An announcement in the October 12 *Gazette* brought one small chapter in the strange case of the Dutcher murders to a close. "High-Profile Lawyer in Springs Barred from Practicing," the headline read. The Colorado Supreme Court Attorney Regulation System had placed Shaun Kaufman, Isaac Grimes's former defense attorney, on inactive disability status. The reasons for Kaufman's demotion were not revealed, but the state rule was clear: "When an attorney is unable to competently fulfill her or his professional responsibilities, because of physical, mental or emotional infirmity or illness, including addiction to drugs or intoxicants, the attorney shall be transferred to disability inactive status."

Rumors had circulated throughout Colorado Springs's legal community regarding Kaufman's unusual, sometimes bizarre, conduct in the courtroom and out. In the Grimes case, it was noted, he had revealed to the press a plea agreement for his client before it had been presented in court, a violation of attorney conduct according to Prosecutor Kathy Eberling.

Summer had passed and Colorado's notoriously brief autumn had breezed by with a quick golden nod. As winter approached, Judge Plotz's patience waned, and continuances were exhausted. Prosecutors and defense attorneys in the Dutcher murder cases geared up for action in at least two of the cases. Once Grimes and Urban entered pleas and were sentenced, they could testify freely to Judge Plotz about the activities of the OARA and their codefendants, Simon Sue and Jon Matheny. Whether their testimonies would hinder or help the prosecutors' cases remained to be seen.

Jennifer Vandresar, awaiting trial for vehicular homicide, dreaded the upcoming season of Halloween, Thanksgiving, and Christmas, bright spots in her life before Tony's death. Charles Dutcher, frustrated by the snail's pace of the court cases and by the slow disposition of his parents' estate, looked toward Bear Trap Ranch and yearned for the time when he would be able to leave the world behind and relocate to the mountain, where he was sure he would be better able to remember his lost family.

At Palmer High School, a new school year was in full swing, the absence of two rising juniors was barely noticed, and the events of September 11 cast a scary shadow over the normally carefree nature of first semester. Days grew short and months stretched long as the first anniversary of the deaths of Carl, JoAnna, and Tony Dutcher approached, a hole in the universe that would never be filled despite all the attempts to explain it, revisit it, and build a semblance of justice around it.

In absence there was no reason, just a void, silver and cold as a wet granite boulder on an abandoned hillside.

CHAPTER 17

In the autumn and early winter of 2001, investigators continued to line up potential witnesses who could help characterize Simon Sue as the leader of a secret paramilitary organization with ties, imaginary or real, to Guyana. A Young Colorado Springs man named Mike told Investigator D. J. Hannigan in October that he'd known Simon throughout high school and that they'd talked a lot together, especially in the Latin class in which Simon had first met both Isaac Grimes and Tony Dutcher.

"I didn't really like him but he always seemed to want to be my friend," said Mike. He described Simon as a pest with a lot of far-fetched stories: of being a policeman in Guyana, arresting people and throwing them in the back of a pickup truck; of being a soldier, a member of special ops ready to carry out missions. Mike said Simon had told him he'd received military training in Guyana, had told him about being attacked by a guy with a butcher knife in Guyana, had told him about the time he'd attacked a drug dealer in Guyana because the man was exposing Simon's girlfriend to his sordid lifestyle.

Simon, reported Mike, had said his family held high-up political and military positions in Guyana and that he had money—opening his wallet and flashing two hundred dollars—weapons, and connections to get Mike anything he wanted, including a job.

Mike told Hannigan he'd watched Simon, Isaac, and Tony Dutcher looking over "military-type" magazines in the back of the Latin class they shared. He said Simon had been interested in guerrilla activities in many different countries but had paid special attention to the political movement and the rise and fall of dictators and leaders in Guyana and Africa. Mike thought Simon advocated a dictatorship and a police state as the most effective form of government and said Simon had also been interested in urban warfare. He recalled that Simon had mentioned a mentor in Guyana, someone he looked up to, and was depressed one day after he'd learned that his mentor had been assassinated. Simon had brought a Guyanese flag to school, said Mike, and had said he was going to petition the embassy to fly the flag in respect for his mentor, a "great man who had helped Guyana."

Simon, said Mike, believed in mixed-race marriages, boasting that he was the mixture of different races. He also boasted that he had several girlfriends in Guyana, a claim Mike doubted.

Mike remembered seeing Simon at school the day after the Columbine High School attacks.

"Simon said if that happened at Palmer, he'd go home, grab his guns and come back and help," said Mike, "but I didn't know exactly what he meant."

After concluding his interview with Mike, Hannigan visited Gabe Melchor, Simon's former friend whose home had twice been burglarized by members of the OARA. Hannigan showed Melchor two gunstocks recovered from the Sue home in the Dutcher case, asking if Gabe could identify them. One SKS stock was identified as being "most like" one that had been stolen from Gabe's home, but the identification was not definitive.

Of equal interest to Hannigan, given what he'd just heard from Mike, were two photos handed over to him by Gabe: one of him posing with Janet Jagan, president of Guyana; the other of him with Michael Shree Chan, late Minister of Trade, Tourism, and Industry of the Republic of Guyana (Chan had died of cancer in January, 2000). Both photos had been taken during the summer of 1999, when Melchor had traveled to Guyana with Simon.

• ◆ •

The tiny South American country, land of rain forest and waterfalls, bordered by Brazil, Venezuela, Suriname, and the Atlantic Ocean, had become more and more interesting to prosecutors as they pursued their case against Sue. Leonard Post had visited Guyana seeking information that might link Keith Sue to the OARA or validate Simon's claims that the organization had ties to Guyana's governing political party, but he had found no evidence of either. Still, Simon's professed allegiance to the country and his use of his Guyanan ties to impress his recruits remained intriguing.

A rudimentary look at the country's history revealed a mixed-race population that included native Amerindians, blacks descended from freed African slaves, East Indians descended from indentured servants brought over to work on sugar plantations during the nineteenth century, and a smattering of descendants of Chinese brought over for the same purpose. A British colony until 1966, independent Guyana had been heavily influenced by covert actions of the CIA, the U.S. State Department, and the British government during the 1970s, propping up the People's National Congress, a party predominantly representing African Guyanese, with Prime Minister Forbes Burnham at the helm.

The U.S.- and British-backed PNC had ousted Guyana's first freely elected minister, Cheddi Jagan, head of the Marxist-leaning People's Progressive Party, which primarily represented Guyanans of Indian ancestry. Burnham had remained at the helm of government until his death in 1985, and the PNC had maintained power until 1992, when Jagan was once again elected and the PPP seized power. Jagan had been president for five years, until his death, and had been succeeded by his wife, Janet Jagan, whose legitimacy was protested by the PNC. A state of emergency had been declared in 1998 after riots spread across the country protesting the PPP. Jagan was only in office for two years and had been succeeded in late 1999 by PPP minister Bharrat Jagdeo.

The rift between African and Indian Guyanans remained as the country uneasily entered the twenty-first century, attempting to establish a place in the global economy, promoting tourism and trade while struggling with basic infrastructure and services like medical care.

Meanwhile, Guyana was plagued by a continuous brain- and dollar-drain as Guyanans seeking a better life fled the country in droves, emigrating to the United States and Canada. The number of Guyanans relocated to North American had reached a half million at the turn of the twenty-first century, while at home the population was only 750,000.

Violence had colored Guyana's contemporary history, most notably in two separate incidents: race riots in 1964 that left thousands dead, injured, and homeless, and the 1978 mass-murder–suicide at Jonestown, a compound settled by messianic American spiritual leader Jim Jones, which had left more than nine hundred transplanted Americans dead.

An Indiana native who had been a charismatic evangelical preacher as a very young man, Jones had traveled to Brazil to build a mission in the early 1960s, establishing relationships with CIA insiders and government leaders before returning to the States. In Ukiah, California, Jones organized the People's Temple, a group that, on the surface, embraced utopian notions of racial harmony and communal living but soon was scrutinized and accused of being a cult that existed to fill Jones's international bank accounts and build his insatiable ego. Among the members of the People's Temple were a majority of disaffected African Americans, many women and children, and a significant number of elderly, whose social security and pension checks were routinely turned over to Jones.

Under attack in the U.S. press, more than one thousand members of the People's Temple relocated in 1974 to a compound in northwest Guyana, following Jim Jones in mind, body, and spirit. A visit by U.S. Congressman Leo Ryan of California and a group of accompanying journalists in November 1978, to look into reports of abuse, turned bloody when a cadre of Jones's followers tracked the Ryan contingent from the compound to an airfield and opened fire on them just as they were preparing to leave. Ryan and four others died, and nine were seriously injured.

Jones, paranoid and reportedly drug-addled, announced to his followers at the compound that their dream had ended, inviting them to come forward and drink from a vat of cyanide-laced Kool-Aid. Many did so voluntarily, and an unknown number of others were force-fed the fatal fluid or killed in other ways. Jones died from a bullet to the head. Ultimately, more than nine hundred dead bodies were counted as the corpses rapidly decomposed in the intense South American heat.

Guyanan government spokespersons were quick to deny any involvement with the cult or the compound, though conspiracy theories multiplied in the decades following the catastrophe: Jones was in cahoots with PNC leadership that had turned away from America toward Soviet partnership and sponsorship; Jonestown was a part of CIA mind control experiments designed to control populations for cheap labor; Jonestown had been established to create a buffer zone on the Guyana-Venezuela border that would be impervious, because the Venezuelans would be reluctant to attack Americans.

Whatever happened there, whether utopian or dystopian, the powerful force of Jim Jones's cultic leadership could not be denied, and Guyana, well off the radar of most of the world, was ripe for such an experiment. Indeed, Jones was not the first American fugitive to establish his power in Guyana. In 1972, David Hill of Cleveland, on the run from the law after he was convicted of corporate blackmail, was granted asylum in Guyana and changed his name to Rabbi Edward Emmanuel Washington. In short order, Hill established the House of Israel, a cultic, quasi-religious organization that recruited hundreds of Afro-Guyanese members. The House of Israel allied with the PNC, and its members were repeatedly involved in violent activities against the PPP.

Simon Sue's loyalty to the PPP was simple and straightforward. Party leaders were apparently Sue family friends, and Simon's mother, Nadia, was of Indian descent. More complicated were the varied cultural and racial in-fluences of his Guyana connection, as confused and confusing, violent and erratic, as the country's volatile history. Whether Simon was fascinated with Jim Jones to any serious degree was not established, but a small piece of evi-dence indicated that, at the very least, he understood the power of the Jones legacy.

In his computer applications class, the last semester of his senior year, Simon designed promotional materials—business cards, a flyer, and a busi-ness letter with logo—for a fictional business: Jim Jones Summer Camp, lo-cated in Jonestown, West Coast Essequibo, Guyana, an "alternative foreign exchange program for minor delinquents that cannot assimilate into soci-ety," designed to develop "mentally fit children." The proprietor of Jim Jones Summer Camp was identified as Reverend Simon Sue. Camp activities would include outdoor recreational activities and an educational curriculum emphasizing fiscal theory, cadre development, Marxist theory, political re-form, and revolution.

It seemed like an insider joke and earned some chuckles. Another assign-ment for the same class, a brief autobiography, echoed the geographic and cultural split in Simon's personality. The final paragraph read, "In the next four to eight years, I plan on going to college . . . and during that period also marrying and building a family. I plan on majoring in Spanish, Political Sci-ence and Criminal Justice. I am not sure if I want to settle down in Col-orado, because I have seen that most people that have never traveled outside Colorado end up dying here. I hope to God that I don't die in this cursed place."

•◆•

In late October 2001, Isaac Grimes climbed into a squad car with sheriff's deputies and was transported from the Park County Jail to the Fremont County Jail in Canon City. The route to Canon City, down Colorado State Highway 9, passed Hartsel, then the turnoff to Guffey. The last remaining yellow aspen leaves trembled at the ends of their branches. The road wound past boulder fields and pine forests, past occasional homes, and through long stretches of national forest before cresting above Canon City.

In reverse, this was the route Jon Matheny and Isaac had taken to the Dutcher home on New Year's Eve ten months ago.

Canon City, dusty and brown, is a city of about fifty thousand citizens, many of them employed in one capacity or another by the Colorado Department of Corrections. Home to several state penitentiaries, Canon City is also the site of the state prison museum, housed in the historic Territorial Prison, a stone fortress that the town had built itself around in the late 1800s. At the Colorado Territorial Prison Museum, visitors can see an actual gas chamber, hangman's nooses used in executions, and a variety of prison contraband and disciplinary tools. Thirty-two redecorated cells are outfitted with memorabilia dedicated to various crimes or to notorious criminals, including Alferd Packer, the famed Colorado cannibal who did time in Territorial, and Anton Wood, the boy who, at age eleven, became the youngest person ever convicted of murder in Colorado.

Eight miles south, the Royal Gorge, a spectacular geological site of massive rock cliffs carved out by the fast-flowing Arkansas River, is bordered by Buckskin Joe's Frontier Town, another tourist attraction, where spectators can ogle the dramatization of a shootout and capture, culminating in a simulated live hanging of the bad guys.

Appearing in Fremont County Court (Judge Plotz was overseeing a trial there and couldn't make it to Park County), Isaac Grimes and his attorneys planned to enter a guilty plea in exchange for future testimony against Jon Matheny and Simon Sue, as carved out in the plea bargain agreement with prosecutors.

Isaac entered the courtroom tall and lanky, dressed in a too-big Fremont County Jail blue jumpsuit, his hands cuffed to a chain around his thin waist. The courtroom was bright and cheery, outfitted with blue chairs, dried flower wreaths, and mountain-themed wall art. As his parents watched from the gallery, Isaac was asked to sign a series of papers and did so standing up, grasping a pen in one hand and steadying that hand with the other against the rattling of chains around his wrists.

Judge Plotz promptly explained the rights Isaac would waive in exchange for pleading guilty: the right to a trial by jury and the right to choose to remain silent or to testify on his own behalf. Plotz carefully explained what the instructions to a jury would be should Isaac waive the plea bargain and stand trial.

"Your plea must be voluntary," Plotz explained. "You must understand the charges and enter into the plea agreement with no coercion, of your own free will in a knowing and intelligent manner."

The charges had been reduced from the twenty-six Isaac had originally faced to three: one count of second-degree murder in the death of Tony Dutcher and two counts of conspiracy to commit murder in the deaths of Carl and JoAnna. The sentence could range from sixteen to forty-eight years on the first charge and ten to thirty-two on each of the second and third charges. The possible sum would be not less than thirty-two years and not more than seventy, as agreed on in the plea bargain.

"Do you understand?" asked Plotz.

Isaac nodded assertively.

"How do you plead?"

"Guilty," said Isaac, his voice strong and clear. Donna Grimes's head collapsed against her husband Rob's shoulder in the midst of the blue chairs. Her hands wiped at tears pouring down her face. She tried to calculate how old Isaac would be, how old she would be, in thirty-two years. Isaac would be older when he was released from prison than she was now.

Judge Plotz set a date for Isaac Grimes's sentencing, and court was dismissed.

On the sunny courthouse lawn, Charles Dutcher called the plea bargain "a necessary evil."

"We can't let the others think they can get away," he said, adding that he hoped Plotz would give Isaac the full seventy-year sentence. "I think they should all get capital punishment. When I look at them, I don't see children.

I see monsters. I see terrorists. If it was 150 years ago, these kids would be hanging from a tree."

Back home in Colorado Springs, Donna Grimes struggled to keep from crying in front of her two younger sons, and she reflected quietly on Isaac's fate.

"I'm real proud of him," she told a reporter over the phone. "He's walking through the depression and he says he wants to be able to atone for Tony's death. He knows he needs to do penance."

Sometimes, Donna said, Isaac speculated what life would be like when he was finally released from prison, knowing that he would be a black sheep in society. Sometimes, she said, he asked Pastor Hedstrom if God really forgives anything. He wondered aloud, sometimes, how to deal with his conscience and the terrible knowledge of what he had done.

•◆•

The week before Isaac Grimes entered a guilty plea, a brief hearing had been held in Fairplay, before Judge Plotz, to set the ground rules for Jon Matheny's trial, set for December 3. At issue was the *Faces of Death* video showing beheadings and footage of throat slashings. The prosecution requested permission to show jurors the video, saying they had proof that OARA members had watched it and other graphic videos to desensitize themselves to violence.

"These videos are what the OARA is all about," said Deputy DA Sean Paris. "This is what the OARA brought to Guffey on New Year's Eve."

Jon Matheny's defense attorney, Elvin Gentry, argued to ban the videos, saying the gory images would jeopardize Matheny's right to a fair trial.

"It is outlandish, gruesome, and extraordinarily prejudicial," said Gentry of *Faces of Death*. "No jury should have to watch it."

Plotz ruled in the prosecutors' favor, allowing the video to be shown in the courtroom. In a second decision, he agreed to move the trial to Salida from Fairplay, where the case had received heavy publicity.

"Fortunately for Park County," he said, "there are not a lot of murders. When there are murders, people note them."

A third issue was raised: whether the original videotaped interview of Jon Matheny at the Colorado Springs Police Department on March 8 could be entered as evidence. In the tapes, Matheny repeatedly denied involvement in the crimes, insisting he and Grimes had stayed in his house all night New Year's Eve and early New Year's Day, insisting he didn't know anything about the OARA and was not a member.

"I've never been to Guffey," Matheny had told investigators at the recorded session. "Isaac was at my house all night. I don't even know those people [the Dutchers]." Jon's mother, Bonnie, who had sat beside him throughout the ninety-minute interrogation, had broken down in tears at the end of the session when it became clear that Jon would be arrested. He had comforted her.

"It's OK, Mom," he said. "The truth always comes out in the end."

Judge Plotz, concerned that Matheny hadn't been properly informed of his Miranda rights—to remain silent, to have an attorney present—sided with the defense on this issue, ordering that the recorded testimony could not be used as evidence. The prosecutors immediately announced their intention to appeal the judge's decision in a higher court. Their case against Matheny relied almost completely on the testimony of others; catching him in a willing lie was central to their strategy.

Gentry requested that Matheny's trial be postponed until April to give him more time to prepare. Plotz granted the continuation.

In November, Glen Urban, who had pleaded guilty of accessory to murder for destroying the weapons used in the crimes, passed his nineteenth birthday in the Park County Jail, where he slept at night and was released into the community to work by day. His sentencing had been delayed while the court sought placement for him in a community corrections facility. Thanksgiving came and went as Glen worked at a Fairplay pizza parlor and his mother, Cathie Cumming, worried about his safety in the Park County Jail.

Tensions were high. Little had been settled in the courts, though hundreds of courtroom hours had passed and thousands of pages of discovery had been gathered in the nine months since the first two arrests.

Isaac Grimes gave his little brothers a new Lego set for Christmas. Donna Grimes remembered the conversation she'd had with him in the jail, just before he pleaded guilty.

"One day," said Donna, "Isaac said he'd been looking through the Lego catalog and had found what he wanted to give his brothers for Christmas. 'Here's what I want to give them,' Isaac told me, 'and here's what I want for myself so don't let them open it.

"'I didn't get to have any fun,' he told me. 'After I met Simon, I didn't get to have any fun.'"

CHAPTER 18

In the early months of 2002, as Isaac Grimes's sentencing approached, skiers bemoaned a drought that deprived them of fresh powder snow. Ice-packed slopes were no fun to slide down, and Colorado's powder was legend—a fine gossamer layer over dense snowpack that left fountains of white in its wake as two-legged adventurers plowed through it most winters. Abundant, frequent snow was regarded by Coloradans as their winter birthright.

But the drought, its seriousness just beginning to be realized, represented deeper problems than dissatisfaction at the slopes.

Reservoirs, fed by melting snowpack in the spring, stood barely half full across Colorado. Snowpack during the winter of 2002 measured just half the normal average. Hydrologists and meteorologists began issuing dire warnings. National forests, parks, and wilderness areas, accounting for nearly 36 percent of the state's acreage, were at high risk for massive tree die-offs. Stream flows, directly dependent on snowmelt runoff, might be so low in the summer that fish populations would be threatened. Ranchers would have to ship their cattle to other states for grazing if the drought continued, killing off grass supplies. Farmers, who depended on water diverted from creeks and rivers, might end up with dry irrigation ditches.

The state's lifeblood seemed to be drying up.

In Judge Kenneth Plotz's courtroom in January, attorneys complained loudly about the dearth of snow and compared bad skiing experiences before settling down to the business at hand: continuing Simon Sue's preliminary hearing one more time. Judge Plotz expressed growing frustration.

"I feel that if these cases [Grimes, Urban, Matheny, and Sue] continue to piggyback each other, we'll never complete any of them," he complained.

Ann Kaufman argued that she needed Grimes's and Urban's testimonies—she hoped to discredit them on the stand—and prosecutors wanted them, too, but for different reasons. Neither boy could testify until after he was sentenced and couldn't incriminate himself further.

Meanwhile, the question of motive in the murders was becoming murkier as more evidence was gathered and more testimony rendered. Grimes had told investigators that Sue wanted the Dutchers dead because they were racists. Sue had told investigators that Isaac and Jon wanted Tony dead because he was a drug dealer. Investigators had speculated that stealing weapons from the Dutchers' large cache was the group's principal goal, though only two guns had apparently been stolen from the home although many others were present.

Privately, others theorized: Donna Grimes believed that when Simon Sue recruited Isaac for the OARA, he had also tried to recruit Tony Dutcher but had been rejected, and Simon didn't take rejection well. Moreover, she believed, the murders had been in large part a test of loyalty for her son, a test that would bind him forever to Simon if he wanted to save his own life. Once Isaac and Jon had killed, and Simon was the only one who knew it, they would be his for good.

At the end of January, Plotz reluctantly agreed to reschedule the continuance of Simon Sue's preliminary hearing to March 19, a month after Urban's scheduled sentencing and a week following Grimes's sentencing. This, he warned, would be the last continuance he would grant.

In February, as Simon turned twenty in the Park County Jail and no snow fell in the Colorado mountains, the Grimes family, their neighbors, and friends again bombarded the judge and the DAs with letters of support for Isaac, begging mercy in the case.

Diana Lantz of Colorado Springs wrote to Judge Plotz:

> I think the timing of this particular case is especially important in light of the terrorist events that have taken place in our country recently. This entire situation is an example of exactly that kind of activity, perhaps on a smaller scale, but certainly the same. When a young, intelligent mind not yet close to being out of childhood can be targeted, brutalized and made to think he has no alternative but to do the evil deeds of others as he is told to do, it is indeed an act of terrorism. Just as President Bush recognizes that terrorism must be stopped by stopping those at the top, my prayer is that you will realize that there are others much more responsible for what Isaac did than Isaac himself. I am praying for you and for Isaac and for the difficult decision that has to be made in his sentencing.

Neighbor Scott Erickson wrote:

> Isaac Grimes was always a very quiet, polite, and respectful child. I hired him a couple times to mow my lawn and he has also helped me with various other small tasks. He has always done an excellent job and has always been eager to learn. . . . I had no idea that he was recently involved with such an evil "cult." . . . These people took advantage of Isaac's weakness, and chose him to do their dirty work for them. It angers me terribly to know that this could have happened to anyone, including one of my own children if they happened to be in the wrong place at the wrong time.

●◆●

On February 12, Glen Urban was sentenced with little fanfare. A few months earlier he'd pleaded guilty to lesser charges of accessory to murder for destroying the gun and the knife used in the Dutcher murders. His mother, Cathie Cumming, spoke on his behalf, urging the judge to consider Glen's full cooperation and to remember he had not injured or hurt anyone.

Plotz pointedly took issue with Cumming's defense of her son.

"What if his destruction of the evidence means that those who committed these crimes might go free?" he said, demanding that attention be paid to the seriousness of Glen's actions.

Glen was sentenced to two years in a community corrections facility, and until a suitable one could be located, he would remain in the Park County Jail. He would be in the custody of the court until his sentence was completed but would be able to work during the days, retiring to the jail at night.

Urban prepared himself for a few more months in the jail that had become his temporary home. He hadn't gotten along well with the jailers in Park County and basically thought they were a bunch of out-of-control gunslingers. Recently, he had been moved out of his isolated cell into the general population of illegal Mexican immigrants being held over until they were transported back to their homeland. Glen liked this arrangement better than being held in solitary, especially late at night, when the men quietly sang songs in Spanish to help themselves fall asleep. He couldn't understand the words but imagined they were about love or beautiful landscapes, sunsets, beaches, mothers' smiles. The guards coined a nickname for inmate Urban: the white prince of Hispanic land.

•◆•

The week before Isaac Grimes's sentencing, on a bitterly cold and windy day marking the first anniversary of his confession and arrest, Robin and Donna Grimes invited reporters into their home in central Colorado Springs. Holding hands and huddled close together at one end of a worn, lumpy sofa, they offered kitchen chairs to the small group gathered in a semicircle. Pastor Keith Hedstrom and Pastor Promise Lee stood in the corner, offering support to the family.

Donna and Rob explained that they couldn't talk about the details of the case, but they wanted to talk about Isaac, what kind of kid he was, what his life had been like in the months before his arrest, and what kind of punishment they thought would be fair.

A reporter asked how Isaac could have been involved in the OARA and in criminal activities without his parents knowing.

"Isaac did a lot of maneuvering and spent a lot of energy to keep this other life separate, and he did it well," said Rob. He explained that his son had believed the OARA was a large network with secret members embedded in police departments and the government. Rob suggested he didn't think law enforcement had taken the potential threat the OARA posed as seriously as they should.

"They told him he would be trained to be a recruiter, that a wife would be chosen for him. He was being trained to be a guerrilla," said Rob.

Donna told reporters the story of how Isaac had his braces taken off in February, before his confession, and the dentist had discovered the enamel was worn from most of his teeth. Months later, after he was arrested, Isaac had told his mother that he'd been throwing up every day for months.

Wind whistled through the front door and the picture window frame, rattling the small ranch-style house and flattening brown grass stubble in the front yard. Donna placed her hand on Rob's thigh as he strained to sit straighter.

"What kind of kid was Isaac before all this?" a reporter asked.

"This was a kid who, when he was six years old, built a scale model of the *Titanic*," said Donna, smiling. Rob nodded proudly.

"Before he met Simon, Isaac read a lot, he played Legos, he camped and went four-wheeling with his dad," said Rob. "He could interact with adults more easily than with his contemporaries. He liked hunting and fishing. Tony camped with us one time. He spent the night with us a lot for two years in junior high."

Two skinny little boys, Isaac's younger brothers, now five and seven, scampered across the far edge of the living room, casting mischievous glances toward their mother. She motioned them with a single finger toward the kitchen and raised the finger to her lips, issuing a silent shush.

"What did you think when you heard your son confess to Tony Dutcher's murder?" asked a reporter.

Donna looked at Rob and dabbed at the corner of her eye with a tissue.

"We couldn't believe we could hurt so bad and not die," she said. "We told him to tell the truth, tell them everything you know." Her mouth curved into an ironic smile. "That was our first mistake."

Rob grimaced. "We told him, 'Isaac, you lied to us!' He said it bothered him every single time but he couldn't do otherwise. He believed he was saving our lives. He told us he wanted to get out [of the OARA] the first summer, but they said he would have to commit suicide in the front yard, then the first family member that found him would be killed, too. Simon had a copy of our house keys. Isaac's bedroom window was broken." Rob shook his head and rubbed his eyes. The story was still as fantastic to him as it was to the group of reporters gathered in his living room. But Isaac's bedroom, now stripped of his belongings and painted a calming pink, still had a pipe, installed by Rob at Isaac's request, wedged in the window, a silent testament to his son's fear.

"Our premise is we want Isaac back," said Donna, seizing the interview and turning it toward the upcoming sentencing. "We're not afraid to have him back. We look at his prison time as a break in his time at home."

"It's like we've lost a member of our family but he's still alive," said Rob, thinking of Isaac in prison. "Some days I wake up and think this never happened, but it did. It's literally one day at a time."

Donna continued. "Our son was hijacked but he's still our son. Isaac is someone society doesn't have to be afraid of. He has a great amount of support from our church and our neighbors. He's a kid who respects truth and respects life. He understands he has to be punished for what he did. But we can't bring Tony back. Isaac's hand did it; his heart didn't do it, his hand did."

Silence followed as reporters stared at their notepads.

"We're hoping for an institution favorable to young prisoners where Isaac can get an education," said Donna. "We've heard good things about Buena

Vista Correctional Facility. Survival is going to be the name of the game for him in prison. I think it's reasonable to hope for the lowest sentence of thirty-two years. He could serve half of it; that would make him thirty-two when he's released."

Heads ducked quickly and pencils scribbled.

The group dispersed against the chaotic wind and the intense cold. Cars pulled away from the curb as Donna and Robin Grimes stood side by side in the picture window looking outward, arms pulled across their chests in tight hugs while two little boys' neatly crewcutted heads bounced up and down on either side of them.

•◆•

Early March, in the tiny town of Calhan, due east of Colorado Springs on the expansive, windblown eastern plains, a fourteen-year-old ninth-grade girl was expelled from school for tucking a .22-caliber pistol into her back- pack along with a box of bullets, and carrying them off the school bus into the school. Her intention was not known. Shooting was a popular pastime in Calhan, but this seemed, possibly, to be something different. She was ex- pelled from classes for a year.

•◆•

The Fairplay courtroom buzzed on March 12 as members and friends of the Dutcher and Vandresar families, and members and friends of the Grimes family, packed the wooden benches and chatted, awaiting the entry of Isaac Grimes and Judge Plotz. In the far back row, Jennifer Vandresar, released on bond and awaiting her own trial, sobbed quietly into a handkerchief as she watched Isaac, several inches taller than he had been a year ago, stride into the courtroom, dressed in a sweater and slacks, his hair cut and washed.

Judge Plotz invited her to the front of the courtroom. Standing there, a crumpled sheet of notebook paper in her trembling hand, eyes swollen, she looked like a teenager, petite and scared. The prosecutors had mounted photographs of Tony and of Carl and JoAnna, Exhibits 1 and 2, so that spectators could see them.

"My son spoke four languages," said Jenny. "He played Bach and Beethoven on the cello. He loved God, his mother, and video games."

She smiled weakly and continued. "The last time I saw him he was happy. He and I were reconciled." At that, she broke down and cried openly, wiping her nose, shoulders shaking.

She looked at Judge Plotz.

"I lost my son. I lost my life. I lost my mind," she said. Plotz knew the circumstances of Jenny's arrest for vehicular homicide. He nodded solemnly. He knew what she meant.

"Sometimes in sleep at night, I tell myself I must feel remorse," she said, struggling for the next words. "I accept [Isaac's] plea, but I call him Manson. I call him Hitler. Prevention is my plea. I will be in court in April to testify at Simon [Sue's] trial. I'm petrified of what Isaac, Jonathan, and Simon are capable of."

Jenny touched a pendant hanging from a chain around her neck.

"The only thing I have are the ashes of my son that I wear around my neck. I wish it was his heart because I know he took mine." With that she returned to her seat in the back row and all eyes followed her. She collapsed forward, burying her face in her hands, willing everyone to look away.

Judge Plotz invited the Dutcher family's comments. From Georgia, Ty Dutcher weighed in with a lengthy, rambling sermon over speaker telephone. Plotz urged him to wrap it up after about five minutes.

"I just want to tell the kid, Isaac, that I'm sorry God didn't get to him sooner."

Charles Dutcher strode forward next. Dressed in tight jeans, a leather jacket, and cowboy boots, his long straight hair flowing loose, he stared straight ahead at Plotz through dark aviator-style sunglasses. His deep, bass voice split the quiet air.

"Tony was my first-born son," he began, turning on his heel to glare at Isaac Grimes at the defense table. He resumed in a low growl: "He was the sunshine of our lives. He followed in his granddad's footsteps, studying self-defense and learning about the military. He was a learning machine. He was confident in his choices. I remember all the notes that kid stuffed in my pockets," he said, stopping to look down as if to capture a memory that had just emerged out of nowhere.

"I talked to Tony about his friends, and Isaac was definitely mad at him," he said, trying to offer something of substance that would impact Plotz's decision on how long a sentence to impose. "Isaac talked to Tony that night. He killed him in a cowardly manner, from behind."

Charles's voice gathered strength as he dealt his final volley: "Murder is murder whether you're young or old, whether it's three or two thousand people. Today's the day to show these kids, to send a message to kids that this is unacceptable."

As he turned to return to his seat, walking between the defense and prosecution tables, Charles mumbled something about a "dead kid," shaking his head. It was unclear to which kid he referred, Isaac or Tony.

A somewhat withered and shaken defense attorney, Kent Gray, stood up to open the defense's case for a merciful sentence. Slight and balding, Gray called Dr. Frank Barron, the licensed clinical psychologist who had evaluated Isaac months before, to the stand.

Barron might have come from central casting, his eyeglasses balanced low on the bridge of his nose, a Freud-ish beard jutting from his chin. Guided by Gray, he walked through his evaluation of Isaac Grimes's psychological state: inadequate development of social skills, immaturity, social isolation, inability to make decisions, social anxiety, no major mental disorder, no evidence of a tendency toward violence or rage, no indication of psychopathy or a criminal mind.

"How did he feel near the end of his affiliation with the OARA?" asked Gray.

"Terrified for his life and for the lives of family members," said Barron. "Simon was skilled in making him feel there was no way out, though he did resist somewhat."

"Was he suicidal?"

"He contemplated suicide before and after the murder of the Dutchers," said Barron. "He was told that no matter what he did the raid would occur spontaneously. He was told his family would be killed in gruesome ways if he didn't cooperate. His recounting to me was very consistent, and his feelings of trauma were consistent with the experiences he related."

Then Barron described post-traumatic stress disorder and Isaac's symptoms: decreased concentration, nightmares, excessive startle response. Many in the gallery—Jenny Vandresar, Charles Dutcher, Donna Grimes, Kathy Creech, and others—shared similar symptoms.

"Someone unable to feel remorse or empathy for others will not develop PTSD," said Barron.

"Did Isaac express remorse?" asked Gray.

"Yes," said Barron, adding that in his prior evaluations of people who had committed murder, it was extremely rare to find indications of empathy or remorse.

Prompted by Gray, Barron addressed the issue of a long-term prison sentence for Isaac Grimes, concluding that it would punish him for what he had done and that Isaac felt that was necessary; he knew he deserved serious punishment. In terms of protecting the community, however, a long-term sentence wasn't particularly useful. He predicted that without treatment for his depression and PTSD, a high likelihood in the Colorado Department of Corrections, Isaac would likely become excessively passive and possibly suicidal.

Barron related a telephone conversation he'd had with Dr. Richard Ofshe of Berkeley, California, a Pulitzer Prize–winning expert in coercion and mind control, following Ofshe's brief evaluation of Isaac Grimes. Dr. Ofshe, said Barron, felt that Isaac's portrayal of what had happened to him was believable, and that with the degree of threat and coercion involved, it seemed to him that even young adolescents with stronger constitutions could have been coerced by Simon to do his bidding.

The prosecution, represented by Assistant DA David Thorson, cross-examined Barron.

"Dr. Barron, you've said that Isaac Grimes was someone subject to outside influences," said Thorson. "We don't know what influences might affect him in the future. How can we predict how and by whom he might be influenced in the future, say, if he were paroled?"

Barron responded flatly. His tests were probably not useful as predictors of future behavior. He acknowledged that Isaac's having killed someone would be a factor in the court's consideration of parole.

Barron left the stand and Gray called Pastor Hedstrom, who characterized Isaac as he had in a letter to Plotz.

"I genuinely liked him and thought he had great potential," he said.

"Is Isaac grown up yet?" asked Gray.

"No," said the pastor, "he's still relatively immature, very idealistic and naive. He's not street-savvy. My sense is that some of the old Isaac is coming back. Where he was previously unable to express feelings, his capacity to feel is returning. He has extreme remorse. None of us are afraid of him doing anything like this again."

Promise Lee was called to the stand, where he was quite blunt about his prediction of Isaac's chances in adult prison. "Not to scare him, but he'll either end up somebody's girlfriend or dead," said the sharply dressed former inmate turned community activist, a small muscular man with a sculpted jaw and lively light brown eyes. Gray introduced him as someone who'd been honored by Vice President Al Gore for his work in criminal prevention programs and prison outreach.

Lee described visiting Isaac in jail to talk with him about taking ownership of his crime and accepting the consequences of his behavior.

"He was hearing voices, seeing figures in his cell, having nightmares and suicidal thoughts and concerns over the safety of his parents," said Lee.

"Still, he took full responsibility for his actions. He was extremely remorseful during our first visit, but he was told by attorneys not to talk about any of this. He talked about the prison time the crime would carry and said he didn't fear that but feared going to hell. He knew the crime was irreversible. He said he wanted to talk to the Dutchers to express his remorse and asked me if it would be superficial to say so in a letter. He was told not to do so. It was eating away at him that he couldn't go to them to ask for forgiveness."

Gray asked Lee what he regarded as personal assets for an inmate within the adult prison system.

"Being a tough guy and having a reputation as a tough guy," said Lee who remembered himself, while in prison, as a tough kid who feared nothing.

"What liabilities do you see in Isaac Grimes as a potential inmate?" asked Gray.

Lee looked at Isaac and carefully controlled the tone of his voice. "It's like putting a goldfish in a bowl of piranhas," he said. "He should be in protective custody because he's labeled as a snitch for confessing and testifying against the others."

"Look, prisons make these guys career criminals," said Lee. "Statistics show that. Isaac is not streetwise at all. Not to scare him, but I just don't know how long he'll live. He's already labeled as an informant. I got a letter recently from an inmate, an adult, who's been locked up since 1994 and has seen kids come through the system, relating the terrible things that have happened to them."

"What can the court do at this point?" asked Gray.

"Punishment is certainly warranted," said Lee. "But Isaac needs resources, schooling, trade training, and mental health care access, preferably at a facility aimed at youth."

Gray thanked Pastor Lee and called Robin Grimes to the stand. Rob didn't mince words and directed his message to Tony Dutcher's mother, not to Judge Plotz.

"It's all a bunch of crap," said the angered father. "I don't know what to think of today. I know my son has done a terrible thing. I cared for Tony. I took him camping. I treated him like a son. If I had my druthers, I'd have kicked [Isaac's] royal butt before any of this happened."

A little more softly, he added, "I know what Jenny was talking about. We've lived with the death threats and the fear. I'd like to say to Jenny that I can't imagine her pain; we only have our own pain. [Isaac's] a kid thinking with a kid's mind. But I believe he has a noble heart."

The floor was opened to concluding statements. Thorson went first for the prosecutors.

"Some of the witnesses here today have offered opinions that the defendant shouldn't be tried as an adult," he said. "Well, we're way past that. Second, the plea bargain we struck with the defendant takes into account his cooperation with law enforcement, his duress, and his status as a good kid. Those are the reasons we agreed to a plea bargain with a cap of seventy years."

Thorson gestured to the photos of Tony, Carl, and JoAnna Dutcher.

"I introduced photos of the victims, because sometimes we forget what was lost," he said. "I considered entering photos of Carl Dutcher lying in the hallway, of JoAnna in the bathroom riddled with bullets, of Tony Dutcher with his head nearly cut off."

"At issue," he said, turning toward the gallery, "is the brutality with which the defendant killed Tony. The autopsy showed he sawed back and forth." Thorson demonstrated a sawing motion with his hand against the loose skin of his own neck. "He severed the spinal cord, not just the spinal column."

"Given the seriousness of the crime, we recommend Isaac Grimes be considered for probation after serving sixty years," said Thorson. "Regarding protecting society, we've heard that Isaac, under not so unique circumstances, chose to do this. We all make choices every day about our welfare versus the welfare of others. Isaac wormed his way in that night. Essentially it was Tony who invited him. He deserves every nightmare he wakes up from; he deserves every year of seventy years."

Gray stood up to make his closing argument. He proceeded slowly, trying to defuse Thorson's vigorous physical demonstration.

"It's true that the choice has been taken away by the legislature, by the district attorneys, to prosecute Isaac Grimes as a juvenile. It's also true that it's easy for any of us to say, 'I could have said no.'"

Gray choked up. "He still was a fourteen-, fifteen-year-old boy when he was involved in the OARA. Our legislature has taken away the ability to have a defense of coercion. But Isaac Grimes faced a tougher decision than you do today, than I ever have. It's not uncommon for people to get involved in cults, in organizations because of their values, then distorted and manipulated. Isaac truly believed he was in that dangerous situation; Isaac *was* in that situation. There was a calculated, planned effort of coercion, of manipulation, combined with the ability to do it due to the presence of weapons."

"Simon Sue," Gray continued, "wore away Isaac's support system. He was told no matter who he went to, [Simon] would find out. He was told to disobey his family; he was told how to dress, where to sleep, where not to sleep. Tell them [about us], Simon said, and they're dead. Isaac was on probation: any mistake and he's dead."

From the far back of the courtroom, Jenny Vandresar whispered, "Poor kid."

"People are still taking these threats seriously," said Gray. "They're sitting in this courtroom in flak jackets. To this day, despite intensive investigation, nobody has been able to prove or disprove the existence of this organization."

Gray shifted his somewhat scattered focus to the sentence at hand.

"The life span of a snitch is less than seven years in prison," he said. "Yes, the court's obligation is to punish, but the court also has discretion to focus on the individual. It's kind of an odd situation today, Judge, for me to ask you to give my client thirty-two years in the hopes that it will save his life. It may not. This boy was coerced by a very sick, dangerous individual and his accomplice. They should be sentenced to seventy years. Isaac should be sentenced to thirty-two years."

Gray sat down next to Isaac at the defense table. Plotz asked Isaac if he had anything to say. The boy stood up. If anything, his comments echoed Thorson's more than Gray's.

"I won't ask for forgiveness, I don't deserve it," he said, looking down at his hands on the table in front of him, his voice shaky. "I deserve every nightmare. I'm sorry to my family for putting them through this, for letting them down. I'm sorry to the investigators, the lawyers, the DAs, the judge. I'm sorry to Charles Dutcher and Jenny Vandresar for causing them so much pain."

"I was never mad at Tony," said Isaac, rebutting Charles Dutcher's earlier comment. "Our drifting apart had nothing to do with the crime."

Isaac looked up at Judge Plotz.

"I can't change anything that has happened. I felt there was no way out of the situation. I thank God that I was caught and that this was stopped."

From the back of the courtroom, Jenny Vandresar's tear-choked voice called out, "Thank you. Thank you."

Plotz took a moment to compose himself, then addressed Isaac Grimes directly, his bushy eyebrows almost touching on his deeply furrowed forehead.

"When I became a judge, I never imagined I'd ever be witness to a situation this bizarre," he began. "The one crime Carl, JoAnna, and Tony Dutcher committed was to be connected to Isaac Grimes. I can't imagine the hurt their family must have to go through. It's hard to imagine, Isaac, that you, sitting before me, caused this. The hurt that you've caused is just unimaginable.

"You're not an adult but you're old enough to know, to be responsible," the judge continued. "My job is to weigh aggravating and mitigating factors to come up with a fair sentence. On the mitigation side, it's good you're young. And your testimony aided law enforcement. On the aggravating side, first, there's the manner in which the crime was carried out. It was heinous. Tony went to bed that night camping out with a friend, assured that he would wake up the next morning. It was a cold, calculated crime. Second, I don't fully buy into the theory that you were completely brainwashed by Simon Sue. You're too smart for that. Third, you killed a defenseless friend. More importantly, you live in a civilized society, and in a civilized society we have to take and accept responsibility for ourselves. You're beginning to take responsibility for your actions, but it's a little too late.

"You've destroyed yourself and it's very painful for me to sit here and watch that. The only good that can come from a crime like this is to prevent it from happening again.

"I sentence you to forty years plus five years' parole, and twenty years plus five parole, to be served consecutively, not concurrently. You'll receive credit for 369 days served, applied toward your total time."

Court dismissed swiftly, and the Grimes family and their supporters stood silently, staring at the front of the courtroom, where Isaac was being prepared to return to his cell in Fairplay. It was impossible to grasp the number that was beginning to take form in their heads. Sixty. Isaac would serve sixty years.

Jenny Vandresar stumbled from the courtroom sobbing, her face buried in her hands, avoiding reporters. Two women who'd been sitting near the back crossed over the center aisle, tapped Donna Grimes on the shoulder, and, one by one, hugged her deeply. One of them was Tony Dutcher's aunt, Jenny's sister, Kathy Creech. The other was Tony's grandmother, Jenny's mother, Jodie Sherer.

Outside, in the bright afternoon sun, Charles Dutcher spoke to reporters on the brown courthouse lawn. "These kids have just got to learn they've got to pay for their actions," he said.

His fury had not been tempered by the length of Isaac's sentence. It didn't bring back his son, his mother, or his father. He could only look forward to the day when Simon Sue and Jon Matheny received equally hefty or greater sentences.

Later that night, at home, Donna Grimes reflected on the day's events.

"Isaac was right," she told a reporter. "There really wasn't anyone he could go to. We were expecting him to serve time. We did not expect Judge Plotz to ignore the medical experts."

Donna said the evening had been tough. Her seven-year-old had met her at the door when she returned home from court, expecting her to be coming home with Isaac in tow.

"It doesn't matter how much information you bring forward. If the judge has made up his mind, the truth doesn't matter," she reflected sadly. "This whole case was built on Isaac telling the truth. And there are the prosecutors, the ones they're going to use as a star witness, calling our son a liar in the courtroom."

"We raise our kids to always tell the truth and be honest," Donna said. "We told Isaac to tell the investigators the whole truth. It was the stupidest thing we ever did."

In less than a week, Isaac would be called to the stand again, this time to face both Simon Sue's defense attorneys and the prosecutors as he told, for the first time in court, the story of the OARA, the Dutcher murders, and the tyrannical leader, Simon Sue. Whether or not anyone believed him seemed less important at this point; he had nothing left to lose. Now he turned his attention to his next destination, the Denver Referral and Diagnostic Center, the DRDC, a maximum-security holding pen where he would be evaluated and sent to a prison deemed appropriate for a sixteen-year-old.

He looked forward to the ride to Denver. After a year in the Park County Jail, he was ready for a change of scenery.

CHAPTER 19

Simon Sue's preliminary hearing, postponed now for nearly seven months, was a chance for the judge to determine whether there was sufficient evidence against the defendant to bring him to trial. Though Isaac had been called by the defense, who hoped to make him look like a liar and an unreliable witness against Sue, he would provide the prosecution its first chance to have the OARA story told by one of its members, hopefully compellingly.

On the Friday before he was scheduled to take the stand, Isaac was suddenly and unexpectedly whisked away from the Park County jail to an undisclosed location. Robin and Donna Grimes were informed that there was a security breach at the jail, and that their family should be on guard at their home in Colorado Springs. Rob called the Colorado Springs Police Department, locked the doors, and waited, not knowing where his son had been taken or why.

Sheriff's officials denied that Isaac's evacuation was the result of an investigation into a diagram they'd found in the jail a few days earlier, in Glen Urban's cell. Glen was designing a transmission for a car and had left his pencil-drawn rendering lying on his pillow when he left the jail for his day job on Friday. A jailer had picked it up and, in consultation with others, determined that it might be a diagram of the jail, intended to aid in a bombing. Urban was rounded up quickly and questioned, and the rumor of a possible bomb plot was proven false. But Grimes was moved out of Park County anyway, allegedly in response to a different threat.

Urban was puzzled but not surprised by the deputy's accusations against him. One day while he was parked in the town library's parking lot, giving himself a haircut with manicure scissors, using the rearview mirror to see what he was doing, he had found himself suddenly surrounded by cops with their weapons drawn. He was accused of plotting to burn down the sheriff's office because he had a can of gasoline in the backseat of his Volkswagen, a junker Glen had patched together from spare parts in his garage workshop.

Glen was taken in and questioned, but not before he had made a call to his mother, Cathie Cumming. Cumming sought help from Investigator Leonard Post, explaining to him that the jailers were constantly accusing Glen of one conspiracy or another. Post called the watchdogs off and got Glen a day's absolution.

On March 19, Isaac Grimes appeared in court, surrounded by sheriff's deputies wearing full body armor and carrying guns. On a dirt hill across the parking lot from the courthouse's back door, where prisoners were brought into court, an armored police gunman aimed a tripod-mounted M-16 at the door. Isaac's appearance was brief, as Sue's attorney, Ann Kaufman, became ill halfway through the day. Grimes was returned to the undisclosed protective location and the jail security breach remained a mystery.

A little over two weeks later, on the day before Simon Sue's hearing was scheduled to resume, Captain Monte Gore of the jail sent a memo to Sheriff Fred Wegener, the courts, the DAs, Glen Urban, and his mother, Cathie Cumming, informing them he'd received notice that a Georgia psychiatrist treating Ty Dutcher had expressed concern over Ty's "strong homicidal thoughts for the individuals responsible for murdering his parents."

Dutcher had voluntarily admitted himself to the hospital for treatment and could just as easily check himself out and drive to Colorado. The doctor said his homicidal rage "permeate[d] his thinking process," and she had felt she must report the situation to law enforcement.

Gore had contacted her and asked if Ty Dutcher had indicated how he might carry out such threats. Dutcher, who said he had military experience and was considered a marksman, had told his doctor, "It would be easy," and said, "One of the guys goes in and out [of the jail] every day." Gore assumed Dutcher was referring to Glen Urban.

Though Dutcher was still fourteen hundred miles away in Atlanta, Gore implemented extra security measures for the inmates associated with the Dutcher homicides, and he temporarily suspended Glen Urban's work release. He needed to keep Urban and Isaac Grimes safe until they'd completed their testimony in Simon Sue's upcoming hearing.

On April 9, Isaac Grimes finally got his full day in court. The temperature was still cool, but the mountain air was filled with birdsong and the promise of spring. Ann Kaufman hurled questions at Isaac while he sat rigid and straight, betraying little emotion except when recounting the murder of Tony Dutcher. At that point, he closed his eyes tightly as if to read the script permanently inscribed on the backs of his eyelids.

"Where did you get the knife?" asked Kaufman.

"From Jon."

"On August 14, you said you got the knife from Simon Sue. Which is true?" grilled Kaufman. Isaac cautiously said the knife could have come from Simon through Jon.

"Why were you and Simon talking about killing Carl, JoAnna, and Tony Dutcher?"

"He said he wanted them to be killed," said Isaac. "He wanted me to prove loyalty to him and the OARA."

Kaufman asked for specifics. When had he said this?

"Mr. Sue [Simon] asked me a lot about the Dutchers, their weapons, whether they were racists."

"Did he ask for specific examples?"

"Yes, I told him Carl Dutcher was prejudiced against Asians. Simon said Carl Dutcher had probably raped Vietnamese women when he was in Vietnam. He told me I should write a protocol for a mission." Then Isaac described the now familiar story of his botched plan and how he had angered Simon with his incompetence. Matheny had been there, he said, and Simon had told him "a mission was going to go forward." Isaac described Simon's tirade with the riot baton.

"He said that Jon and he had planned to take me over to Jon's and shoot me," said Isaac. "He went into various things about killing my family. He says I'm a traitor; I'm plotting against him."

Kaufman tried to get details about the protocol and about the officials in Guyana Simon had said he'd contacted, but Isaac was no more specific than he'd been in the past. His plan had been unacceptable to Simon. Ten days before New Year's, Simon had called him a traitor again, this time by phone, and had renewed his threats.

Grimes described the first time he and Jon had gone up to the Dutchers and aborted the mission. He described a night he'd spent at Jon's when they were supposed to go up again but didn't. He described the final plan, communicated by Simon over the phone, and how it had almost worked exactly as planned except that Tony had wanted to sleep outside, on the hill.

"Did Tony have any idea he was about to be killed?" asked Kaufman.

"No," said Isaac.

Kaufman brought up a number of incidents, earlier in Isaac's OARA career, when he hadn't followed Simon's orders, implying that his actions with the Dutchers had been committed of his own free will. She pointed out that when he'd disobeyed Simon in the past, nothing had happened to his family, thus discrediting his claim that he'd done what he did to protect his family.

Isaac quickly countered, "When I didn't show up for the burglary, as I was ordered to, Simon and Jon waited for me at my house with a gun wrapped in a Guyanese flag. They took me to my bedroom, pushed me with the gun, and told me I'd screwed up. The threats got worse over the months. I felt following Simon's orders to kill the Dutchers was the only way to save myself and my family. This was my last chance."

Isaac struggled to keep his gaze aimed directly forward, at the podium where Kaufman stood, her thick notebook of notes and documents propped open in front of her. He avoided meeting Simon's eyes at the defense table, just a few feet away.

Asked what he believed about a Guyanese political organization now, Isaac was adamant.

"I believe it's possible that my family is in danger. I believe it's possible that there are family members of the Sues who may be involved in the U.S."

"Did Simon ever tell you anything about violence associated with politics in Guyana?" DA David Thorson asked in cross-examination.

"He showed me stories in the Guyana newspaper," said Isaac.

"Why did you go through with the murders and why did you never contact the authorities?" asked Thorson.

"I was afraid," said Isaac. "It's easy to talk about it in the courtroom today. When you have a gun pointed at you, it's different."

"Were you brainwashed?"

"A professional would have to make that determination. Certainly I was manipulated over the months."

Isaac Grimes relinquished the stand. A sheriff's deputy, his free hand ready at his holster, led Isaac away from the courtroom.

Glen Urban took the stand over the objection of Thorson, who argued Kaufman was calling him strictly for discovery, a process that was supposed to happen outside the courtroom so that no big surprises would be revealed to either side unawares. Kaufman said she'd called Urban pertaining to the racketeering and organized-crime charges Simon Sue faced. The judge allowed Urban's testimony.

Urban, visibly nervous, made faces, wiggled in his seat, tugged at this hair, and grew redder by the minute as he explained his position in the OARA. He told how he'd met Simon, how Simon had explained the organization to him and the nature of Urban's role as mechanic.

"When did you know what you were involved in?" asked Kaufman.

"I was at the police station on March 8, being questioned by some sheriff's deputies, when Agent Sadar of the CBI burst into the room. He said, 'Simon says he gave the gun to Glen.' That's when I figured it out."

"But you knew you were involved in a military organization prior to that," said Kaufman.

"Yeah, but the military doesn't call itself 'Killing People Incorporated,'" he said, eliciting the only laugh of the day from those gathered in the courtroom.

Judge Kenneth Plotz was quick to issue his decision about whether there was sufficient evidence to hold Simon Sue over for trial on felony charges.

"The court finds probable cause, the presumption is great, and the proof is evident," he said. "What I recollect most clearly is the testimony of Isaac Grimes, his testimony of what he did, his testimony of the abuse that was perpetrated on him. The court declines to set bond. Arraignment is set for June 17."

•◆•

In mid-May, Isaac Grimes finally said good-bye to the Park County Jail and boarded a sheriff's van for the Denver Reception and Diagnostic Center, where he would be held until the Department of Corrections determined where he should be permanently placed.

The hour-and-a-half drive down State Highway 285 to Denver offered a welcome view of brilliant blue skies. Missing, however, were the dense snowcaps normally still in evidence on the surrounding mountain peaks. Snowmelt had been early this year. Before summer had commenced, the landscape was already brown and sun-scorched, or perhaps it had never turned green this arid spring.

Settled in at the DRDC, Isaac wrote his dad a letter:

Hey Dad:

I called Mom this early night/morning and I have to say that I don't know what it is or what's going to happen but I love you and am praying for a good prognosis. [Isaac's concern stemmed from news of Rob's increasingly serious back problems.]

> I just got back from rec. It's real hot and muggy in the pod area. I can do ten pull-ups in a row (without a jump start) under or over handed—my all time record. . . .
>
> Did I tell you that I'm hooked on coffee? Yep, ah gots th' chronic. It's good! My first cup, two weeks ago, tasted like coffee, but I was intrigued. . . . Now, I've had another and it's good! I had it with sugar but I think it's better without.

Father and son often exchanged ideas about new taste experiences. Rob had worked as an executive chef before his back injury. His former boss, Chris Pulos, had called him a "wizard" in the kitchen. Isaac had worked briefly, before his arrest, in the kitchen of a fine-dining restaurant in Colorado Springs, where he'd begun to learn some of the basics of sauces. In jail, he'd read more and continued to share an interest in the chemistry and alchemy of food and drink.

> Something real cool happened yesterday. The guy across the way was yelling to deputies when they were passing through the hall (I'm in seg now, again.)

Seg was administrative segregation, a part of the facility set off from the general population, generally reserved for troublemakers or those with special needs. In Isaac's case, seg was where he could be separated from the general population of older adult males.

> . . . Anyway, he'd keep yelling after whoever had passed through the door and went into the booking area. . . . So he kept doing it for a while and I took some deep breaths—in, out, in out—real slow and deep. I kept doing it until the next time he yelled and kept yelling, then [I took a breath in] real deep, then I yelled, "SHUT THE HELL UP!" real firm and strong. And he stopped for a couple hours. It made me feel really good, so I took a nap.

It isn't good sleepin' in here though. It's hot—real hot, and if it isn't real hot, I'm wide awake and it's pleasantly cool going on chilly.

Isaac launched into a long discussion of the value of gold, a filter he was inventing, a drawing of a gremlin he'd made for his little brothers, and a serenity prayer he'd copied for his dad.

> Have you ever had a really good pencil? You know, not too long, not too short, eraser erases well, wood and lead are just right. I have one of those right now, an Eberhard Faber No. 2 HB. While it isn't a day pass, it's one of those satisfactory little pleasures.
> I'll sign off now. Take it easy, have fun and don't eat the meatloaf.
> Love,
> Isaac

Donna and Robin Grimes treasured what they called Isaac's "quirkiness," his odd sense of humor and his unusual perception of the world around him. They were happy to see it intact in letters like this one.

While most inmates are processed within thirty days of entering DRDC, Isaac Grimes was there for nearly three months awaiting placement. He asked his mother for a hundred dollars, money he quickly learned he needed to buy protection and favors, to keep himself safe.

•◆•

In early June, the central part of the state, including massive sweeps of forest from South Park to Fairplay and east toward Denver, burst into flames in what turned out to be the largest wildfire in the state's history, the Hayman fire, so named for the section of the Pike National Forest where it first began.

Sixty miles away, in Colorado Springs, the view of Pikes Peak was smudged by smoke hovering in the mountain air. Some mornings, the scent of wood smoke woke those who slept with their windows open. In Fairplay, sheriff's deputies watched reports of the fire's spread carefully, in case the jail or any of the town's buildings needed to be evacuated. The fire burned steadily the first day, then raced across seventeen miles on the second day, fueled by record low relative humidity and wind gusts up to sixty miles per hour. Some two thousand firefighters from across the West rushed in to help contain the rapidly expanding inferno.

On June 16, a visibly shaken Governor Bill Owens, State Attorney General John Suthers, and officials of the National Forest Service held a press conference announcing the arrest of the alleged fire starter, Terry Barton, thirty-eight, mother of two daughters, a forestry technician for the forest service. The extreme drought across the state had spurred a strict fire ban in all national-forest camping areas. Patrolling one of those areas for illegal fires, Barton had started a small fire in a campfire ring, and it had grown swiftly out of control.

A large-boned woman with precisely curled platinum blond hair, Barton told investigators she'd been distraught over letters she'd received from her estranged husband and had stopped to burn them that day. Instead of eradicating evidence of her ruined marriage, she had set loose a fire that ultimately burned more than one hundred thousand acres, nearly one hundred square miles of forest, destroying the hundreds of homes, outbuildings, and commercial buildings in its path. The final cost to the state was over $39 million; the cost to those who lost their homes was immeasurable. The environmental tally would take years to calculate.

The Dutchers' land at Bear Trap Ranch, well out of the path of the Hayman fire but close enough for discomfort, lay crisp and brown throughout the summer of 2002. Carl Dutcher's pond sank several feet lower than usual, the water murky and gray. Charles Dutcher drove out regularly to check on the land, glancing cautiously up the hill toward the rocky area where Tony's lean-to had once stood. There were no signs of life.

At the end of July, Isaac Grimes was moved to Sterling Correctional Facility and placed in an administrative segregation. He wrote his parents, saying how much he had enjoyed the view of cornfields on the way to Sterling, cornfields as far as the eye could see.

"I like the flatlands and cornfields and everything else, like grain elevators, tractors(!) and big stacks of hay bales. If Iowa and Nebraska are pretty much like that, they rock!" Isaac wrote.

At Sterling, he soon learned he was housed in a ward with a group of white supremacists. Rumor was they had him framed in their crosshairs for his crime of killing a white man while under the influence of a mixed-race South American. He retreated into the familiar place of terror he'd inhabited over the past year and a half, afraid of ever meeting his next-door neighbors face-to-face.

Instead, he focused on an eight-legged friend on his windowsill. He wrote his mother from Sterling:

Dear Mom,

It is ok here. . . . Right now I'm on Level 1, which means I only get one visit and one phone call a month. . . .

I wear DOC [Department of Correction] greens and boots (no laces) and the blankets are nice (not like DRDC's holey-weaved ones). There's a spider web and spider outside my window. I've named the spider Oliver. He's representin' the OSM—Orange Spot Mafia, and has seen it all—prisoners coming, prisoners going and all that stuff. Oliver can suck the guts out of a bug so quick, and is on top of anything that hits his web like a Green Beret with a garrote.

•◆•

August brought the promise of rain, with monsoon clouds gathering overhead each afternoon, and the certain end of a disastrous summer. Gearing up for trial, Simon Sue's attorneys—Ann Kaufman and her partner, Rick Levinson—filed motions in Judge Plotz's courtroom asking that Simon's trial be moved out of Park County; asking that all evidence linking Simon with the OARA be disallowed in court; and requesting that Simon's initial March 8 interview with investigators be withheld from jurors.

Simon entered the courtroom smiling and animated.

Over DA Thorson's objections, Plotz quickly capitulated to the request that the trial be moved, pointing out he had already ruled that Jon Matheny's trial be moved and he owed the same fairness to Sue. For that he received a polite nod from Simon.

Kaufman, wearing a butter-yellow suit, summoned CBI Agent Dave Sadar to the stand, trying to establish grounds for suppressing the statements Sue had made and Sadar had taped over a year ago, the evening of Isaac Grimes's confession. If she could prove Simon's testimony had been coerced or illegally obtained through improper government conduct, she could have the incriminating tape withheld, a key defense victory.

Kaufman depicted Simon as a young man manipulated by power figures, taken in for questioning as a suspect in a criminal case, deprived of his Miranda rights, and involuntarily held. Sadar patiently answered questions from her and the prosecution, describing the interview from his point of view, then relinquished the stand to Colorado Springs Police Detective Delmar Wedge, the white-haired twenty-six-year veteran who'd given Sue a ride to the station that night and briefly participated in the interrogation.

Wedge's depiction of the evening's events departed from the picture Kaufman was trying to paint. Sue had been remarkably friendly, said Wedge. He'd even thanked Wedge for getting him out of the house. Sue had made small talk with the cop, telling him he'd played chess with his boss, Chief of Police Lorne Kramer.

"Did you tell him he would be videotaped?" asked Kaufman.

"No."

"Why not?"

"It just didn't happen."

The defense and prosecution volleyed accusations: Kaufman said Sue had been forced to testify; Thorson and Deputy DA Sean Paris depicted him as eager to speak to someone. Kaufman argued that Simon had not been given a chance to waive his Miranda rights; Paris argued that Simon had not been under formal arrest and had been informed of such by Sadar.

Kaufman depicted the police entry into the Sue house as being loud, covert, and aggressive, carried out unusually late at night, drawing Sue from a deep sleep.

"Mr. Sue is never told he has a choice about being [at the police station]," said Kaufman of the taped interview. "He's never told he can leave, never told he can ask for counsel, never told he can have his parents there if he wants."

(A spectator in the courtroom whispered loudly, "He's an adult. He's eighteen.")

Kaufman entered a string of similar law cases into the record, concluding that Simon's statement was "completely involuntary."

"Sadar and Wedge have already developed beliefs: If what Simon says agrees with Grimes and Matheny, then he is telling the truth. If not he's lying." She argued that both Sadar and Wedge had been coercive, scaring the boy into confessing his involvement. She strongly urged the judge to suppress the evidence.

Paris spoke forcefully for the prosecution.

"The key question is whether [Sadar and Wedge] are there to ascertain the truth or get an arrest. Simon Sue attempted to manipulate the interview. He's not an eighteen-year-old boy, he's an eighteen-year-old man organizing a very vicious group in Colorado Springs. He'd already been interviewed by Sadar at Palmer High School on January 19. He spoke freely. There was no indicia of custody during that interview or the one in question. It was not custodial and there was nothing to indicate coercion.

"We reject the view that the law burst into Sue's house, that Simon was sleeping deeply when the police entered. Mr. Sue's behavior belies the fact that he's merely an eighteen-year-old boy, out of his league. He's a very controlling person who has a good grip, who had control in most moments of the interview. Nine-thirty at night is not unreasonably late. The police proceeded properly. They were not overly aggressive or scary. Mr. Sue eagerly, and I use that word intentionally, adopted Detective Wedge's suggestion that the interview take place at the Colorado Springs police station.

"He was never told he was under arrest. He was never threatened. He was never told he couldn't leave, and indeed, he left the interview, was driven home and was not arrested."

Paris asked that the motion be quashed.

Judge Plotz rendered his decision.

"I observed that interview," he said. "I find this is not your ordinary eighteen-year-old boy. It's clear to the court that he was not in custody. Regarding voluntariness, he was not arrested. He was never told he would be arrested. Yes, he was not advised of his rights by police, but it's impossible for me to find that he was not in control of the interview. He was voluntarily participating; his mannerisms make this clear. This was indeed voluntary. The motion to suppress is denied."

The defense then entered a motion that all evidence naming Simon Sue leader of the mythical OARA, and any suggestion that he ordered the other members to kill to test their loyalty, be disqualified from the case.

A zip disk allegedly containing OARA records, obtained from Isaac Grimes's computer and turned over to the Colorado Bureau of Investigation by prosecutors, had accidentally been destroyed by the state crime lab. The defense argued the disk could have contained information exculpatory of their client. The prosecution said the information could just as well have contained damaging evidence against Sue that would have strengthened their case. At issue was whether the prosecution should be held responsible for the mishandling of evidence by the state crime lab.

Plotz said no, delivering strike two of the day to the defense, denying their motion. Also denied the defense was access to Dr. Frank Barron's psychological evaluation of Isaac Grimes, confidential material Plotz refused to make public.

•◆•

Simon faced a second colorless autumn in the Park County Jail waiting for his upcoming arraignment, when he would plead innocent to all the charges piled up against him. With Glen Urban now moved to ComCor, a community corrections facility in Colorado Springs, and Isaac Grimes housed at Sterling, Jon Matheny was the last OARA lieutenant left under the same roof as Simon.

Matheny's tactic appeared to be delay at all costs. In September, his attorney, Elvin Gentry, asked for permission to withdraw from the case, citing irreconcilable differences with his client. No specifics were offered.

"Guess I'll have to waive my right to a speedy trial," Matheny calmly told Judge Plotz.

In October, Matheny represented himself in court, asking that the criminal case against him be dropped because he had not received a speedy trial. He rejected the court's appointment of Public Defender Nick Lusero, citing a conflict of interest due to Lusero's prior knowledge of the case.

Plotz listened with frustration and amazement at the endless twists in the cases of the four defendants in the Dutcher murders. He said the court had until November 20 to try Matheny, but he admitted the trial would probably be delayed while a new attorney was familiarized with the massive body of discovery. As the second anniversary of the Dutcher murders drew near, the defendant accused of gunning down Carl and JoAnna was nowhere near ready for trial.

•◆•

That same month the nation's attention was drawn to another young man, a soldier of sorts dubbed the "American Taliban." John Walker Lindh, son of a prosperous Catholic father and a liberal Buddhist mother, had been captured by American soldiers in Afghanistan in a fierce gun battle nearly a year before, following the terrorist attacks of September 11. Lindh had come to Pakistan as a teenager to study Islam and had joined the Taliban at twenty. They had trained him in weapons identification, maps and topography, battlefield tactics, and explosives. His hair matted and his face smeared with dirt, Lindh was carried out of Afghanistan on a stretcher and sent to prison in America, where he faced charges of consorting with the enemy and conspiracy to kill U.S. nationals.

On October 4, 2002, he accepted a plea bargain and a twenty-year sentence offered by federal prosecutors, pleading guilty to lesser charges and agreeing to cooperate with investigators seeking information about Al Qaeda and the Taliban.

Lindh, twenty-one, wept openly and apologized for fighting alongside the Taliban. "Had I realized then what I know now . . . I would never have joined them," he said. He condemned Osama bin Laden's actions against the United States and bin Laden's distortion of Islam, saying, "[I] never understood jihad to mean anti-American or terrorism."

Lindh's attorney told reporters, "He was a soldier in the Taliban. He did it for religious reasons. He did it as a Muslim, and history overcame him."

His father said, "John loves America. And we love America. God bless America."

•◆•

The week before Thanksgiving, in Colorado Springs, Jennifer Vandresar prepared to face a jury that would decide her fate for driving down the wrong side of the highway and killing an innocent man.

On Monday, November 18, the courtroom was filled with potential jurors. Public Defender Todd Johnson comforted his client frequently as her demeanor shifted from zombielike to distraught. An assistant district attorney asked potential jurors if they would be able to set aside sympathy for the mother who'd lost her only son to murder in a highly publicized case.

A jury was formed and the trial began on November 19. Prosecutors cited lab results showing a positive result for methamphetamine in Vandresar's bloodstream at the time of the crash that had killed Stuart Edwards, and a blood alcohol level more than twice the legal limit. There was also evidence Vandresar had used Ecstasy earlier in the evening before climbing into her car and driving the wrong direction down I-25. Jurors were shown autopsy photos of Edwards, who'd been thrown from his car and had died of blunt-force trauma to the head and chest.

"This is a case about taking responsibility for your actions," the prosecution told jurors.

"Jennifer Vandresar is responsible for an accident but she is not guilty of a crime," countered Public Defender Johnson in his opening remarks. Vandresar was indeed debilitated by drugs and alcohol, the Ecstacy ingested accidentally, he argued, and she was distraught over the murder of her son and the degradation of her job. When she took the wheel that morning, she was beyond making judgments or calculations of any kind, including judging her own condition or actively killing anyone.

Johnson told the jury Jennifer Vandresar drank "to escape a degrading, depressing job" and to mask the pain of losing her son and her husband in the same year. She'd had a headache and asked another dancer for an aspirin. The pill turned out to be Ecstasy.

Prosecutors called Jacob Weaver, an eyewitness, to the stand. Weaver had driven his car parallel to Vandresar's on the morning in question, headed in the same direction but on the correct side of the road. He had tried to get her attention while a passenger in his car called 911. When Vandresar's car crashed into Edwards's, Weaver had pulled over to the cement median, jumped over, and pulled her from her car.

"She seemed confused and more concerned about her car than about Edwards," said Weaver. "She started hitting me and telling me it was all my fault. I said, 'It's not my fault; you're the one who did this.'"

Colorado Springs Police Officer Robert Patterson testified that he'd told Vandresar about Edwards's death later at Memorial Hospital. He recalled her crying for "about three minutes" after hearing that Edwards had died and that she would be charged with vehicular homicide.

On the second day of the trial, Jennifer Vandresar testified. She described the nightmares and delusions she'd endured daily since Tony's death, preceded by her husband Paul's suicide. She admitted she had taken prescription drugs to help her sleep until she overdosed on sleeping pills and her prescription was canceled. Then, she said, she'd started using alcohol to numb the pain.

"I'd lie awake at night and think of how my son died, and I'd think my husband's ghost was coming to kill me," Jenny said. She described her depression over a recent breakup with a boyfriend and her job at Déjà Vu, a nightclub that featured nude dancers.

The prosecutor, on cross-examination, jumped on Jenny's characterization of herself as an unhappy stripper.

"Isn't it true, Ms. Vandresar, that you've worked in strip clubs and starred in pornographic films for more than fifteen years?"

"Yes," said Jenny, struggling for composure.

"You're giving this jury the wrong impression, aren't you?"

Jenny admitted she'd worked in strip clubs and appeared in movies and magazines, including *Hustler* and *Penthouse*.

"I did it to support my son," she said, "but since his death I found it degrading to be grinding against some stranger for money." Jenny cried softly, then continued, "I sold my body for my son, so he could have everything. Then my life fell apart when he was killed. He was everything to me."

From the stand, Vandresar, dressed in blue, mascara dripping down her cheeks, apologized to Stuart Edwards's family members.

"I know what it's like to lose a child," she said. "I would never do anything like that to anyone. I have a very high regard for human life."

On Day 3, the jury deliberated for five hours before finding Jennifer Vandresar guilty on four counts: drunken vehicular homicide, criminally negligent homicide, driving under the influence, and reckless endangerment of a child. The reckless endangerment charge stemmed from minor injuries sustained by a child in another car at the crash site.

In summation, the defense called the wreck "a tragedy, not a crime." The prosecution said, "If everyone who was having a bad life went out and drank and drove and did drugs and drove . . . that would be anarchy."

Upon hearing the jury's decision, and considering what would be an appropriate sentence, Stuart Edwards's mother, Kay, said she sympathized with Vandresar's personal hardships, but probation would not be punishment enough.

Jenny was released on bond, knowing she faced up to twelve years in prison. Awaiting the judge's sentence, she returned to her sister's house, where, two days after her conviction, she sat down for Thanksgiving dinner with her niece and nephew.

If Tony had lived, his final semester in high school would have commenced come January. He would be old enough now to enlist in the military, his lifelong dream. Instead, January 2003, the second anniversary of his death, would be the month when Judge Richard Hall sentenced his mother to ten years in prison.

"You've suffered a lot of things that most people don't encounter in their lives," said Hall. "That might explain your actions, but it doesn't excuse them."

Jenny stood tall in the courtroom, just minutes before she was transported to the Women's Correctional Facility outside Canon City. "I'm taking responsibility for what happened," she said. "However, I know I would not be here had they not killed my son."

•◆•

The drought of 2002 turned into the drought of 2003 as snow failed to fall, Jennifer Vandresar faced turning forty in prison and a lifetime without her son, and Simon Sue and Jon Matheny awaited trial.

If Charles Dutcher had his way, the nightmare that had begun in January 2001 would finally end in the new year, leaving him to grieve in peace.

If Isaac Grimes could make it through another day at Sterling penitentiary, then maybe he could figure out how to save his life—or end it for good.

Cathie Cumming breathed a sigh of relief that her son Glen was finally back in Colorado Springs, and Bonnie Matheny tried to make her daughter Heidi's Christmas and New Year's celebration as normal as possible.

Donna and Robin Grimes prayed for a new year with less back pain for Rob, some normality at home, presence of mind for Isaac, and justice, finally, for Simon and Jon. Some days the story of the OARA slipped their minds; then they remembered that they needed to keep it alive for a few months longer, at least until the last two members had received their final orders.

CHAPTER 20

The youngest inmate at Sterling Correctional Facility didn't stay there long enough to turn seventeen.

After three months in administrative segregation, locked down twenty-three hours a day, seven days a week, denied contact visits with his family, able to hear only the tortured voices in his own head, Isaac Grimes decided to end his life. He told his mother later that he tied his bed sheets together and fashioned a noose. He hoped to go swiftly. But when the moment came to cut off the stream of air to his lungs, he couldn't bring himself to do it.

He was a failure at living and a failure at dying. He couldn't kill himself and he couldn't bear staying alive. A prison psychologist, called in to examine Isaac when his suicidal wishes were reported, immediately recommended a transfer to the Department of Corrections mental health facility, San Carlos in Pueblo, Colorado.

San Carlos is a modern, 250-bed operation on the grounds of the Colorado Mental Health Institute, formerly the Colorado State Insane Asylum, designed to house the developmentally disabled and severely mentally ill. The prison section serves a small fraction of the thousands of inmates in the DOC in need of acute and long-term mental health services.

Isaac moved from lockdown in a massive prison filled with hardcore adult offenders to lockdown in an adult mental ward, a slight improvement. He was evaluated and offered a choice of antidepressant medication as well as an antipsychotic drug to help him sleep. His parents could visit more easily since Pueblo was just fifty miles down the road from Colorado Springs, but they still couldn't touch him. Contact visits were not permitted to prisoners in administrative segregation.

In early February 2003, Simon Sue entered a plea of innocent to the long list of felony charges piled up against him, and it looked as though he would be going to trial. But two short weeks later, on the deadline date prosecutors had given for accepting a plea bargain, to everyone's surprise the defense announced that Simon would plead guilty on three counts of conspiracy to commit murder plus one count of violating Colorado's organized-crime act.

The weather was bitter on February 25, the day Simon entered his plea. The South Platte River was frozen solid, and bison huddled alongside the highway bisecting South Park, steam pouring from their nostrils.

Defense Attorney Rick Levinson arrived at the courthouse in a flurry, throwing off a thick wool overcoat. "Are we first?" he asked the prosecutors already seated at a front table. "I'd like to get back before it snows."

Simon Sue, thin and drawn, his cheeks hollow, was escorted in and took a seat next to Levinson. His parents sat in the gallery looking miserable. Broad men in jeans, sheepskin jackets, and boots spread out on the sparsely filled benches, their hats removed and set aside. No members of the Dutcher family were present.

DA Dave Thorson addressed Judge Kenneth Plotz first, asking that "extreme indifference" be added to the conspiracy charges as well as an element of "universal malice."

"On what grounds?" asked Plotz.

Thorson said Sue, in this pre-sentencing interview, had admitted directing Jon Matheny and Isaac Grimes in a burglary of the Dutchers and admitted saying that if anyone got in the way, they should be killed.

Levinson clarified. "Mr. Sue specifically denied ordering Grimes and Matheny to kill the Dutchers, your honor." Plotz nodded and knitted his eyebrows.

"Mr. Sue," he said gently, "do you understand that by accepting a guilty plea, you are giving up the right to a jury trial?"

"Yes, sir," Simon said, his voice weak.

"That you are giving up the right to testify or to remain silent?"

"Yes."

"That you are giving up the right to appeal?"

"Yes, sir."

"How do you wish to plead?"

"Guilty."

Levinson threw an arm around his client's thin shoulders and patted him before he was led out of the courtroom.

Nadia Sue leaned forward in her seat, her mouth open as if to call him back.

Reporters gathered around Levinson in the courthouse lobby as gray clouds gathered outside, a storm boiling up from the west.

"It's a difficult decision [to plead guilty], but we all think it's the best solution for Simon in the end," he said. "There is a significant risk whenever you're charged with a felony that you could end up doing life in prison. You always weigh the possibility of being incarcerated for the rest of your life against having a release date."

Levinson reminded reporters that Simon hadn't committed first-degree murder, nor had he pled guilty to murder. "What happened to the Dutcher family is very unfortunate, and what happened to Simon and his family is very unfortunate. Hopefully this is the best road for everybody."

Nadia and Keith Sue rushed past the crowd, avoiding reporters' questions.

Dave Thorson loped down the hall on long, thin legs and stopped for a brief comment.

"Three down and one to go," he said, unable to contain a grin.

•◆•

March delivered the state a massive blizzard that collapsed roofs in some communities, blew roof-high drifts in others, and brought welcome moisture to all. Fairplay deputies cleared snow and rescued stranded travelers. Coloradans stayed home from work and school, shoveled, snowshoed, and thanked the snow gods. And in living rooms, restaurants, and offices across America, people huddled around the television, obsessively watching non-stop television coverage of an event on the other side of the world.

President George W. Bush announced Operation Iraqi Freedom, a military invasion designed "to disarm Iraq of weapons of mass destruction, to end Saddam Hussein's support for terrorism, and to free the Iraqi people." On March 17, Bush delivered an ultimatum to Iraqi dictator Saddam Hussein and his two sons, Uday and Qusay: Leave the country or else. Three days later, he ordered 120,000 American troops into Iraq in a combined land and air attack promoted as "Shock and Awe." Television viewers watched slack-jawed as missiles launched from ships in the Persian Gulf, split the sky, and exploded in Baghdad. The sight of bombs exploding precisely on target became arguably the most watched spectator sport in America.

A month and a half later, on May 1, Bush marched onto the aircraft carrier *Abraham Lincoln,* decked out in a full military flight suit and announced the "end of major combat operations" in Iraq. Behind him, a banner announced, "MISSION ACCOMPLISHED." In June, Uday and Qusay Hussein were killed in a fourteen-hour firefight with elite American military forces. To prove their demise to the Iraqi people and to signify the fall of Hussein's reign, the American government released photos of the brothers' bloodied, bullet-holed heads and torsos. The images were broadcast on television stations across the world and printed in most major newspapers.

Those who'd never seen a close-up of a dead person's face recoiled at the sight. Those who had couldn't help but remember the dead faces they'd seen before.

•◆•

On August 27, 2003, both the *Denver Post* and the *Rocky Mountain News* published a photo of Charles Dutcher in a white T-shirt, his long hair streaming, his arms spread wide, embracing a weeping Donna Grimes and a grimacing Robin Grimes on the Park County Courthouse lawn. Charles's wife, Rhonda, stood crying in the background.

Charles Dutcher had offered the first comments to the crowd gathered for Simon Sue's sentencing hearing, a day-long affair. Sue had entered the courtroom looking gaunt and thin. A large contingent of family, neighbors, and friends were assembled on his behalf.

"Simon Sue has finally admitted, after two years, that it was a hit, not a burglary," said Charles. He told the judge that Tony's mother, Jennifer Van- dresar, had declined to come to the hearing today because it would require her staying overnight in the same jail as Simon Sue, something she couldn't bear to do.

Sue's attorney, Ann Kaufman, presented a three-prong strategy to con- vince Judge Kenneth Plotz to give her client the lightest possible sentence. She set out to deconstruct the notion of Isaac Grimes and Jon Matheny as "automatons under the complete sway of Simon Sue, not individual, voli- tional people who came to Mr. Sue for their own needs." She would debunk the prosecution's notion that Simon had not taken responsibility for what he'd done, and she would present the "extraordinary other life of Mr. Sue" through a string of character witnesses.

A stranger in the courtroom who'd not heard prior evidence in the case might indeed have thought she was witnessing an episode of *This Is Your Life* celebrating the multiple talents of a remarkable young man.

Kaufman first called Thomas Hallenback, past president of the Colorado Springs Coin Club and assistant treasurer of the American Numismatic Soci- ety, headquartered in Colorado Springs. A distinguished-looking, well- dressed gentleman, Hallenback recalled the twelve-year-old Simon Sue who used to come into his coin shop to view foreign coins. The coin club, of which Simon became a member, had about fifty members with an average age close to sixty.

"He was treated special and encouraged to continue," said Hallenback. "He brought his collection of several hundred different varieties of coins."

"What was your reaction when you heard of Simon's arrest?" asked Kaufman.

"Disbelief and shock," said Hallenback.

Keith Smith, Simon's math teacher at Palmer High School, was also called to the stand and said he'd gotten to know Simon his junior and senior years "as a student and as a person."

"He took an interest in me," said Smith. "We don't have a teacher's lounge, so I often went to the commons area. Simon stopped me one day and asked questions about me. I considered him a student and a friend; that's unusual for me."

Simon, said Smith, was easygoing, easy to approach, and well liked and "never seemed to get in trouble with other teachers."

"When you're a teacher you always have kids you're concerned about, but never Simon."

"What was your reaction on hearing of his arrest?" pressed Kaufman.

"Beyond shock," said Smith. "I didn't think it was even possible." He paused to compose himself. "I do think there's good in Simon."

Rose Trigg, a cheerful silver-haired woman, took the stand next. The wife of a prominent retired Methodist minister in Colorado Springs, Trigg had met Simon while substitute-teaching at Palmer High School over a five-day period. She exuded affection for her favorite student.

"The very first day I noticed Simon," she said. "I found that he engaged with the teacher. My first impression was so strong. I had a lot of experience with adolescent boys, and Simon set the tone for the class. I think what I saw was so genuine, so sincere."

When she heard Simon had been arrested and accused of being involved in the Dutcher murders, Trigg said she couldn't believe it was the same person she knew; she thought there must be a mistake. She called his attorney. She called a teacher at Palmer, who shared her amazement.

Trigg turned toward Judge Plotz and appealed to him directly. "[Simon's] life can be reclaimed. I think, Judge, that Simon will prove your faith in him."

One of Simon's former chess mates, David Goodale, a handsome U.S. Air Force Academy senior, described his friend as "very respectful," a boy who "went out of his way to get more knowledge, a mentor to younger chess players—one of the most loyal, caring friends I ever had."

Thorson cross-examined.

"Chess itself is a metaphor for war, isn't it, Mr. Goodale? The king hangs back and sacrifices his pawns. Is that a fair interpretation?"

Goodale agreed it was.

Neighbors took the stand, expressing their love for Simon. Cynthia Allison, the mother of one of his closest friends in elementary school, presented the judge a photo of her son, Simon, and two other boys fondly known as the "group of four."

Simon's brother, Marlon Jagnandan, a law student at Denver University, testified for the family. Marlon glanced over at his brother, and both he and Simon began to cry.

"Simon was very loving," he said. "I was very concerned about getting into law school and taking the LSATs. I was distraught and Simon cheered me up.

"We used to hunt; our dad's brothers in Guyana hunt. We tried to go every year. We played Teenage Mutant Ninja Turtles, video games. We listened to West Indian music.

"I think being named after my grandfather, a philanthropist in Guyana, meant a lot to him. . . . He loves to read, to enrich other people. He reads the Bible all the time." Simon the Hindu who'd reportedly told Isaac Grimes to renounce his Christianity had apparently broadened his religious horizons.

Marlon was handsome and sharply dressed in a gray suit, his black shoes shined. He looked at his brother lovingly.

"I'll be there for him," he said. "Simon is extremely remorseful about what happened to the Dutchers, and I am, too."

Simon's aunt took the stand and praised him as a "good conversationalist" and a good listener. His other brother, Brian, a uniformed staff sergeant in the U.S. Air Force, testified to Simon's good character and his pride in his Guyanan heritage.

Then Simon's mother, Nadia, nervously took the witness chair. A petite, fine-boned woman with a sweep of shiny chin-length black hair, she shared her son's lush lips, smooth skin, and almond-shaped eyes. In a hushed voice, she described her son as a premature, lactose-intolerant baby with acid reflux disease. She described him as a hard worker with two jobs. She said Simon had been teased and treated badly in the past for being so small and for being a racial minority in an all-white neighborhood.

Kaufman asked her if she was aware of the gun collection in the Caramillo Street house.

"I knew [my husband] Keith was a sportsman," she said. "Keith taught Simon that guns were a good investment."

Nadia said Simon's fiancée from Guyana was planning to come to America to marry him in January.

"When Simon gets out of prison, I plan to be there for him," Nadia told the judge. "Personally, I don't believe Simon was responsible for this crime."

She addressed the surviving Dutcher family.

"I ache for you. I hurt for you," she said, and the pain on her face attested to the truth of her statement.

Keith Sue did not take the stand.

Ann Kaufman set out to characterize Isaac Grimes, the boy whose word had gotten her client arrested, as "a grossly unstable, dangerous person." Chief among her witnesses was Karla Flynn, a manager at the Carl's Jr. fast-food restaurant, where Grimes and Matheny had worked. Flynn said Grimes had a propensity for dead baby jokes and joked about how it would feel to get stabbed. He and Matheny were like brothers, Flynn said, but Sue never hung out with them.

This statement of Flynn's was disputed by an interview with the prosecution's investigators recorded at an earlier date. At that time she had told them a small, dark-skinned young man frequently came into the restaurant to talk with Grimes and Matheny, but the prosecutors didn't bring the inconsistency up.

Flynn said Matheny had brought a big Rambo-type hunting knife to work, and that on December 31, both boys had shown up dressed in camouflage and taken out a huge order of food. When she had asked what they were doing, Matheny had told her they were going hunting.

"Isaac got quieter after New Year's," said Flynn. "I sometimes saw him crying to himself after January 1."

Craig Cox, a private investigator who worked for Kaufman, also reported Grimes's morbid behavior at Carl's Jr., recollected by a couple other employees. Cox had found that in 1998 Matheny had been involved in an online magazine, *Bad Apple,* in partnership with Jeffrey DeMers and Gabe Melchor, two of the Colorado Springs kids whose homes had been targeted for burglaries by the OARA. Antiestablishment, antipolice, antiracist, antihomophobic, and anticapitalist, *Bad Apple* had aimed for the punk audience in the city.

Cox had analyzed Isaac Grimes's computer communications and had found many searches for Guyana that started showing up after February 2001. He cited an e-mail to a girl Grimes had met in a Rage Against the Machine chat room he'd signed "in Karl Marx, Comrade."

All of this was to show that Grimes and Matheny had set political views and weapons interests independent of Simon Sue. Kaufman quoted a letter from Pastor Keith Hedstrom, characterizing a younger Isaac Grimes: "He will never fit in with his peers; he had very set military and political views at age twelve."

Thorson stood up, stretched his long frame, and faced Cox from the prosecutors' table.

"Wouldn't a Guyana [Internet] search two months after the murders be consistent with having doubts about Mr. Sue?"

"Not in my opinion," said Cox.

"Mr. Cox, isn't it true that there are any number of reasons someone might be conducting computer searches?"

"Yes."

Thorson leaned on the podium and delivered the prosecution's summation, a scorching revisiting of the evidence against Simon Sue.

"To the extent the defense is trying to shift the blame, the defense has delivered less than they promised," he began. "What little we have heard shows that [Grimes and Matheny] were easy marks for someone of Mr. Sue's intellect. They were disaffected youth. Overwhelming evidence has been presented that [Mr. Sue] is charismatic, and we've all seen how charismatic people can use that asset for good or for evil. Maybe up to a year or so before he was arrested, he used it for good. But starting in 1999 and 2000, he used it for his own gain—monetary gain and a power trip. He used it for evil.

"His acts and what he has admitted doing wipe out all the testimony of these people who knew him before that."

Thorson cited the presentencing report, an interview with a probation officer conducted a month earlier to evaluate Simon's culpability and his character. In that report, Simon had said "I am the leader of the OARA."

"He admitted to writing the oath," said Thorson. "He said the OARA was 'a scheme I developed to get money out of these guys. Jon was getting a little bit more suspicious, so I had to tell lies.' The burglaries were pursued to feed the lie. [Mr. Sue] said 'it was just the bait to build up a lie more, to build up weapons.'

"What was his motive? To keep control over Jon and Isaac, especially their money."

Thorson related Sue's admission that he "probably" threatened to kill Jon Matheny on another occasion, and his complicity in both burglaries of Gabe Melchor's house, including the one that netted the NHM90 reportedly used in the Dutcher murders. He recounted that in the presentencing report, Sue had admitted he'd said, "Yes, if there's anyone involved that gets in your way, yes, you'll have to kill them."

He referred to the December 9, 2000, report captured from Isaac Grimes's computer and accused Sue of destroying all others. He recounted the tactics and demands of the leader of the OARA, the required inspections of his underlings' rooms, his claims that guns would be sent to Guyana, his instructions in ambushing someone with a knife. Thorson said Sue had admitted pointing an assault weapon at Grimes, taking back the rifle and uniform he'd issued to him, and ordering him to pay back two thousand dollars.

Thorson described Sue's direct involvement in the planning of the Dutcher raid, including "sweating Isaac on it" and "lying that analysts [from Guyana] looked over the protocol." He pointed out that the guns stolen from the Dutchers had been recovered from the Sues' Caramillo Street house, that the orders to destroy evidence and the alibi had all come directly from Simon.

"Was the primary driving force [of the OARA] greed or power?" asked Thorson. "It doesn't matter. A few hundred or thousands of dollars isn't the price of three lives.

"This is an ego that got out of control. Mr. Sue was the leader of an organization of his own creation, using his charisma and his intelligence to read and recruit people. He took them for money, then got them so indoctrinated, so afraid, they'd do anything he told them to do."

Thorson retired, rubbing the stubby white whiskers on his rough face.

Kaufman stood to deliver the defense's summation. She ordered her notes on the podium, set her shoulders, and began.

Regarding the plea bargain agreement, she said one of the considerations in accepting it was the remote possibility of Simon's getting a fair jury trial after 9/11.

"What he did was terrible," she said, "unforgivable in many ways, inexplicable given who he is. But he cooperated completely with law enforcement. In federal court, he'd be rewarded for that. He's a better witness for the prosecution than Mr. Grimes would ever be."

Kaufman suggested that by the time of the Dutcher murders, Simon Sue, who was in Canada, had backed out of the OARA, leaving Matheny in charge. She pointed out that when Simon was in charge, he had made sure no one was at home during raids. She scoffed at the notion of Grimes and Matheny as disaffected youths, characterizing Matheny as "independent, involved in school, sophisticated enough to fire his attorney," and Grimes as "a kid with a violent predisposition who wanted to be part of the OARA, who needed to believe that the OARA was real and part of a larger thing." She said even Dr. Barron didn't know the real Isaac Grimes.

Regarding reputed death threats made by Simon, Kaufman said "mutual death threats were going around," pointing out that Jon Matheny had threatened to kill Isaac Grimes and Glen Urban if they "spilled the beans" during the cover-up of the murders.

Kaufman revisited the gruesome homicide scene.

"This isn't the way people afraid to kill, who don't want to kill, kill people," she said.

She reminded the judge of the statement he'd made at Grimes's sentencing, that he knew Grimes was bright and impressionable but not out of control.

"If Simon had done what Isaac said he did, why didn't Isaac tell somebody while Simon was out of the country? He was too smart; he had to have known the OARA was a lie."

Kaufman characterized Matheny as a kid who was "into criminal burglarizing activity well before he hooked up with Simon Sue," and as a troublesome inmate who'd tried to order hits on both Grimes and Sue while in jail.

"Simon Sue never put together a plan for a homicide," said Kaufman. "I think it's true that Mr. Sue never did a bad thing in his life before making up the OARA.

"Does what he did in his life up to age nineteen not count? He was unusual in the amount of good he did. He's trying to own up to what he did; that's part of rehabilitation. He's going to come out to a caring, intelligent family that will take care of him. He seems to be amazingly redemptable. Can all these people be wrong? He doesn't have any of the hallmarks of the Charles Mansons of this world."

Kaufman urged Judge Plotz to consider the unfairness of assigning Simon equal culpability to "the beheader—the cold-blooded murderer" Isaac Grimes. She asked that the court give Simon forty years—a hefty sentence that "doesn't unduly diminish the crime, but recognizes that he has come clean."

Kaufman relinquished the floor to her client. Simon stood up at the defense table, hunched over and skeletal. "I stand here in shame," he choked out through tears. "I've deeply disgraced my family. I'm terribly sorry. I've ruined many lives. I've failed everyone. I'm here to account for my actions. I'm not here to ask for forgiveness. I will do my damnedest to come back to society and give back to society what I owe them." Simon looked the judge in the eye with this last statement, then sat down.

"Mr. Sue," said Judge Plotz, his angular face twisted like that of a Picasso figure, "it broke my heart this morning to see the picture of you and your fourth grade friends. You were a smiling boy.

"It also broke my heart to pick up the paper and see that Tony, JoAnna, and Carl Dutcher had been murdered. There is no reasonable explanation that has been provided from anyone to explain what happened. What went on in your mind to allow this to happen, much less to engineer it? I'm sad for the victims, for your family, for you. What cause was advanced? Why? What did you get out of this? What did you hope to get out of this?"

Plotz scanned the notes on his desktop.

"I watched your interview with the CBI agent, and I saw a cold, calculating person, a different person than the one I see here today. I believe that there are indeed two Simon Sues in the world, including the Simon Sue that conspired to kill three innocent people."

Plotz said he feared Simon could commit such crimes again and he thought rehabilitation was unlikely.

"On the three counts of conspiracy to commit murder, I order you to serve three terms of forty-five years concurrently. On the Colorado Organized Crime Act charge, I order you to serve eight years consecutive with the others."

Court was dismissed, and reporters rushed to file their stories—fifty-three years for the mastermind in the Dutcher killings, seven years less than for Isaac Grimes, the confessed killer of Tony Dutcher. On the courthouse lawn, photographers from the *Denver Post* and the *Rocky Mountain News* captured the moment when Charles Dutcher put his arms around the parents of his son's murderer, sharing their relief that Simon Sue had finally been sentenced and their bitter regret over all that had happened.

An angry and animated Charles addressed reporters' questions.

"Like the judge says, we still don't have a reason why," he said. "[Simon] should have gotten the death penalty. I think forty or fifty years is a pretty long time to be in prison. I'll be at all the hearings. I'll be sure they never do get out."

"How did you feel about the string of character witnesses who spoke on Mr. Sue's behalf?" a reporter asked.

"Where were all those teachers for my son? That's what I want to know," he said. "I don't have a family. I sit up on that mountain by myself. I think it was pretty much up to Simon, that he controlled the situation. I thought all those character witnesses were a little overdone there.

"What he did up on that mountain, that's the real Simon Sue. If he could do this as a child, imagine what he could've done as an adult."

Dutcher retreated to the parking lot, his mirrored aviator sunglasses glinting in the scorching afternoon sunlight. The Sue family remained in the courtroom, absorbing condolences from friends but feeling no consolation.

CHAPTER 21

Six weeks later, in early October 2003, Jon Matheny entered a guilty plea to three charges of conspiracy to commit first-degree murder and one count of violating Colorado's organized-crime laws, eliminating the possibility of a trial. The real possibility of Simon Sue's testifying against him was apparently the deciding factor in the acceptance of a plea deal.

The prosecution team had worried that without physical evidence, jurors in a trial might not believe Sue's and Grimes's testimony against Matheny. Not wanting to risk losing the conviction, they'd offered the deal.

Matheny, who'd faced thirty charges, including three first-degree murder counts, would avoid a possible life sentence and, assuming good behavior, could be eligible for parole after serving half his sentence.

Both Isaac Grimes and Simon Sue had fingered Jon as the shooter who gunned down Carl and JoAnna Dutcher, but no physical evidence placed him at the scene. In his presentencing report, Matheny admitted helping to plan the killings and driving Grimes up to the Dutchers', but he stopped short of admitting to killing anyone.

The sentencing hearing was held on December 1. Low clouds hovered over Fairplay on a dry, crisp day. Leonard Post arrived at the courthouse, looking uncomfortable in a stiff suit. The DA's full team was assembled, jovially shaking hands with sheriff's deputies. Dave Thorson coughed a wet smoker's cough and turned red in the face, exchanging small talk with a court reporter dressed in jeans and cowboy boots. Over two and a half years, the mood in the courtroom had become familiar, almost friendly. Donna and Robin Grimes arrived and were greeted by a deputy who had guarded their son in the Park County Jail. "Please tell him I said hello," said the officer.

Jon Matheny, dressed in an orange prison jumpsuit and body armor, his hands bound in front of him, entered the courtroom, his head cleanly shaved. There were no representatives of the Sue family there, but many Matheny family members, including Jon's sister, Heidi, crowded the wooden benches. Public Defender Patrick Murphy presented the case for the defendant, asking for the minimum sentence of forty-eight years. Prosecutors wanted the maximum of eighty.

District Attorney Ed Rodgers spoke for the prosecution team on this day that capped thousands of hours preparing cases against the four members of the OARA. His suit hung loosely over his thin frame, looking as if it had been worn for a few days.

Leonard Post was called first by Rodgers, to reiterate the now familiar litany of evidence supporting Jon's participation in the OARA and in the planning of the Dutcher murders. Ed Rodgers directed Post through Matheny's presentencing report, in which Jon admitted being in charge of transportation and helping make the final plan for the raid on the Dutchers.

"He was calling the shots, was the person with weapons, had charge of Isaac Grimes while Simon Sue was in Canada. Is that correct?" asked Rodgers.

"Yes," said Post.

Then Rodgers tracked back to Jon's initial interrogation on March 8, 2001, when he told CBI Agent Sadar he had no knowledge of the OARA, nor was he a member, when he repeated the alibi all four boys had shared since the crime, statements that painted Matheny as a liar.

Rodgers plodded through much of the old evidence and Judge Kenneth Plotz scolded him for presenting information he'd already heard in court at least two times before. Rodgers resumed, saying he'd considered offering photos of the victims at the scene.

"I have seen those photos and I assure you I remember them," said Plotz.

Rodgers called a string of Dutcher family members and friends, including Rhonda Dutcher, Charles's wife.

"The holidays have been a nightmare for us since the murders," she said. "They're the anniversary of deaths. This has ruined everybody's lives. Jenny's in prison. James is a basket case. . . . It's unfathomable. I want [Jon] to serve eighty years. Please put him away for a long time."

Jenny Vandresar spoke next, also dressed in an orange prison jumpsuit, her feet chained. She had been transported to Fairplay from the women's prison in Canon City and was accompanied in the courtroom by a female guard.

"JoAnna always cheered me up with comic strips," she remembered. "They were good people until this little boy with a big gun hunted them down. Conspiracy to commit murder is not the truth; murder is the truth. Isaac confessed and got sixty years. The only person saying Jon didn't do it is Jon. We all know what he did. All I've wanted to hear from the beginning is 'I did it' and 'I'm sorry.'"

Charles Dutcher addressed the court next.

"My father was awarded the Vietnam Service Medal, a Bronze Star, and a Good Conduct Medal. My mother raised three boys by herself while he was in the field. She went to school. In her later years, her life was her grandkids. Tony was the first-born. Ever since Isaac got a plea bargain, I've had to play all these games in court, and I don't like it," he said. Charles's voice began to shake. He cut his comments short and returned to his seat.

Rodgers presented victim impact statements from Carl's sister, JoAnna's sister, and James and Ty Dutcher, then rested the prosecution's case.

The defense called an investigator for the public defender's office and presented Exhibit A, a CBI lab report.

"Agent Swanson collected over one hundred items looking for fingerprints. How many were found?" asked Murphy.

"Forty-four," said the investigator.

"Jon Matheny's prints were turned over to investigators. Were any matches found?"

"No."

Murphy presented defense Exhibits B and C: lab reports on hair and fiber analysis and DNA testing, nearly one hundred more tests. No matches had been found with Jon Matheny for any of them.

A line of character witnesses for the defendant was called, including Verna Buhr, Jon's former boss at the Garden of the Gods Club, where he had worked for two summers in the kitchen and pantry.

"I taught him how to make angel food cake for his mother," said Buhr. "I never heard him cuss, say bad words, or be mean."

Timothy Ingrassia, a friend since freshman year in high school, described Jon as "really nice, laid back. He helped me get my first job." Ingrassia had lived with the Mathenys for a summer and had observed Jon with his sister, Heidi. "He loves his sister very much; he did everything he could for her."

"Did Jon have a special relationship with animals?" asked Murphy.

"He loved animals. He brought in strays," said Ingrassia.

Alexander Haarbrink, a social studies and foreign language teacher at Palmer High School, who'd had both Jon and Tony Dutcher in two of his classes the semester before the murders, testified. Though Jon had a hard time with his classes, he had stayed after class and put in special effort, said Haarbrink. A former chaplain in the Los Angeles Juvenile Detention Center in the 1980s, Haarbrink felt that "Jon was absolutely not a juvenile delinquent."

Haarbrink described the tense two weeks before Tony Dutcher's slaying.

"Tony and Jon were both in two of my classes. Jon was polite, as if he wanted to please and Tony was a happy kid, always friendly. Both became withdrawn several weeks before the tragic events." Haarbrink, who had asked the counseling office to test Jon for learning disabilities and had been frustrated in his efforts, said he'd reported the change in the two boys' demeanors to the counseling office.

"I told them the kid [Jon] was beyond depressed," said Haarbrink. "I went to the assistant principal. Jon had told me he was very concerned about his sister, who was in special education at Palmer. He said, 'I might have to leave for an emergency.'

"Those two weeks were a cold, unhappy time," he said. "Tony was sitting every day like this, with his head in his hands. Jon was white as a sheet, not saying a word."

Rodgers cross-examined for the prosecution.

"Mr. Haarbrink, were you aware of a group called the OARA in October 1999?"

"No."

"Were you aware that Jon Matheny was being trained to kill people?"

"No."

Jon's mother, Bonnie Matheny, a petite woman with black hair curled under at the ends and round ice blue eyes, walked to the front of the courtroom. She looked remarkably like Jon.

"Ms. Matheny, can you please characterize your daughter Heidi's medical diagnosis for us?" asked Murphy.

"Heidi is developmentally delayed, with fine and gross motor handicaps and autistic tendencies," said Bonnie, smiling wryly. She knew that these terms would mean little to anyone who'd never met Heidi.

"And what is Jon's relationship with his sister like?"

"Jon has watched out and cared for her all his life," said Bonnie. "He was eighteen months old when she was born. He always made sure no one teased her."

"Was it always easy?"

"No. As a small child, she could only rock and grunt. Jon was the only one who could calm her down."

"Can you tell us a little about Jon's love for animals?"

Bonnie laughed. "My house was overrun with critters: lizards, frogs, dogs, rabbits, birds, fish. I was always telling him not to bring another animal home, but he would anyway."

Bonnie described her son as an attentive grandson who had often gone over to check on his grandmother, a kid who had repaired the backyard fence, who had grown his own vegetable garden. She described him as a boy who had taken on the role of responsible caregiver in his home, a boy who loved his mother and sister and wanted to be the man in the house who made everything OK.

"Did he have any violent tendencies?"

"No, not ever. We have never had weapons in our house. We don't watch violent movies in our house because my daughter can't handle it."

Murphy asked Bonnie Matheny if she wanted to say anything else to the court.

"Mr. Post has said that Jon didn't have a heart," she said, looking past the prosecutors' table to Post, sitting on the front bench behind them. "What [Jon] was thinking about at that time was that his sister was in school with Simon Sue and he had to protect her. I want to say that I can't believe all the families in this room have had to go through this terrible mess."

Rodgers stood to cross-examine Bonnie. His shoes squeaked as he crossed the short distance to the witness stand.

"Ms. Matheny, are you aware that your son admitted in the presentencing report to stealing guns?"

Bonnie paused and looked down, then gave Rodgers a defiant look, her blue eyes flashing.

"I've been counseled by attorneys not to refer to specifics in the case."

Bonnie stepped down and returned to her seat and put her arm around Heidi, who was rocking and had begun to moan softly. She quieted at her mother's touch.

Ed Matheny, Jon's dad and Bonnie's estranged husband, took the stand. He was a thin man, dressed in a tweed jacket, khaki slacks, and leather moccasins.

It didn't matter what question Murphy asked Ed. He was here to complain about what he viewed as the sloppiness of the investigation and the weak evidence against his son.

"They never even executed a search warrant on our house," he said. "I have been reading the evidence in the case, and having read all three versions of Isaac Grimes's stories, I can't put together his stories with the physical evidence. They're incredible! He carefully folded up his bloody jacket, then laid down on the couch to wait for Jon to pick him up?" Matheny threw his hands up in the air, incredulous.

Judge Plotz interrupted him.

"Mr. Matheny, your son pleaded guilty and I accepted that plea. The court's job is to impose sentence on these counts. Is there anything you'd like to say about that?"

"Jon was not a problem," said Matheny. "He didn't drink, smoke, or stay out late. He pleaded guilty to conspiracy, not murder. He never had a trial."

Jon's grandmother and aunt testified, saying what a good brother, son, nephew, and grandson he was, and a packet of letters written in his support was presented to the judge.

Plotz called a break. Jon turned to face his family. "Hey, Heidi, what's up?" he said, waving his chained hands over his shoulder, and his sister smiled widely.

Charles and Rhonda Dutcher stood in the aisle, talking with Jenny Vandresar. She appeared to be medicated, her words slightly slurred. They spoke of her isolation in prison, where she was currently housed in a lockdown unit.

"I'm kind of happy just alone," said Jenny. "I don't care, you guys. I've given up. And I don't say that so you'll feel sorry for me. I just don't want you to worry." Rhonda hugged her while Jenny's guard watched on.

At the end of the break, Rodgers took the podium to make the prosecution's summation. As he spoke, he shook his head in disapproval and pointed his finger in a scolding manner.

"I have never seen anything like this," he said. "It doesn't get any worse. Matheny's culpability should earn him the full eighty years in the Department of Corrections.

"He was a charter member of the gang. He was financing the operation. Who knows where this thing would have gone if these kids hadn't been caught? He committed five burglaries of his own admission. He was an enforcer for the OARA, part of an out-of-control organization, running around threatening members of his own group. He helped organize these murders, and afterward he was still threatening others. He's admitted basically everything we've charged him with in relation to the OARA. He provided transportation for OARA operations; he made it possible for it all to happen.

"It would not have happened without him. Grimes didn't have a driver's license and Simon Sue was afraid to drive. In the presentencing report, Jon admits to planning these homicides.

"Matheny used a fabricated alibi until now. He never came to the table. Grimes and Sue did, to explain to these families why this happened. Jon provided the knife to Grimes to murder Tony Dutcher. He admitted, 'I put it in Isaac's backpack.' Jon Matheny stole the assault rifle used to kill Carl and JoAnna Dutcher."

"Who actually killed Carl and JoAnna Dutcher?" asked Rodgers. "The defendant himself, according to Simon Sue, admitted to killing these people. Simon's statement taken at the police station on March 8 [2001], upon initial questioning, was the same story as Isaac Grimes's.

"Why should we believe Jon Matheny now? We shouldn't because he has lied all the way through, denying he knew anything about the OARA. Mr. Matheny has shown no remorse. In the presentencing report, he said, 'I was just doing my duty.'"

Rodgers shook his narrow head angrily.

"[Jon] said, 'Look, this is how it went. We intended to kill them all. Yes, I committed those burglaries. Yes, I was second in command.'" Rodgers tsk-tsked his way back to his seat and Murphy stood up to deliver the defense summation.

"One thing Mr. Rodgers said needs to be corrected," he said. "The Dutcher family needs to know that my client is remorseful about these events. In the presentencing report, the probation officer's evaluation of him says his strengths include empathy, remorse, responsibility, and insight into the crimes. He has been counseled not to show remorse by attorneys, because initially he faced first-degree murder charges."

Murphy consulted his notes, fingered the lapel of his jacket, and continued.

"You see things here that are hard to explain. How does a seemingly normal, intelligent young man find himself in a situation like this? His mother loves him in a ferocious manner. He's dedicated to his family. You can tell that he's a kind person, a person who brings in stray animals. He had friends; he wasn't a loner. He was a dedicated student, a hard worker. He was as good a kid as you can imagine in 1999.

"What happened? In two words: Simon Sue.

"Simon had such a power that he could convince these normal kids to do his bidding. My best guess is that in comes Simon Sue, telling tales of an exotic country, of good guys versus bad guys. This gave Jon some sort of structure and purpose. It had nothing to do, initially, with killing people in Colorado.

"Simon Sue was no normal teenager. Mr. Thorson of the prosecutor's office characterized him this way: 'He had a talent to pick out people, to relate to other people at different levels. . . . He got them so afraid of him that they unquestioningly did what he asked them to do.'

"Simon Sue threatened Isaac Grimes and Jon Matheny. During the first inspection in 1999, when a couple things were wrong, Simon held a gun to Jon Matheny's head and said, 'You or your family will die.' This is according to Jon. Simon admitted it's possible he told Isaac Grimes that if the raid on the Melchor house didn't take place, Matheny could die.

"The more terrifying factor for my client was his sister, Heidi. She was on the same campus with Simon Sue every day." In the gallery, Heidi grew more agitated as Murphy continued, her voice rising in a moan, her hands ticking.

"Those who doubt Simon Sue's influence need only ask: How could a normal kid become involved in this kind of activity?"

Murphy urged Judge Plotz to sentence Jon at the low end of the scale, arguing that Grimes had admitted killing and Sue had clearly been the mastermind, the enforcer of the group. Jon, on the other hand, had consistently denied killing the elder Dutchers, to his previous attorney, to the probation officer, and to Murphy.

"There is no physical evidence that shows Jon Matheny in that trailer," said Murphy. "The fact is, we are not going to know who killed Carl and JoAnna Dutcher. I'd ask you to not sentence him as if he killed the Dutchers."

These were the words Charles Dutcher had dreaded hearing aloud in the courtroom. *We are not going to know who killed . . .* Charles believed he knew who had killed his mother and father and he was sitting less than twenty feet away. He nearly bolted from his seat, but Rhonda held onto his arm, held him back. Jenny turned to look back at him, as if his rage had seared the back of her head. Knowing who had killed Tony hadn't made it any easier for her to lose him. Would not knowing have been worse? It was hard to imagine anything worse.

Murphy retired to his seat, and Jon Matheny stood up beside him, his broad back to the gallery, his deep-set round eyes aimed at the table below him.

"I'm sorry that they lost three people, that my family lost me, that the Grimeses lost their son, that the Sues lost their son," he said, reading the words, then sat down.

Judge Plotz cleared his throat and sat up straight in his chair. He was a marathon runner, and the cases of the OARA members had been a marathon judicial run. He was tired.

"Many people think there should have been a trial and that the ends of justice have not been met in this case." He glanced at Ed Matheny. "Since the facts are so contested at this hearing, it would have been good to hear all the testimony."

He turned to face Jon.

"It doesn't make much difference to me whether you or Grimes or Sue, for that matter, pulled the trigger, Mr. Matheny." Plotz measured his words carefully. "The details of these murders are horrible. The horror spreads, like when a stone is thrown into a pond, and it keeps spreading."

Plotz said he was concerned that Matheny could be influenced to commit crimes again and said he believed he presented a danger to others. He expressed his concern that Jon hadn't cooperated in the investigation. If he was less culpable than the others, Plotz asked, why hadn't he come forward?

"From what I can see, your silence hasn't protected your mother and father, you or your sister," said Plotz.

"I search for something good to come out of this. I keep looking at this case, and I find nothing that tells us how this could have happened.

"I've accepted the plea bargain. For the three counts of conspiracy to commit murder, I sentence you to forty-eight years, the sentences to be served concurrently. For the organized-crime count, I sentence you to twenty years, the sentence to be served consecutively with the others. You have a right to appeal the sentence."

Jon Matheny had been in jail for exactly one thousand days, for which he would receive credit for time served. If the sentence stood, he had around sixty-five years left to serve.

Charles Dutcher bolted from the courtroom, strode through the courthouse door, and furiously shook a cigarette from its pack. He stood on the lawn and smoked in the cold December air, a plume of condensed exhale mingling with a column of gray smoke above his head. Reporters gathered around him.

"Mr. Dutcher, why did you agree to the plea bargain?" asked one. Prosecutors had to have the victims' family's approval before offering a plea bargain. Charles had been consulted in the plea deals of all four defendants.

"To go to trial was too risky. There's a possibility he would have got off," said Charles. "I believe Jon did it. There's no reason for Isaac not to confess to killing Mom and Dad if he'd already confessed to Tony's murder."

"Does it bother you that no one was convicted of killing your parents?" someone asked.

"Yes, it bothers me. But we were safer this way to make sure they didn't hit the streets." He pulled a long drag from his cigarette. "Eight hundred years wouldn't be enough to punish them. . . . Yeah, occasionally my father would say the word *gook* and that pissed off Simon. But we'll probably never know the truth about why they did it."

Charles grew angrier as he talked. "Jon opened fire on my mother like he was in the bush. Hell, their dog was the sole survivor." He smiled weakly as he remembered the dog's name for reporters: Jean Claude van Damme. The toy poodle, he said, had never stepped foot outside the trailer until the murders, except when he was perched on JoAnna's shoulder. Van Damme was addicted to Carl's cigarette smoke. Charles rubbed his cigarette butt into the dirt with the toe of his boot.

A reporter asked if he felt all of the boys were equally guilty.

"I view Isaac differently than the others," he said. "I believe if not for him, the others wouldn't have been caught."

His voice softened a bit, and three long tears traced a path down Charles Dutcher's hard, expressionless face. "I was supposed to be up there that night, but I had to work. The property was finally opened up and released to me today. It's been locked up for three years. I'm gonna go up there and fix it. I got no friends. I'm gonna go live on the mountain where my boy's ashes are spread."

"Tony was going to be a translator in the Rangers," he said. The U.S. Army Rangers were an elite special operations military regiment.

"He would've graduated this year. They pretty much took my only reason for living."

As the last reporter turned to go, Charles offered one more statement.

"Just remember him," he said. "Please remember Tony."

PART FOUR

Reckoning

CHAPTER 22

As the five-year anniversary of the Columbine High School massacre approached, Denver journalist Dave Cullen offered a reconsideration of why Eric Harris and Dylan Klebold opened fire on their schoolmates and plotted to blow up the school back in the spring of 1999.

Based on an extensive FBI report in which a team of psychiatrists and psychologists had analyzed both boys' personalities and motives, Cullen concluded in *Slate* magazine that previous notions of the boys as "Trench Coat Mafia" outcasts or boys taking revenge against bullies should be discarded. Instead of asking what drove the killers, he said, we needed to view them as "radically different individuals with vastly different motives and opposite mental conditions"—Klebold the hotheaded, depressive suicidal kid who "blamed himself for his problems"; Harris the sweet-faced and well-spoken but cold and calculating psychopath, the "mastermind and driving force" of the planning and the attack.

Klebold, the psychiatrists argued, could never have pulled off the attack without Harris. Harris, they concluded, "was not a wayward boy who could have been rescued. Harris, they believe, was irretrievable." As with most psychopaths, also called sociopaths, Harris was surmised to be lacking a conscience, empathy, or remorse for his actions.

In 2004, another kind of reconsideration was under way in the case of Isaac Grimes. Donna Grimes, who'd schooled herself in the language and theory of cultic behavior and mind control tactics, had sprung into action as "Maze Mom," her e-mail handle, determined to convince Judge Kenneth Plotz to reconsider the sixty-year sentence he'd handed down to her son.

Donna posted a letter on the Internet, appealing for support for Isaac:

> It was a crime beyond belief. It was a crime that Isaac, of his own voli-
> tion, could never have committed. The forensic psychologist testified
> that Isaac had severe PTSD, believed he needed to be punished, was ex-
> tremely remorseful and in his 15-year-old mind had no other option
> than to commit murder. The psychologist testified that Isaac had no so-
> ciopathic tendencies and had been physically and mentally tortured.
> Judge Kenneth Plotz said, "I don't buy this story," and sentenced Isaac
> to sixty years.
>
> Isaac is currently in Colorado's prison for the serious mentally ill in
> 23-hour lockdown due to his youth. He receives drugs for depression
> but no mental health care. Five months ago, he was seen by another psy-
> chologist who specializes in cultic abuse. This doctor reports that he has
> an acute case of PTSD which will turn into psychosis if not treated. . . .
>
> In this day of terror phobia, it is ironic that Judge Plotz would not
> believe it would happen here.

The "other psychologist" mentioned in the letter was Dr. Cathleen Mann of Denver, a forensic consultant and licensed counselor hired by the Grimes family and their new attorney, Dale Parrish, to evaluate Isaac. Donna and Robin Grimes felt that Kent Gray and J. B. Katz had not represented Isaac aggressively enough at his sentencing and were enthusiastic about his new attorney. Parrish was an openly religious lawyer who prayed with his clients, someone the Grimes family believed would go to the mat for Isaac. Donna Grimes organized a fund-raising campaign to help pay for Parrish's services, including an evening presentation at Ascension Lutheran Church in Colorado Springs, where the Grimeses outlined their needs and introduced Parrish and Mann to their home congregation.

Their hope, they told church members gathered on a July evening, was to get residential treatment for Isaac at Wellspring Retreat and Resource Center, a treatment center specializing in the rehabilitation of victims of cultic abuse.

"Isaac's crime was committed at the direction and under the coercion of a cultlike group, which, through threats against him and his family and the exploitation of his sensitivity, intelligence, and loneliness, got him to do things that no one would have expected him capable of doing," Donna told the congregation. "His path to redemption, difficult enough given the horror of the crime, is compounded by the effects of mind control that come with cult involvement."

Pastor Keith Hedstrom told church members they could support Isaac in a number of ways: pray for him and his family; write to him; write to Judge Plotz and District Attorney Ed Rodgers to express support for Isaac; contribute to the Grimes defense fund, supporting a resentencing effort in the courts that would be very expensive; or offer a pledge to help pay the costs of the Wellspring treatment. As part of their appeal, Hedstrom explained, the Grimeses hoped to get permission from the court for Isaac to participate in the program. They had long ago depleted their savings.

Dale Parrish briefly addressed the crowd. A good-looking, fit man with a thick mane of black hair and a sparkling smile, Parrish wore jeans and a silver belt buckle under a western sports jacket. He toted a *Cowboy Bible,* a customized New Testament with sketches of bucking-bronco riders on the covers. He encouraged the congregation to write letters to Isaac, the judge, and the DA.

"Isaac did not receive the kind of caring, visionary defense he needed," said Parrish, hinting at one of the tacks he might take in asking the court for reconsideration.

"There are two ways of reconsideration, beyond the initial threshold decision of being sentenced as an adult," he explained. "One, we can try to convince the judge to show mercy. Two, we can demonstrate that something was done improperly by his legal counsel and needs to be fixed."

"This was one of our lambs that the wolves grabbed and took away from the fold," said David Snell, a church member. He urged his fellow church members to raise the five thousand dollars needed for Isaac's treatment and take that information to the judge, to show the level of support for Isaac within his church community.

It was a risky strategy. So-called brainwashing defenses, used to explain incomprehensible behavior, had not been successful in criminal cases, dating back to the watershed Patty Hearst case of 1976. Nineteen-year-old Hearst had been kidnapped by members of the Symbionese Liberation Army (SLA), a revolutionary group in San Francisco, and held captive in a closet for two months, where she was raped, tortured, and indoctrinated.

A photo of Hearst carrying a rifle at a bank robbery was distributed by the SLA as proof that she'd become a fellow gun-toting revolutionary urban guerrilla. Hearst was captured, arrested, and tried for bank robbery. Her attorney, F. Lee Bailey, argued she'd been coerced into performing criminal acts but the jury didn't buy it, instead finding Hearst guilty and sentencing her to seven years in prison.

Hearst's sentence was eventually overturned by President Jimmy Carter, and President Bill Clinton pardoned her.

In Colorado, a defense of coercion in a felony case had long been disallowed by the courts. But the Grimes family hoped to appeal to Judge Plotz's heart if not his mind, convincing him that Isaac had been under the undue influence of a charismatic cult leader when he killed Tony Dutcher, and that he was of a tender, impressionable age when the crime occurred. Those factors, combined with Isaac's confession and cooperation with law enforcement in the investigation of the rest of the group, might weigh in Isaac's favor in a reconsideration hearing. Defense lawyers routinely filed for reconsideration when a stiff sentence was handed down, hoping to get years knocked off.

An online petition was posted under the banner of a group called Betrayed Innocence, addressed to "local, state and federal courts of Colorado and assorted politicians," urging officials to recognize that Isaac was of a young age, that he had been under duress and mind control, and that he was a strong candidate for successful rehabilitation.

Nearly four hundred people signed, most of them advocates against the adult prosecution of juveniles. "How can you figure putting a child into a state facility for sixty years is going to help in any way, shape or form?" one signatory asked. "I believe it will do him more harm than if he were to be sent to a juvenile facility or to receive professional help."

People from the United Kingdom, Australia, and across the United States signed the petition. "An adult can be brainwashed. What makes the public think a child couldn't?" asked one signer. A petitioner from Canada asked, "When will it ever stop? Why on God's green earth do kids get more time than adults? Go figure . . . it has to stop!"

Two dissenting voices were registered: One, an unnamed teen from Colorado Springs, said, "He had a choice, he made it, he took the life of his best friend, the court was harsh, but he did what he did and there is no changing that." The other, Ty Dutcher of Raleigh, North Carolina, son of Carl and JoAnna Dutcher and uncle of Tony Dutcher, wrote his message in all capital letters:

THE BOY HELPED KILL MY FAMILY. WHERE WAS MY PARENTS AND TONY'S JUSTICE? I GUESS THAT DOESN'T MATTER BECAUSE OH YA—IT DIDN'T HAPPEN TO YOUR FAMILY, DID IT? WALK IN SOMEONE ELSE'S SHOES BEFORE YOU ARE QUICK TO JUDGE. CLOSE YOUR EYES AND THINK. I DO EVERY NIGHT BUT I CRY. TY

Classifying the OARA as a cult and Simon Sue as a cult leader might have seemed a stretch for some who had dismissed the whole thing as a hoax designed to fill Simon's pockets with the money of his underlings. But Cathleen Mann argued that so long as a number of clearly defined elements were in place, a cult was a cult was a cult, regardless of its size or ultimate intentions.

"First, there is often a self-appointed leader who inspires devotion, and who makes decisions and limits choices in a top-down, authoritarian manner," said Mann in a position paper defining cults. "Second, the cult leader (usually enlisting the help of current adherents/followers) practices deceptive recruiting, where a potential client/adherent/follower is not provided with the informed consent or information necessary to make a rational decision about affiliation or 'joining.'"

In the case of the OARA, both Isaac and Glen Urban had told investigators they believed the group was one thing when they enlisted and soon found it was something different altogether.

Third, said Mann, the group or its leader practices a form of unethical mind control, also known as coercive persuasion, thought reform, or undue influence: "This is a deliberate attempt to alter the reality of a person by manipulating his or her environment." This attempt might be aided by control over diet and intake of food, sleep deprivation, physical threats, or other methods such as the alienation of a person from her or his former life and interests, or deliberate alienation from family members who do not subscribe to the cult's teachings.

A cult leader, according to Mann, might "deliberately create disinformation about critics or defectors . . . by attacking peripheral friends or family members of the involved adherent/follower." Cult leaders demand sole allegiance, said Mann, only to themselves, not to others.

After visiting Isaac Grimes, Mann told the Grimes parents that she saw in Isaac many typical characteristics of a person exiting a cultic group.

"Once they realize they've been in a cult and done some bad things, they react in predictable ways," she said, "often going to the other extreme of extreme legalism or extreme religiosity."

The Grimeses were concerned that Isaac had consistently and methodically weaned himself from all outside influences while locked down in his cell, getting rid of his television and radio and reading only his Bible. And while he had always been a boy who liked to discuss his Christian faith with his parents, now his religious ideas were becoming more rigid and inflexible, more sharply focused and somewhat obsessive.

It was a phase, Mann assured his parents, that Isaac would pass through, assuming he got the care he needed. In the extreme isolation of lockdown, his reality checked only by himself, Isaac had turned his Christianity into a cult for himself, in which he could be saved if he followed certain rules in a certain way or read Scripture in a specific way that allowed no dissent or interpretation. It was a way to comfort himself.

But it's difficult when you come out of a cult to rehabilitate yourself, Mann warned. "You need someone to explain to you what's happened to you, how sociopaths operate."

Mann had not met or evaluated Simon Sue, but she observed in Isaac's story about him the general characteristics of a successful cult leader. "They are usually sociopaths, socially adept, glib people who know how to manipulate, who learn this through trial and error. All successful cult leaders are pretty highly intelligent, and appear to have a vast amount of knowledge. They express interest in you, tell you how special you are, use a lot of flattery."

What had been in it for Isaac and the other boys was "a sense of specialness, uniqueness that comes from being involved—this big secret," said Mann.

In formulating Isaac's reconsideration of sentence, Attorney Dale Parrish repeatedly told Mann he had a problem believing that any of the claims about the OARA were true. Mann told him it didn't matter whether the organization as Simon described it existed or not, whether it was empirically true or not. "The fact is that it was used to manipulate and seduce."

If there were any doubts about the level of fear created by Simon Sue, Mann dismissed them. "When you're in these kinds of groups it gets exhausting to constantly be striving to serve the whims of the leader, to keep it a secret, to engage in the things they want you to do," she said. "[The boys] were so spent and exhausted doing what they thought they had to do to survive. That's not a justification; it's just the reality. They're fearful. They're operating from a position of exhaustion and survival."

•◆•

In October 2004, four soldiers stationed at Fort Carson in Colorado Springs were charged with murder for suffocating Iraqi Major General Hamed Mahwoush to death while interrogating him in Iraq. The soldiers had reportedly slipped a sleeping bag over the general's head, then turned him over from his back to his stomach. One account accused the soldiers of sitting on the general's back, causing his asphyxiation. Two other Fort Carson soldiers awaited courts-martial proceedings for drowning an Iraq civilian in the Tigris River.

These events drove home widely televised reports of torture and prisoner abuse at Abu Ghraib prison in Iraq, where American soldiers had taken hundreds of shocking digital photos showing themselves sexually, physically, and mentally humiliating and abusing Iraqi prisoners. One photo showed a smiling young U.S. Army specialist giving a big thumbs up over a corpse. As public enthusiasm for the war diminished, long after President Bush had declared "Mission Accomplished," these incidents raised serious questions about the nature of the mission, its leaders, and the tactics employed to achieve victory.

And on October 17, 2004, the U.S. Supreme Court began considering the constitutionality of the death penalty for sixteen- and seventeen-year-old criminals. Mental health professionals briefed the court with what was considered a "novel" scientific argument: Juveniles should not be executed because their brains are still developing and they are therefore not as culpable in their actions as an adult criminal with a fully developed brain. "The old idea was that adolescence was a social phenomenon, not biological," said

Dr. Jay Giedd, chief of brain imaging in the child psychiatry branch of the National Institute of Mental Health. The images Giedd and his colleagues had developed showed adolescent brains in dynamic stages of change.

•◆•

Isaac Grimes, now nineteen, first incarcerated at age fifteen, wrote Judge Plotz in anticipation of his upcoming reconsideration hearing:

Howdy, Your Honor!

The first thing I want to say is that no matter what happens today, you have my undying thanks for giving me a 60-year sentence back in March of 2002. That was such a blessing because without having that long sentence I wouldn't have been forced to see that I couldn't live life on my own—I needed (and still need) God's help. Having a long sentence on top of everything else forced me to pursue a personal relationship with God which total [*sic*] changed me inside. . . . I can honestly say that I have never felt better and I have never been better—even though I'm in prison!

What do I think is a fitting sentence? Well, JUSTICE would be a death sentence. I wrongly took an innocent life, and no amount of fines or fees or incarceration time can pay for that—only by my being executed would JUSTICE be done. A life for a life.

But there is a thing called MERCY: not to strike without need. Society does not need to have me in prison. I am no danger to anyone, and rather than costing taxpayers thousands of dollars every year sitting in prison I am very much willing and wanting to be a productive positive contributor to society. . . . Quite simply, to say that anything less than a life for a life is even partial payment is an insult to the value of human life—it is an insult to the memory of Anthony Dutcher.

Isaac explained that his attorney wanted to ask the judge to let him out in May 2006, reasoning that five years served in solitary confinement equaled ten years under normal circumstances, but Isaac couldn't agree with that option. Instead, he made a recommendation "just about unheard of in the Unites States."

> I ask for four years imprisonment, plus five years mandatory parole and house arrest . . . plus any other measure the court sees fit to make sure that I am no danger to society, such as monthly interviews and progress reports by Dr. Mann. I also ask that the court order I go to Wellspring until they are satisfied that I can indeed cope with the outside world. I don't ask this because of anything I've earned or deserved—I ask in the name of MERCY—and I promise that whatever sentence you give me, even if you leave my sentence at 60 years, I will continue to do my best to be a positive contributor to the world around me and the world at large. Thank you.
>
> Isaac Grimes

Dale Parrish worked with Donna and Robin Grimes, formulating his strategy for the hearing. He hoped to show the judge how Isaac's truthfulness had made the other prosecutions possible. He hoped to show a kid whose world had changed when he met Simon Sue. He hoped to open a window into Isaac's head, to show that first time in Simon's bedroom, Jon standing sentry at the door with his arms across his chest, Simon reading out the rules of the OARA. He hoped to demonstrate to Judge Plotz that "every boy has his own path to manhood. At fourteen or fifteen, you have kids ranging in appearance from nine or ten to those with muscles and whiskers talking about the Marines," said Parrish. He hoped to show what was unique about Isaac Grimes. He felt good about the date God had delivered for the hearing, December 27.

•◆•

On the Monday just past Christmas, frozen silver fields lined Highway 24 past Woodland Park. Between Lake George and Florissant, signs were up for the annual antique and classic tractor pull. The South Platte River formed a winding frozen S through the flat valley: An ice skater could jump on the river at Hartsel and glide all the way down to Lake George.

Radio stations broadcast after-Christmas specials, sales on everything from sofas to skis. In Fairplay, the diner on the main drag had changed names and fares three times over the three years since Isaac Grimes was first arraigned.

The Park County Courthouse was chilly inside as the Grimes family and their supporters assembled on the hard wooden benches. No Dutchers were here, no Sues, no Mathenys. Rob Grimes, nearly crippled by sciatica, looked forty pounds lighter than when his son had first been arrested. Donna still looked fresh and young. Her nature was to smile and cut jokes; humor was her coping mechanism, something Dale Parrish had warned her off. He'd chosen Rob, the more predictable of the two, to take the stand on Isaac's behalf.

Sean Paris, focused and wired with nervous energy, sat alone at the prosecutors' table. Dave Thorson, dressed in outdoor gear, sat in the back of the courtroom observing his young colleague.

Isaac Grimes, seven inches taller than he'd been at his first court appearance three and a half years ago, was escorted into the courtroom, shackled and bound. He was thin, his hair spiky and short, buzzed around the ears, and he wore plastic-rimmed prison-issue glasses, each lens the size of a coaster.

Dale Parrish opened the hearing for the defense.

"I seek to convince you that this is an appropriate case for a consideration of mercy for a number of reasons," Parrish told Judge Plotz.

He introduced the concept of adolescent mitigation, not an excuse or a plea designed to completely exculpate his client, but a consideration of reduced blameworthiness due to impaired decisionmaking and unusual circumstances. He cited several examples of case law and introduced several exhibits: an overview of the gathering at Ascension Lutheran Church in support of Isaac Grimes; all newspaper articles pertinent to the case; a December 22 letter from Tony Dutcher's aunt, Kathy Creech, asking the judge for mercy in his reconsideration of Isaac's sentence; letters from several others, including a letter from Betrayed Innocence addressed to the judge and the DA; Department of Corrections reports on Isaac Grimes; and two photos of Simon Sue posing with weapons.

"This case is notable for many reasons," said Parrish. "First, the aspect of mind control or cultism. It has been likened by people related to the case to Charles Manson or Jim Jones. This language was signed off on by a probation officer in Isaac's presentencing report, who said, 'He has related his fears several times; it appears he sincerely believes his family would be killed.' The probation officer noted that aspects of these fears were corroborated by materials seized from Simon Sue." As an example, Parrish offered the flyer for Jim Jones Summer Camp, proprietor Reverend Simon E. Sue, addressed to the Colorado Springs Chamber of Commerce Division of New Businesses.

"Second," Parrish continued, "the court must consider the age of Isaac Grimes at the time he came under the influence of Simon Sue. It was his first time out of the neighborhood when he left for Palmer High School at age fourteen. His first semester, he had lunch with Tony Dutcher. Second semester, he had lunch with Simon and later with Jon and Simon.

"Third, we come to this reconsideration, we believe, with the support of the Dutcher family: James, Charles and Rhonda, Kathy Creech.

"Fourth, when Isaac confessed on Thursday, March 8, 2001, there was a breakthrough in the investigation." Parrish argued that the prosecution might not have solved the case without the assistance of Isaac Grimes.

Finally, he argued, the court needed to take into consideration his client's extreme duress, his fear of retaliation against him or his family if he tried to get out of the OARA. To support this point, Parrish offered Glen Urban's and his best friend Anthony Jacobs's interviews with prosecutors, in which both boys expressed similar fears.

"Neither Isaac nor his parents have ever tried to downplay or trivialize the seriousness of his behavior," said Parrish. "Indeed, the first time Robin and Donna Grimes spoke out was a year after Isaac's initial arrest. They told the press, 'My son was afraid.'"

Parrish reminded Judge Plotz that at Simon Sue's preliminary hearing, he had said "the most compelling evidence [against Simon] was Isaac Grimes's testimony."

Parrish called Rob Grimes to the stand. Rob hobbled up the single step to the witness stand and carefully lowered himself into the chair.

"Mr. Grimes, were you present at the March 2 sentencing hearing for your son?" asked Parrish. Rob said yes, he had been.

"Was Judge Plotz given all the information needed to ensure a fair consideration of a sentence at that time?"

"In my opinion, no," said Rob. "Lots of items were left out by previous counsel, mitigating factors. Isaac was born May 30, 1985. His elementary and junior high schools were four blocks from our home. Palmer High School was three and a half miles away.

"As a kid, Isaac was mainly just friends with Tony. He had difficulty making friends. He was soft-spoken, polite, something of a loner, but he was a typical teenager until his association with the OARA."

Parrish asked Rob to describe the circumstances at home during the time Isaac was in the OARA.

"I broke my back in August 2000," Rob said, as straightforwardly as if he'd said he'd broken his arm.

"Can you describe your son's level of maturity freshman year in high school?"

"He was young for his age. He was book-smart but didn't have much common sense. His best friend was Tony Dutcher. Tony was smart, too." Rob described their mutual fascination with the military, how neither had a girlfriend. "They fit together as odd men out."

"I noticed Isaac was very uncomfortable and reserved about attending high school," he said. Later, he had become withdrawn from his family and was supposedly playing chess on Wednesdays after school.

"He rode to school with his sister, a senior. We thought he'd be all right. He'd never lied to us." Rob described being disabled after he broke his back, spending a lot of time in bed awaiting surgery around the time Isaac started his sophomore year. At that time, Isaac had spent more and more time with Simon at the Sue homes.

"Mr. Grimes, in May 2001 Isaac accepted a plea bargain. Were you consulted by his attorney?"

"No."

"Was your wife?"

"No."

"How old was Isaac and what were his circumstances at that time?"

"He was fifteen. He was here in the Park County Jail, in close proximity to Simon and Jon, and he was afraid of both of them. I'd just had reconstructive spinal surgery."

"Did Isaac's attorney consult you before the plea hearing in which he pleaded guilty?"

"Yes," said Rob. "They told us, 'This is the best we can get. We'll hope for a reconsideration.'"

Parrish offered Robin Grimes a chance to speak directly to Judge Plotz.

"I think he's changed now," he told the judge. "We'd like to take care of him. When Isaac was arrested, he begged Leonard Post to make sure his family would be safe. He was genuinely afraid for his life.

"We talk by telephone a lot. He's quirky. Please show mercy on our son. Although he did unspeakable things, he was bound by evil."

Plotz listened carefully, then called a recess. As the crowd in the gallery stood, Donna Grimes leaned forward to get as close as she could to Isaac. The guard reached his hand out between them. "No touching, no hugging," he said.

Following the recess, Sean Paris cross-examined Robin Grimes for the prosecution.

"In April 2000 your son was in the OARA, a group whose purpose was to perpetrate crimes not sanctioned by the law, yes?"

"Yes," said Rob.

"It was a gang?"

"Yes."

"Your son became a member."

"Yes."

"You told us Simon told your son to slash your daughter's tires. Do you rely on that fact?"

"Yes."

"Your son visited the home of Carl and JoAnna Dutcher. Carl taught Isaac and Tony to make knives. The knife he made with Carl ended up on a knife rack in your kitchen. Was your son comfortable with knives?"

"Yes."

"The summer Simon Sue left for Guyana, Isaac was left in charge and Jon was on probation. Weapons were taken from him and some were given to Isaac during this time. Isaac devised a raid on Gabe Melchor's house. When Simon returned, the raid was not done. Isaac selected the Dutchers as the object of the next raid. Isn't that true."

"I don't think that has been established."

Parrish volleyed.

"Mr. Grimes, did Isaac want out of the gang?"

"Yes."

"Is it true that Glen Urban also wanted out?"

"Yes."

"Had threats been made to more than one member if they wanted out?"

"Yes."

"Had Isaac been forced to do other acts?"

"Yes."

"Thank you, Mr. Grimes."

The defense called Cathleen Mann to the stand and quickly established her credentials in issues of mind control, undue influence, cults, and their effects on families. She had first been contacted by a national advocacy organization, then by Robin and Donna Grimes, who had asked her to examine their son and look into his case. She had met Isaac at San Carlos and reviewed the case using legal databases.

Mann was a heavyset woman with practical shoes and a practical manner. She told the court she'd studied the neuropsychological development of young adolescent males, specifically the most recent research showing adolescence to be a time of "present orientation and risk taking" when "judgement is most often extremely poor."

"The most salient thing that struck me is that adolescents have a tough time with individuation, with separating out from family and keeping things good," said Mann.

When Mann had met Isaac Grimes, then eighteen, he had presented as much younger than eighteen. She told the court her observations: He had been socially isolated at Palmer High School; he was delayed socially; he had poor skills at developing relationships; she thought he had possible social anxiety disorder.

Judge Plotz yawned and rubbed his eyes.

"Ms. Mann, were you involved in a cult in the past?" asked Parrish.

"Yes, from 1989 to 1991," she said, "I was recruited into a cult. Later, after studying psychology I became an expert in cultic studies."

"And can you tell us what constitutes a cult?"

"Of course. There are four criteria: First, a self-appointed charismatic leader. Second, the practice of mind control, thought reform, or undue influence, isolating people from their support groups, alternating between punishment and reward, confusing them. There's usually secretiveness involved and the dynamic of making someone feel special. Third, there's deceptive recruiting. Fourth, deliberate and continuous implantation of dependency and dread."

"Ms. Mann, at Mr. Grimes's sentencing hearing, Judge Plotz said, 'You're too intelligent for that,' referring to mind control. How do you respond to that?"

"It has nothing to do with intelligence; in fact, it's important to understand that smart people are more vulnerable."

"Ms. Mann, how would you characterize Isaac Grimes's current mental and emotional condition, considering that Dr. Barron previously diagnosed him with severe post-traumatic stress disorder?"

"Isaac's condition is deteriorating in his current setting. And the PTSD, if untreated, presents a serious risk factor. If he goes untreated, he could become psychotic."

Parrish, in a well-rehearsed line of questions, introduced Wellspring as a potential treatment center for Isaac Grimes and presented printouts from the Web site to Plotz.

Sean Paris rose to cross-examine Cathleen Mann.

"Ms. Mann, to your knowledge is the campus of Wellspring a secure site?"

"Probably not," she conceded.

Mann was released from the stand and replaced by Leonard Post, called by the prosecution. Post looked nervous and miserable, his head hung low, his eyes avoiding Isaac and the Grimeses' side of the courtroom. In one week he would retire from the DA's office.

Paris wasted no time.

"Mr. Post, did Isaac lie to you?"

"Yes, early on, prior to the acceptance phase of the initial March 8 interview, he was deceptive for an hour and a half and truthful for two and a half hours."

Dale Parrish cross-examined Post.

"Was there evidence at Simon Sue's house that corroborated what Isaac Grimes told you?"

"Yes."

"Was the threat of retaliation real?"

"I believe Isaac thought it was real."

All the witnesses had been called. Parrish began his summation. He outlined Isaac's term of incarceration under the standing sentence, the dangers to him in prison as a young man and as an informant who'd cooperated with police against his fellow defendants, a snitch. The mere fact that he was a snitch, said Parrish, was an indication that he didn't have a criminal mind.

"And now he's dealing with a place he may not survive. Isaac Grimes was the youngest inmate in the state prison system when he entered prison at sixteen and was sent to Sterling. He was segregated there for his own safety, then transferred to San Carlos, where he is still in a segregated unit, locked in his cell twenty-three hours a day. Segregation is intended to protect him from other inmates. His case manager has said she believes he will be raped or killed when he's placed in the general population," said Parrish.

He asked the judge for mercy as he reconsidered Isaac's sentence.

Parrish returned to the defense table and took a seat next to Isaac. Sean Paris strode to the podium and faced the judge.

"This court should summarily deny the motion to reconsider Isaac Grimes's sentence," he said. "The motion was allowed to linger for thirty-two months after a 120-day filing period." The idea that Isaac Grimes had not promptly pursued reconsideration inferred that it had been undertaken only after Attorney Parrish entered the picture, at the request of Grimes's parents, as a way to manipulate the court's earlier decision. It was a technicality, but an important one.

"Let's talk about the brutality of the slaying," said Paris. "Yes, sixty years is lengthy, but his acts are fully deserving. The thirty-two- to seventy-year range was agreed upon in the plea deal considering the seriousness of the crime.

"Why did Isaac go the extra mile? That doesn't fit the defense theory. He killed with enthusiasm and zeal. Why? Grimes made many of his own choices. The teenager was once left in charge of the gang while Sue was out of the country. He was the one who selected the Dutcher family as targets, and he attacked Dutcher with such enthusiasm and zeal that he nearly decapitated Tony as he lay in his sleeping bag.

"The level of betrayal is beyond words. Isaac Grimes brought a knife to a game of Scrabble.

"A stint at a chalet in the mountains of Ohio is adding insult to injury. Duress in this society is not a defense for first-degree murder—that's a matter of policy we have to adhere to, a matter of common law for one hundred years."

Isaac Grimes was given a chance to address the court before the judge rendered his decision. He stood up at the defense table and scanned the notes he'd been making throughout the proceeding.

"I have respect for Mr. Paris's job," he said, "but I abhor the misrepresentation of the facts by the DAs." Sharp breaths were drawn around the courtroom—by Isaac's parents and by those there to defend him. There was no predicting what he would say next.

"Ever since March of this year, it has been the best year of my life. I'm right with God; I'm right with my family.

"There was a discussion of X number of years, but to say that any number of years or a fine of any kind can equal a life is ludicrous. The only truly fair punishment for what I did is death. I would deserve it." The sharp intake of breaths turned to breathlessness. Donna Grimes looked down. Dale Parrish looked down. Robin Grimes looked down. Judge Plotz looked straight ahead with growing interest.

"Send me home," he implored the judge. "Wrap me up with any restrictions you like and I'll do it. Just send me home. I'm so sorry these horrible things happened."

Isaac sat down and stared straight ahead.

"Mr. Grimes," said Plotz, "in reconsidering your sentence, I am still taking into consideration rehabilitation, punishment, and the safety of the public.

"What you do unconsciously is distance yourself from the act. You say, 'I regret that these things happened.' But it was a very personal thing because of your friendship with Tony Dutcher.

"I believe that, especially with you, there is some potential for good. You forced me to think about that. Regarding cult behavior, the bulk of what we've heard here today we've heard before. I've thought about it a lot.

"But all the evil behavior in our society, in civilized society, doesn't absolve personal responsibility. If it did, anyone could claim they were members of a cult. It doesn't justify to Tony Dutcher what happened, that his life was taken.

"I believe you were on the extreme of those adolescent behaviors talked about in court today, and that's why you're still a safety risk. Cult behavior is something of a mystery to me, but it doesn't excuse you. All of that doesn't make it possible for me to send you to Wellspring, to ask for probation.

"I am concerned about the danger of prison, but I can't order you released and sent to a juvenile facility or given parole. It's a serious concern, but it doesn't fall within my jurisdiction. It's the responsibility of the Department of Corrections.

"Nevertheless, you were the youngest, and you should not be the defendant who receives the highest sentence," Plotz said. "I made a mistake in sentencing you to more time than Mr. Sue. So I'm ordering a five-year reduction on the count of second-degree murder and a five-year reduction on one count of conspiracy. That will make your sentence lesser than Mr. Sue's. You'll receive 369 days' credit for the Park County time served. That makes your sentence fifty years with one year off for good behavior."

Dale Parrish couldn't hide his elation at the judge's decision. As Isaac Grimes was led from the courtroom, Parrish began making calculations. Half of fifty years, if Isaac got half his sentence remanded for good behavior, would be twenty-five years; he could be as young as forty-three when he emerged from prison. That was something, but not enough. He declared he'd file another motion for reconsideration.

Plotz had avoided the scrutiny and potential scorn of the judicial community by, at once, rejecting the mind control defense and chopping ten years off Isaac's sentence as an expression of fairness.

Isaac Grimes went back to San Carlos embracing his fifty-year sentence, vowing to spend it repenting for the unforgivable sin he'd committed. Tony Dutcher and his grandparents had been dead for nearly four years. Time had little meaning anymore to Isaac, less than it did even to the dead, who were preserved forever in memory. He wished he could disappear into his cell with the knowledge of what he'd done and simply be forgotten.

CHAPTER 23

Charles and Rhonda Dutcher spent Christmas and New Year's at the Bear Trap Ranch house, where they were settled in for the winter. Sometimes they were snowed in for days, until a neighbor plowed the road. Charles drove the rugged road to Cripple Creek several times a week to cook in a restaurant. Rhonda kept a few chickens in a pen next to Carl's former gunshop. They cooked on a hot plate, hauled in water, and heated the place with a woodstove.

Charles liked chopping wood. It made him stop thinking.

Up the hill behind the trailer, little evidence of Tony's lean-to remained four years after his death. Inside the house there were still plenty of reminders of the night Carl and JoAnna had been gunned down: bullet holes, bloodstains, ravaged plumbing, and, Rhonda believed, ghosts. Sometimes, she said, JoAnna joked with her at night.

Photos of JoAnna still colored the walls of the small living room. Carl's big brown armchair was Charles's roost; he was the man of the house now. Beneath the ponderosa pine at the side of the house, its bark ragged and vanilla-scented, stood a tombstone memorial to his lost family, surrounded by orange boulders and a thick bed of pinecones. Above it hung wind chimes that tinkled through the long winter nights. A walking stick stood leaning against the tree, and beneath it, a bright festoon of artificial flowers, a silk bird of paradise—the only spot of color in the drab winter landscape.

•◆•

In February 2005, Isaac Grimes terminated his relationship with Dale Parrish, his parents, and the real world. He'd retreated deeper and deeper into his study of the Bible after the reconsideration and had determined that the people who cared about him worshipped God in a manner that was impure. Parrish was tainted because he listened to Christian rap, an abomination according to Isaac's doctrine. His parents and the folks at Ascension Lutheran Church were far too lax in their interpretation of God's word. The only way to protect himself was to divest himself of impurities.

He wrote Parrish:

Dear Dale Parrish,

As you know, my family and church and I have had disputes over proper doctrine. As they have refused Biblical truth (see Rev. 3:1–6), I cannot accept their aid anymore. I am not their enemy nor do I want to see any harm done to them but I cannot accept their aid because in doing so I would be giving the impression that refusal and distortion of the Word is a small matter. To do so would be a grievous offense against God.

As you know, I have no income (well, about $6 a month), and so I am unable to pay for your services. If I owe you anything, please keep a record and one day I will pay you back. I do not know when or how, but I know God will provide. The fact that I can't pay for your services means, quite naturally, that they must be terminated. I have great appreciation for all of your help and pray that this will be a painless, mutually respectful parting. Thank you.

Sincerely,

Isaac Grimes

Although Isaac's case manager had determined he would benefit from taking meals outside his cell and was no longer a suicide threat, he cloistered himself more tightly than ever and remained segregated by choice, wrapped in the arms of the only God that could keep his demons at bay.

Simon Sue appeared before Judge Kenneth Plotz on February 28, asking for reconsideration of his sentence. The court had already ruled that his plea bargain could not be rescinded; now he would argue that the sentence he had been given exceeded the normal range for conspiracy. He had parted ways with defense attorneys Ann Kaufman and Rick Levinson, citing conflict of interest, and had immersed himself in the law since entering Sterling. He entered the courtroom looking older and physically fit, sporting a neatly trimmed beard. At the defense table, he flipped through a thick law text flagged with Post-Its and furiously scribbled notes. His court-appointed attorney, an attractive young woman from Denver, was barely familiar with his case. Simon called the shots, conferring with her at length each time she addressed the judge.

Nadia and Keith Sue sat in the courtroom with Rose Trigg, the silver-haired substitute teacher who'd testified for Simon at his sentencing, and her frail, elderly husband, Gerald Trigg, the former head pastor of First United Methodist Church in Colorado Springs.

Simon's attorney argued that his sentence should be thrown out because it exceeded legal guidelines. Sean Paris, for the prosecution, said Simon had agreed to a forty- to sixty-year range as part of the plea deal. Judge Plotz observed that Simon had said he'd read and understood the plea agreement when he signed it and denied the motion. Court was quickly and efficiently dismissed.

Leaning on a walker, Reverend Gerald Trigg hobbled forward from the gallery toward the judge's bench. The court reporter stopped him and asked if she could help.

"I need to speak with the judge," he said. "I must speak with the judge."

"Sir, you can't be in this part of the courtroom. If you want to see the judge, you'll have to make an appointment with him in his office," she said gently.

Trigg painstakingly turned around and headed for the back of the courtroom in a slow, measured gait, shaking his head and mumbling to himself. He stopped to rest in the hallway, leaning against a vending machine, crying softly.

A newspaper reporter asked if she could help him.

"This is wrong," he said. "Terribly wrong. That is the finest young man I've ever met. The judge needs to understand. I know him. I've prayed with him. I trust that young man so much I'd let him babysit my grandchildren. The judge has got to understand."

Trembling, Trigg composed himself and waited for the Sues and Rose, then joined them for the ride home to Colorado Springs. Simon returned to Sterling to plan his next appeal.

• ◆ •

As soon as Judge Plotz had reduced Isaac Grimes's sentence from sixty to fifty years, DA Sean Paris petitioned the Colorado Court of Appeals to overturn the judge's ruling. In October 2005 a three-judge panel set aside Plotz's ruling and remanded the case back to Park County. At issue was the length of time between the initial motion for reconsideration and Grimes's appearance in court requesting a reduced sentence. To keep the ten-year reduction, Grimes would have to prove that he hadn't abandoned the motion over the nearly three years it had languished.

Shortly after the turn of 2005 into 2006, the fifth anniversary of the Dutcher murders, Isaac Grimes appeared in court without an attorney. He was thin and pale, dressed in a prison jumpsuit, thin white socks, and slippers, his skinny ankles shackled. His absurdly large glasses shielded most of his bony face. The courtroom was devoid of families; Isaac's parents had decided not to come to court when they realized he would be representing himself.

A grandfatherly sheriff's deputy, who'd escorted Isaac Grimes into the courtroom many times, checked purses and bags at the courtroom door. Judge Plotz, retired now from the bench, returned to Park County to take care of unfinished business. Sheriff Fred Wegener, broad and crew-cut with a bushy moustache, sat at the prosecution table with Sean Paris. Isaac sat alone at the defense table, flanked by a sober-looking prison guard.

"Mr. Grimes, you are present without counsel," said Judge Plotz, opening the hearing. "You are incarcerated. The court will provide an attorney if you can't afford one."

"No, your honor, I do not want an attorney," said Isaac.

"The court needs to know if the delay in filing the motion for reconsideration was excusable. It's significant to you because it means a difference in the length of your sentence. An attorney could investigate the reasons for delay. Without an attorney, you are waiving the benefits of that representation. Do you understand that?" Plotz spoke gently to the young man, who still looked as if he'd barely ever shaved.

"I understand."

"Are you currently taking drugs, alcohol, or prescription medication?"

"No." Isaac had taken himself off all antidepressant medication in recent months as part of his purification regimen.

"I find that you are competent, that you understand the explanation I gave you. Your waiver is voluntary and I will accept it today."

Isaac nodded gravely, a bow of respect aimed at Judge Plotz. Plotz looked back at him with an expression that communicated affection mingled with sorrow.

"Mr. Paris, have you received a letter from Ms. Jennifer Vandresar?"

"Yes, your honor," said Paris, holding up a copy in the air.

"I'm going to request that it be read aloud to the court," said Plotz. He asked Paris to provide a copy of the letter to Isaac. As a court reporter read the three-page handwritten letter aloud from the podium, Isaac bowed his head and read along.

It was a petition for mercy, a mother's cry for the son she'd lost and his boyhood friend who'd lost himself. Jenny's letter drew a picture of Isaac Grimes as a good boy whose goodness had been taken hostage by Simon Sue. She asked Judge Plotz to show mercy for her son's killer. The courtroom, sparsely populated by media representatives, was hushed as the passionate, articulate plea came to an end. On the front bench, Leonard Post stared straight ahead, his face reddened, his eyes rheumy and wet.

It was as if a warm blanket had been thrown over the chilly courtroom. The woman who'd read the letter folded the yellow pages carefully and returned to her seat, a soft smile on her face. Plotz composed himself and proceeded.

"Who has the burden to proceed?" he asked.

Isaac Grimes fielded the question. "It doesn't matter," he said. "I'm not going to argue anything Mr. Paris has to say."

Plotz spoke again in a kind voice, the voice of a teacher explaining a difficult concept to a student.

"The Colorado Court of Appeals has remanded the decision to decrease your sentence by ten years, with direction. You are required to show why the delay of thirty-two months was reasonable. Do you plan to argue in any way the reasons for the delay?"

"No, sir."

"Why not? Mr. Grimes, this is your time, your life." Plotz's eyes urged Isaac to defend himself. But he would not.

"I'm not concerned with my sentence length and won't appeal it for any reason," said Isaac, his voice calm and measured.

"Then I'll have no choice but to vacate that order," said Plotz. "Does that not matter to you?"

"No, your honor, it doesn't matter to me."

"Are you going to call any witnesses?"

"No."

"Will you present any argument?"

"No."

"Then I'll ask Mr. Paris to proceed."

Sean Paris meticulously outlined the time of the delay in question, making a technical argument, concluding that the defense had delayed the reconsideration for self-serving purposes. Nothing had prevented Isaac Grimes from proceeding, he said. Delays that resulted from the court's or the defen-

dant's inability could be forgiven, but the courts forbid a defendant's manipulation of a delay to serve his own purposes. Isaac Grimes's mental condition or the fact that he was being held in the state prison for the severely
mentally ill was not mentioned.

"Basically," Paris concluded, "the defendant took no steps to move the reconsideration forward within the required time frame and didn't indicate
any reason outside his control that prevented him."

Judge Plotz interjected. "During the times of the delay, Mr. Grimes was
represented by counsel. He didn't control the proceedings then. Should he
suffer additionally because of possible poor judgment of counsel?"

"With the late filing of a motion for reconsideration, neglect can be
brought out by an attorney," Paris explained. "That was not done in this
case. Both attorney and client must be involved in efforts to move forward. If
they don't, the burden shifts to another branch of government." A boy who
had purged his life of attorneys and legalities had no recourse, according to
the law.

"Mr. Grimes, was the long delay justified? Are there any reasons to justify
the delay?" Plotz pleaded.

"I haven't really paid attention to points of law until this time last year,"
said Isaac. He had accepted a plea bargain, had testified against Simon Sue,
had pleaded guilty, and had accepted a sixty-year sentence, but he hadn't
really paid attention to points of law. "I just did what they told me to do.
What Mr. Paris said is irrelevant. I don't plan to contest my sentence."

"A year from now, five years from now, you will not be able to change
your mind," said Plotz. "Do you understand?"

"Yes," said Isaac.

Judge Plotz handed down his ruling, reiterating the legal points and once
again emphasizing the "horrible tragedy" of the case.

"Mr. Grimes has taken the burden of his representation onto his own
shoulders," he said, locked in eye contact with Isaac. "There really are no
reasons for the delay. I am without jurisdiction. I have no ability to reduce
your sentence so I reinstate the original sentence of the court, sixty years."

Isaac left the courtroom steady and unruffled. Plotz left in a flurry. Triumphant, Paris strode to the courthouse lobby.

"Is this Isaac's last chance?" a reporter asked.

"I hope we're done with the last of the legal proceedings against Isaac Grimes," Paris said, pulling on his overcoat. "These crimes, this is the sort of horror one seeks out on a Saturday afternoon in a movie theater, not a real-life drama to be played out in Guffey, Colorado."

•◆•

Two days later, following a snowstorm that bathed Fairplay in white, a weary Judge Plotz took the stand again to respond to another Colorado Court of Appeals decision, this one requiring that Jon Matheny be resentenced. Matheny's sixty-eight-year sentence, the appeals court had ruled, fell in the aggravated sentencing range, though the district court had made no findings that extraordinary aggravating factors had existed.

Matheny walked into the courtroom broader and taller, his head shaved, his muscled arms tattooed. Public Defender Patrick Murphy argued that Jon had never been convicted of a violent crime, had shown remorse for his participation in OARA activities and for the Dutchers' losses, had "kept his nose clean" in prison, and thus had shown rehabilitative potential.

It wasn't fair that Jon had gotten a harsher sentence than Isaac Grimes or Simon Sue, said Murphy. Grimes had confessed to killing, and Sue was believed to have masterminded the murders, coercing the other two boys to do his bidding. Jon Matheny had never confessed to murder, only to conspiracy.

"I'm going to be forever sorry," Jon told the court. "It's been five years now, and I've grown up a bit since I was a kid. That night is forever going to be with me. I've got a sixty-eight-year sentence and no way of getting out. I'd like to ask for some sort of leniency. There's nothing I can do to take that hurt away."

Judge Plotz glared at the defense table. He had no intention of yielding, and he'd done his math before entering the courtroom. He would reduce the sentence, but only by enough to make sure it couldn't be contested in the Colorado Court of Appeals again.

"I have to consider the consequences of your actions," he said to Jon. "This was not the theft of a loaf of bread or even a robbery. It's the terrible deaths of three people. I saw the pictures, and although it was several years ago, they are still burnt into my mind. What do I tell Tony Dutcher's father, who has lost his son and both his parents in one night?" Plotz didn't say he was convinced Jon Matheny had shot Carl and JoAnna Dutcher, but he did say he had not been convinced otherwise.

"From all the evidence I've heard in this case, you're more culpable than the two others in two of the murders," he concluded. "It seems to me you are more culpable than Mr. Grimes."

Plotz shaved significant years off the penalties for each offense but ordered them served consecutively rather than concurrently. He added twenty years for stealing guns under the Colorado racketeering and organized-crime statute, to be served concurrently with the other three sentences. The total reduction in sentence was two years. Jon's new sentence was sixty-six years in adult prison.

Bonnie Matheny watched her son leave the courtroom. She visited him every week in prison and marveled at his strength. He comforted her with his resolve. "Get used to it, Mom," he told her. "Accept it. I'm basically doing life."

God had gotten her through unimaginably dark days before and would get her through many more. Her church offered her solace. She wouldn't give up on Jon ever. She drove home to Colorado Springs marveling at the beauty of the Earth, the glory of the skies. Her mantra was a prayer for her son, for his release and for her own.

CHAPTER 24

The Pike National Forest between Colorado Springs and Fairplay had seen death and devastation, restoration and revival, since the Hayman fire of 2002.

The largest wildfire in the state's history had killed the forest canopy in a large portion of the 138,000 acres that burned and had sent flames racing across the forest floor in others, destroying all groundcover in its path.

Four years later, hikers reentering the area now found lush wildflower growth, the seeds fed by nutrients in the ash, and thousands of new aspen shoots emerging in an area where mature aspens had been mysteriously dying off for years. Some wildlife species, like the American bald eagle, had departed the area for lack of shelter. Others, like the three-toed woodpecker, had been newly drawn to the ecosystem of dead trees and the bugs that eat them. In some areas the ground was covered with fine gray dust that one hiker dubbed "cremation soil," where, apparently, all seeds and root systems had been incinerated. The forest had become a laboratory for plant scientists to study the aftermath and recovery possibilities of a disastrous fire event.

The years following the New Year's Eve murders of Carl, JoAnna, and Tony Dutcher forced everyone involved—the perpetrators, the families of the dead, the families of those sent to prison, neighbors and friends, lawyers, and investigators—to contemplate the loss of life, the violence and sorrow unleashed at Bear Trap Ranch that night. At the same time, they had to learn how to move forward. Nothing would ameliorate their losses, they found, but the living must breathe and move and search for new ways to grow.

•◆•

On a blustery winter afternoon in February 2005, Glen Urban remembered the days of the OARA, his arrest, and his time in the Park County Jail. His two-year community corrections sentence completed, Glen now worked in Colorado Springs on a department-store loading dock. His felony conviction had followed him wherever he went, he said. It was a record he'd have to live with for a long time.

Wiry and alert, shy and nervous, Glen wore a dark green camouflage jacket. His shaggy, sandy hair stood up around his head. He'd grown a goatee.

He smiled sadly, remembering senior year in high school and his recruitment into the OARA.

"I thought it was some kind of extreme Boy Scouts," he said of Simon and his group. "What appealed to me was that they were actually going to *do* something." High school was a bore. Simon was talking about building things, learning things, going to foreign places.

"The thing that impressed me about Simon was how smart he was, how much he knew," said Glen. "He told me the next big war would be with terrorist cells, then 9/11 happened." He shook his head and looked down, then chuckled nervously.

He recounted what he had thought the OARA was until he learned differently.

"The goal of this thing, the OARA, would be to improve the quality of life of everyone in it. I thought I could excel and be rewarded for it, and I thought I could do that better in a group than on my own."

He also saw it as "a revolt against free trade," a rebellion against the American economy, which was based on demand for consumer products, not on making people's lives better. He vaguely remembered a conversation with Simon referring to the OARA as being similar to a medieval guild, a highly regimented organization in which the members provided for one another's needs while learning and performing a trade. Glen's trade had been mechanic. Simon had provided him with tools and tasks to perform.

"I guess it's like the military," he said. "They set your goals for you, tell you what to do. That appealed to me then."

Glen grew more sober as he recalled the days before Jon's and Isaac's arrests, then his and Simon's. Simon had grilled him and the other members, telling them what the CBI would ask them when they were interrogated, and drilling them in how they would respond.

"They questioned me twice," said Glen. "The second time, on March 8, when Isaac confessed, they told me about the crime, uh, the Dutchers. . . . That was a kind of tough one there. Simon told me that if I didn't give the cops this alibi, he would hunt me down, hunt my family down, and kill us. I figured I'd have to run away if he came after me."

That he hadn't graduated high school still bothered Glen four years later. He had been fired from his job at the public library and forbidden to enter Palmer High School once his name was linked to the crimes.

"I guess I can't blame them," he said, "but I didn't kill anybody."

Glen reflected briefly on Simon Sue, still to serve fifty-three years in prison.

"I think [Simon] just wanted to do something great. He thought the world was going to underestimate him. If he was going to earn the respect of people, he'd have to do something big."

Glen rubbed his forehead, thinking hard.

"He proposed the idea that we steal from thieves—that made it morally justifiable. It was a strange way of thinking. Once he said to me, another Simonism, 'Everyone is equal at gunpoint.' That's when I knew he was crazy. There's a fine line between insanity and brilliance."

• ◆ •

Leonard Post's Salida home, where he's lived for thirty-nine years, is a study in serenity. Sparsely furnished with handcrafted wood pieces, open and breezy, the small bungalow near the center of town has a perfect view of the mountain that provides the scenic town's backdrop, embroidered with a giant S formed of boulders. Post's children live nearby; a daughter who teaches at the local elementary school frequently walks over for lunch.

In April 2006, Post recalled the investigation into the Dutcher murders. Sitting at a spacious kitchen table sipping coffee, the former sheriff of Salida was a broad, thick-chested man with silver hair, a ruddy complexion, and large, rough hands. His voice was gentle and deep as he remembered finding the deceased Dutchers on January 3, 2001.

He'd been heading to Guffey to look into a shooting in town when he received a second call about another suspicious death.

"It was very strange," he remembered. "You very rarely got those calls. I arrived at the Dutchers' at around 2 p.m. I saw them, Mr. and Mrs. Dutcher, and it was obvious to me a real violent act had occurred. I saw what I thought were defensive wounds. . . . I started on getting a search warrant for the house. There was a lot of traveling to get a judge. . . . Then, around 4:30, it was getting dark, and I looked up the hill and saw what appeared to be a structure. I found Tony's body and I thought, 'Do we have a murder-suicide on our hands?' There were a lot of things going through my head."

Post and the Park County deputies assigned to the case had surmised this was an unusual homicide nearly immediately.

"My struggle was to answer the question: Why did this happen? What was the motive? Three things usually motivate a murder: sex, money, or revenge. I was starting to get some bad feelings about it.

"It took us about three days to collect hundreds of pieces of evidence, including Carl Dutcher's big gun safe, filled with major weapons. He had a federal firearms license. . . . We looked for something out of context. It could be a burglary gone bad, but it didn't appear to be. There was no forcible entry. The people who came up here went up to kill these people rather than steal from them."

Post sipped his coffee and drummed his fingers on the tabletop.

"I thought the crime was planned, but not organized. The clues at the crime scene tell you what kind of personality you're looking for. We knew we were dealing with a disorganized personality—the definition of a kid, I guess."

Post admitted he and Park County deputy Bob Horn had disagreed on who was the primary suspect. Horn held the family in suspicion and targeted Charles.

"I didn't," said Post. "Nothing fit."

But the Dutcher sons had to be eliminated as subjects, so investigation into the family members had continued. Post didn't like it. He had attended the funeral, watching Isaac Grimes, whose name had come up several times and with whom he'd already spoken once. Then he and Dave Sadar had interviewed his friends, Glen Urban, Simon Sue, and Jon Matheny, at Palmer High School.

"Sadar and I were comfortable working together," said Post. "I broke him in in Wheat Ridge, Colorado, years before. We knew each other's habits. On hearing the boys' alibi, my reaction was everything fits together too conveniently. There was something about Jon Matheny that didn't appear to be truthful. Simon Sue was a nervous talker. We were still not getting the facts we needed."

Well into the end of February, Post and Horn still disagreed on whom to target. Post thought the Dutchers were secondary at best. Isaac was the strongest suspect; Post knew he'd have to break Isaac's alibi down.

"We decided that among the four, Isaac was the weak link. Two reasons: He was the youngest and he had a conscience. Donna Grimes was beginning to feel uneasy in her heart. She told me, 'I know my son,' then asked, 'Could he do this?'"

Post had set up the March 8 interview with Isaac. He wanted his mother there. If anyone could make him tell the truth, it was her. Post's eyes filled with tears as he recalled the interview.

"It was heartbreaking. You should have seen her face. She watched her son die right there," he said.

Post said he had been sad, but not surprised, on the day he'd heard about Jenny Vandresar's car crash and subsequent arrest. "Jenny was in shock from the first night. I saw her depression. I told her I needed her to help me get through the case. It was classic depression, up and down by the day. You could tell, though, she was going downhill."

Post had held fast to his belief that Jon Matheny was the gunman who killed Carl and JoAnna Dutcher.

"When we interviewed him on March 8, after Isaac, I expected him to say, 'Yeah, I took Isaac up there but I didn't do anything.' But he denied everything, held to the alibi. His mother, Bonnie, said, 'No, this couldn't be. He was sleeping in his bed.' He pulled the wool over her eyes so bad. I know she thinks I'm the devil and I understand why: I took her son away from her. You want to believe your kids. She can't imagine that Jon could kill."

Post had challenged Jon's persistent silence about the case. Even in his plea agreement, he had never made an admission or implicated anyone. Simon had said of him, "Yeah, he killed the old-timers." Glen and Isaac had both identified him as the shooter. He had admitted, finally, taking his car up there. Why had he gotten his tires changed? Why would he destroy his clothes? Why would he clean his car so carefully? What about the calls from his house to Simon in Canada on New Year's Eve and the following morning? Why, when he had been put on the spot, facing life without parole, would he not tell the story if he was innocent?

"I think Jon has the ability to kill again," said Post. "He's probably gang-affiliated in prison. He came to court tattooed." Post said informants in the Park County Jail—inmates who were, admittedly, unreliable witnesses—had told him Jon had bragged about the crime.

Post said he would go to his grave believing that if not for Simon Sue, the murders would not have occurred, even though the Dutchers had been the target because of the Isaac connection.

"Simon always portrayed himself as being the leader. There was no one above him," said Post. "He knew how to pick people who would follow him. I believe he intentionally chose them for specific reasons. Look, he comes out and shows these assault rifles to these kids. There's probably not twenty families in Colorado Springs with these kinds of weapons. It doesn't surprise me that they were impressed.

"I felt Simon's level of remorse was just below Matheny's. His story at the presentencing interview was that he did this to manipulate the other boys for money. He said he didn't think they would kill anybody. But if they didn't do it, what would have happened? He'd squeeze them for more money as he had in the past. They were his and he knew it."

Post said he still regretted that Charles Dutcher had ever been considered a suspect. He saw Charles as one of those people who never have any luck in the world.

"Everybody lost somebody in this; Charles lost everybody."

Post's grown son dropped in to ask his dad a quick favor. They discussed plans to pick up a boat trailer later in the afternoon. Father and son were amiable, relaxed, and easy with one another. Post said he was glad the case was over, at least for now.

"I've come to the attitude that we'll take it as it comes," he said. Afternoon sun glinted through a wall of glass bricks in the adjoining room. Post squinted into the bright light. "Our office is never gonna back down."

•◆•

September 2006 placed two peripheral participants in the Dutcher murder cases in the news.

Sheriff Fred Wegener, the broad-shouldered, thick-necked, crew-cut lawman who'd been at the crime scene the first day and had appeared in court numerous times, faced cameras from national, state, and local news outlets on September 27, after ordering the Park County SWAT team to storm Platte Canyon High School in hopes of ending a hostage situation.

Dwayne Morrison, a bearded man in a blue hooded sweatshirt, carrying a camo backpack, had burst into the school earlier in the day, fired a few shots, and taken a group of girls hostage, claiming he had a bomb. Students had been evacuated from the school a little after 2 p.m.

Around 3 p.m., Sheriff Wegener confirmed that two females were being held hostage inside the school. Four others had been released, one by one. Wegener had decided to enter the school and save the remaining two after the man cut off negotiations. The SWAT team, using explosives, had burst into the classroom where the hostages were being held. Morrison had shot at the officers, then had shot the girl he was using as a human shield, then himself. The second hostage had escaped without being injured, at least not physically. Dead were Morrison and sixteen-year-old Emily Keyes. Everyone in the small town of Bailey knew Emily. She had a twin brother. She had been a waitress at the popular Cutthroat Café.

Wegener was visibly shaken at the press conference.

"I'm still somewhat shocked this can happen in a rural county," he said. Platte Canyon High School, "Home of the Huskies," sat in a picturesque winding canyon about halfway between Columbine High School in Littleton and Fairplay. Wegener had a son at the school.

Wegener said Morrison "did traumatize and assault our children," implying the assault was "of a sexual nature."

"This is something that has changed my school, changed my community," he said. "My small county is gone. I've gone from upset to angry that this man has done this to our community, has done this to our children."

Earlier in the month, in Colorado Springs, a death notice had appeared in the *Gazette*. Marlon Jagnandan of Denver, the handsome law student who'd testified at the sentencing hearing of his brother, Simon Sue, had died in his Denver apartment at age thirty. He had passed the Colorado state bar exam just a few months earlier.

Sorrow trumped sorrow for Nadia Sue. She still hoped for a successful appeal in Simon's case and was angered that his defense attorney, Ann Kaufman, hadn't held out for a trial. She believed a jury would have found Simon innocent of the charges made against him in Judge Plotz's court: that he masterminded the Dutcher killings, that he strong-armed and brain-washed Isaac Grimes and Jon Matheny. Those boys were not automatons, she argued, but criminals who acted of their own free will.

"I never heard of the OARA until Grimes and Matheny were arrested and charged," she said. "It was nothing more than a boys' club, kids' fantasies."

Nadia and her husband Keith had urged Simon to accept a plea bargain in 2003, but years later she regretted that advice.

"Keith and I convinced Simon to take the plea, not knowing it was for conspiracy to commit first degree murder," she said. (Attorney Kaufman declined to comment on the Sue case and the resulting plea bargain.)

As often as possible, Nadia made the long drive from Colorado Springs, across the bare plains to Sterling, to visit Simon. From jail, he filed prolific legal motions. In prison he had become a passionate student of the law, and his mother believed that he would eventually prevail in his efforts to free himself.

She couldn't allow herself to believe otherwise. She had lost her youngest son to prison; now another son was gone. The long arm of tragedy that reached out from the Dutcher home at Bear Trap Ranch had forever changed the lives of everyone it touched.

•◆•

Christmas approached. Bonnie Matheny set up a plastic nativity scene on the small square of lawn in front of her white stucco bungalow in the Old North End. Inside, wood floors gleamed beneath a row of tall south-facing windows dressed in crisp white curtains. Hers was the kind of house with cats on the windowsills, black cats gazing silently at the outdoor winter scene from a warm perch. Tyra, a short-haired bulldog mix with a bald patch on her side belly, paced back and forth from kitchen to dining room, her toenails clicking on the hard floors.

"She's one of Jon's strays," said Bonnie, patting Tyra on the neck.

Heidi sat in the living room watching television. Beyond her, Christmas tree lights sparkled red and green.

Bonnie's pale skin matched the cream color of her Irish knit sweater. A gold Scottish cross hung from her neck. Her blue eyes were light and cool as an iced-over pond.

"Simon reminded me of Eddie Haskell on *Leave It to Beaver*," said Bonnie, imitating Simon's cheery greeting: "Well, *hello*, Mrs. Matheny!" She'd thought it a bit odd, but it hadn't raised her suspicion. Simon's dad had sometimes come over to the house to help Jon with his car. Bonnie had talked to Nadia Sue on the phone regularly, trying to track down Jon. She liked Nadia, thought her a lovely woman.

She recalled that Isaac Grimes had been around a lot. Jon had driven him to work and picked him up most days. She hadn't thought anything of it; that was the kind of friend Jon was. Besides, she had known the Grimes parents had their hands full with two little boys at home, Rob laid up with a back injury, and Donna working. She had known Rob Grimes for years; before he'd been injured they'd worked together at the Garden of the Gods Club, where, for a time, he'd been executive chef and she'd been pastry chef. She remembered him as an outgoing guy with a great sense of humor.

Bonnie spoke about the night of Jon's arrest.

"I met him there, at the police station, on March 8. He was being held in a room and couldn't leave. Instead, they arrested him. We were in there two and a half hours. I tried to leave twice and take my son. It was horrible. I shook for hours afterward."

Jon's interrogation on March 8 had become a contested issue in court when it appeared he was still heading for trial. Judge Kenneth Plotz had disallowed the interview as evidence, and prosecutors had argued before the Colorado Supreme Court, asking that Plotz's ruling be overturned. Elvin Gentry had represented Jon in the case. At issue was whether the police violated Jon's Miranda rights when they obtained statements from him by means of custodial interrogation without first advising him of his rights. The defense had to show that he was, in fact, in custody during the interview; the prosecution had to prove that he was not.

Dave Sadar's account of the interrogation went like this: He went to Carl's Jr. and asked Jon if he could come down to the police department with him. Jon drove. They talked, not about the case but about cars.

Jon called his mom and she arrived at 7 p.m. The interview was videotaped. Sadar told him, "You're free to leave at any time and you're not under arrest. . . . You could answer or not answer any questions we ask you. . . . If you thought an attorney was in order you could ask for one. . . . Since you're a juvenile and your mom is here, any time you want to talk to her in private, we'll see you're afforded that opportunity."

According to Sadar, at no time during the interview had the defendant or his mother asked to leave. Police moved in and out of the room while the interview took place. Finally, Jon leaned forward, placed his hands on the table in front of him, and repeated the alibi one last time: He'd met Isaac at Carl's Jr., then driven to Glen Urban's garage, drunk some rum, returned home at 9 p.m., and stayed there until 6 or 7 the next day. At that point, convinced this version of events was untrue, Leonard Post had arrested Jon. It was 8:30 p.m., one and a half hours after the interview had begun.

Plotz had argued it was clear that the officers had intended to hold Jon from the beginning and had ordered the interview suppressed. The Colorado Supreme Court found that Matheny had not been in custody within the meaning of *Miranda* until Post formally placed him under arrest. Had he gone to trial, his prearrest statements would have been admissible.

Bonnie said it was true she disliked Leonard Post: "He had a vendetta against my son." She described her fears for Jon when he was in the Park County jail.

"He wasn't allowed outside once in three years," she said. "He was in solitary confinement until he turned eighteen. Once, a badly beaten guy was brought in and left in holding. No doctors saw to him. Jon saw it. I was terrified for his safety from phone call to phone call."

She hauled out a photo album and proudly displayed a number of photos of Jon taken at the Limon Correctional Facility, where he was now incarcerated. He was bulked up, arms as big as tree trunks, his head shaven. He smiled, looked healthy. The dark circles around his eyes had lightened. Bonnie saw her son's physical transformation as a triumph in learning how to survive prison.

"They clean doorknobs for two hours, then work out all day," she said, critical of the lack of real jobs for most inmates. "You have to keep your body strong. You have to keep your mind strong. Jon reads history, economics, and health books. He earned his GED with a 100 percent scored on three sections. He has earned a single cell. He's lucky to have a real job working in the warehouse processing food shipments. He's a very talented artist." He hoped to be a graphic designer when he left prison. But the only outlet at Limon, the art and hobby shop, was reserved for those inmates who'd been there for three years without a write-up. The tattoos, she said, scoffing at the notion that they represented gang activity, were part of his artistic expression.

She pulled a sheaf of letters from the album. Neat, curving penmanship was illustrated with meticulously drawn cartoons. One letter, illustrated with a beautiful orange and pink sky and a bold yellow sun read:

Dear Mom and Heidi:

Every day I look out and see the sunrise, because I know you are at home looking at the same sky.
    Love,
    Jon

Bonnie's heart went out to the many young men she saw in prison each week when she visited Jon. She had realized shortly after he arrived there that for most inmates, the visits and telephone calls and cards stopped coming shortly after they were incarcerated.

"They're just boys, young men, and nobody comes to see them anymore." A group of them, friends of Jon's, called her Mom, she said. To provide a forum for their artwork, she had started a Web site where greeting cards, prints, and posters drawn by inmates with whatever materials were at hand, were displayed and were available for sale.

Bonnie said she awaited the day Jon would return home as a result of victory in the Colorado Court of Appeals. Her faith lay in the belief that Jon had been represented illegally in at least four instances before his plea bargain. If Jon's current sentence stood, he wouldn't be eligible for parole until he was in his fifties and could possibly be in prison until he was an elderly man in his eighties.

When she heard he'd accepted a guilty plea, she said, she went nuts.

"His attorney will say I was a raving lunatic," she laughed. "I was furious with him. He was kind enough to come and sit with me as I lashed out at him. Jon tried to calm me and said, 'Mom, you're going to have to accept that I am going to prison.'"

Bonnie said she wasn't sure Isaac Grimes remembered what had really happened on the night Carl, JoAnna, and Tony were killed. She had read his accounts of the murders and found them to be inconsistent. She believed his ability to recount the gruesome events might have been impaired by the trauma he'd experienced.

"Whatever happened," she said, "he's the only one who knows, and now he's checked out. I know where Jon was. And I know there were lots of guns in both of those houses." She referred to the Sues' Caramillo Street house and the Dutcher home.

Lawyers had advised her not to speak specifically about the charges against Jon, Bonnie said. But she knew that he had genuinely feared for her life and Heidi's when he first went to jail. Bonnie said she hadn't answered the phone for weeks; she'd been afraid of who might be on the other end. Only once had Jon spoken to his mother about his involvement with the OARA.

"He told me, 'When it first started, I thought it was something good. Then, when I knew it wasn't, I couldn't get out.'"

Bonnie said her church gave her strength, and recently she'd become engaged to a man she'd met there. The new man in her life, she said, loved her and could handle all that she brought with her, including a disabled daughter and a son in prison.

"I'm blessed," she said, a smile creeping across her face as she looked toward the coming new year, when her life would change once again.

•◆•

Nearly six years after she'd lost her son, Jenny Vandresar was finding insight into a new life through training and therapeutic programs at the Denver Women's Correctional Facility, where she was serving the remainder of her ten-year sentence.

Parole had been denied at the first hearing in September 2006, but Jenny would be up again in a year's time.

Meanwhile, she worked every day in the prison's K-9 unit, training dogs in an innovative program that used inmates to train animals from humane shelters and animal rescue organizations. Supported by adoption fees, the program offered a last chance for many of the dogs that entered, as well as for some of the women who trained them. Some of the dogs were beautiful purebreds, some were mutts; all were given veterinary care and extensive behavioral training. Inmates who completed the Prison Trained K-9 Companion Program left the prison with skills and certification that could translate into good jobs on the outside.

At Denver Women's, Jenny had also participated in another rare treatment program for substance abusers. The Level 6 Therapeutic Community, or TC, was a seventy-two-bed comprehensive treatment program that addressed all aspects of a substance abuser's history and offered individualized recovery plans for each participant. The eight-month program had stripped Jenny down, then built her up again, said her sister, Kathy Creech.

While in TC, Jenny had begun writing Donna and Isaac Grimes, asking Isaac how he was doing but not bringing up the subject of Tony or anything that might upset him. With Donna she shared stories of her own life on the inside.

She had wanted very much to testify at Isaac's final resentencing hearing before Judge Plotz, when the ten years had been added back onto his sentence, but there had been too many obstacles in the way. She knew that Isaac had decompensated and turned more inward at that time, rejecting contact with his parents or anyone. She had felt her forgiveness could help him. Under Colorado law, it was the victim's right to attend the hearing, but typically, a victim was brought in by the prosecution. Jenny had been asking to appear for the defense. It had proved to be impossible to arrange transportation, security, and permission to appear. Still, those who had heard her letter read aloud in court had never forgotten it.

Kathy Creech had told a *Denver Post* reporter that her sister remembered Isaac as "a charming, intelligent kid with a good sense of humor" and "she didn't want to see him discarded.

"There is a concern that she won't be taken seriously," said Creech, "because people don't understand. How could a mother ever forgive the person who killed her child? But she's really very concerned about Isaac, and hearing about his mental health really compelled her to try to reach out and help in any way she can, even if it's just to say, 'I forgive you.'"

In a letter to another reporter, Jenny had written, "Tony was the most wonderful person I ever met and my life is richer for having known him. As for Isaac, in his heart he's a good boy. He's just very sick right now."

•◆•

"I believe it's genuine. She's delightful. I consider her a friend. She likes to crochet; I like to knit," said Donna Grimes of Jenny Vandresar. A slight wave added to her thin brown hair, Donna wore silver hoops in her ears, ironed jeans, and a red sweater on a brilliant January 2007 afternoon. She sat in a colorful coffee shop, recounting her family's setbacks and progress over the past six years.

She could barely remember much of what had happened around the end of 2000, a critical time for Isaac, she admitted.

"I had two toddlers at home at the time, I worked, and I had a sick husband," she said. "Honestly, I barely knew my own name."

Isaac, she said, had been reduced to medium security for the past two years but continued to isolate himself and take his meals in his cell. A new psychologist at San Carlos had recently told the family "he has been so driven inside his own head, it will be a long time coming back." Recently, Donna said, he had been transferred to another unit, where he would have to come out for meals and would have an art class. Whether he would participate remained to be seen.

"He really began to decompensate around the time of reconsideration," said Donna, referring to the hearing where Dale Parrish and Cathleen Mann had urged Judge Plotz to reconsider the length of Isaac's sentence. "I think he was convinced God was going to set him free. He went back to jail and took himself off all medication. He was on Reperidol, an antipsychotic med that helped him sleep, and Effexor, an antidepressant.

"There was nothing we could do. When he was convicted, we lost legal custody. He was a ward of the court. We couldn't enlist a lawyer on his behalf; he had to hire and fire his lawyer. The alternative, when he began to falter, was to petition for legal custody of him. We talked to the people at San Carlos, and they said the criterion for legal custody was whether he was harmful to himself or others; he wasn't either of those. He was adamantly opposed.

"When he came to court for the second part of reconsideration, after the court had ordered that the ten years taken from his sentence be reinstated, his case manager told us, 'He understands the criteria: You can have an attorney or not have an attorney.' He chose not to have one."

Donna said she worried about the time when Isaac would leave San Carlos and enter the general population of one of the larger adult prisons in the system.

"They've told him he can't stay there forever," she said. "They're gonna fix him up good enough to put him back in another prison, where he'll be killed. I'm sure if he hadn't been transferred to San Carlos, he'd be dead."

If Isaac survived, he would be eligible for parole in 2028, the year he turned forty-three, but could conceivably be in prison until he was seventy.

A bright spot in her life, Donna said, was her friendship by correspondence with Jenny Vandresar.

"She first wrote both Isaac and me about a year ago, saying she wished she had spoken up for Isaac earlier in the court proceedings. She said she did what the prosecutors told her to do at the time. She asked for our forgiveness. Can you imagine?" Donna wrote Jenny back, and though Jenny had continued to write Isaac, he hadn't answered her letters.

"Jenny and I get together by mail and order him a special food package four times a year," said Donna. "Recently I sent her some yarn for a project. She wrote me saying she hoped I didn't feel I needed to pay her for her support of Isaac, that it was given freely, with no expectation of anything in return. I wrote back: You're a good woman and a good woman needs yarn."

She saw it as a sign of good health that Jenny enjoyed using her hands and making things. "I knew I was getting better when I wanted to bake again," Donna said. She'd made blueberry muffins for Rob and the boys just that morning.

Donna cited other miracles in her life, including her church's continued support of Isaac and the entire family.

"Our church is still paying our defense costs. We still owe thirteen thousand dollars, and every month a check goes out from donations raised. Whenever we go to court, we'll come home to find that someone has sent us a Safeway card to buy groceries."

Donna said her little boys, now nine and eleven, mentioned their brother every day. They sent him drawings and letters on special occasions.

"We've told them that if anyone asks about Isaac, they can talk about it or not," she said. "One of the boys told a woman recently that he has a brother in prison. She was very kind and talked to him about it."

From jail, Isaac had at first sent his little brothers pages of math problems to work on. They would solve the problems and send the pages back to Isaac to be graded.

"The last normal letter he sent to the family was to his youngest brother on his birthday the year before last," said Donna. "Last year was the first year Isaac forgot his birthday."

Donna let loose a tear and her voice cracked slightly.

"Almost every day when we do our Bible reading and prayer time at night, one of the boys says, 'God, please have your hand on Dad's back and on Isaac's brain.'"

•◆•

Charles Dutcher moved quickly from grill top to dish pantry in the kitchen of the Crystola Inn. He'd taken a new job in the Highway 24 roadhouse, a traditional beer and pool joint near Woodland Park. He dished meatloaf, barbecue ribs, steaks, burgers, roast pork, mashed potatoes, and gravy to hungry road warriors and regulars. He wore a baseball hat, his long hair pulled back in a tight braid.

The years he'd spent on the mountain, honoring the memory of his father, mother, and son by trying to love the place they loved, had taken their toll. He'd put a fireplace in and chopped wood. He'd pulled up ruined carpet and replaced it. He'd alienated himself from the world as best he could. Occasionally, when a Park County sheriff's department squad car would drive down Apache Trail, he'd holler at the top of his lungs at the cops he believed were still watching his every move.

"My father told me one day he didn't understand why he always had to be the asshole," Charles remembered. "He said he always tried to do the right thing. He looked at me and said, 'Son, when I'm gone, you're gonna be the asshole.' He was right."

Charles laughed softly and scraped at the grill, throwing on another burger.

"I tried to do something I couldn't do," he said.

On that mountain he'd lost a son so young his death certificate read, "Occupation—Student. Place of business—High school." He'd lost a mother who always told her son she loved him no matter what. He'd lost a father who did not.

Charles had finally left Bear Trap Ranch and his father's land behind. He'd sold the acreage, including the hillside where Tony's ruined fort lay, to next-door neighbors. He'd moved to Woodland Park, near the path of the Hayman fire, close enough to the wilderness to catch sight of a deer or an elk, and far enough away from the noise and lights of Colorado Springs.

"I can't be a recluse forever," said Charles. "I'm ready to be part of the world again."

Charles Dutcher knew something about the cost of a lost life, a life that could never be replaced. He had walked through fire and he'd been burned. But he was alive, and although he would always carry the memory of his losses with him, he was free.

NOTES ON SOURCES

Chapter 1

Denver Rocky Mountain News, "4 Slayings Stun Small Town," by Robert Sanchez and Sarah Huntley, Jan. 4, 2001.

Multiple interviews with Charles Dutcher.

Colorado Bureau of Investigation, Report of Investigation, Jan. 12, 2001.

Park County Sheriff's Office Continuation Sheet, filed by Deputy Mike Valdez, Jan. 3, 2001.

Chapter 2

Interview with Kathy Creech, Sept. 2006.

Videotaped interview with Jennifer Vandresar and Kathy Creech from Teller County Sheriff's office, Jan. 3, 2001.

Multiple interviews with Charles Dutcher.

Chapter 3

Colorado Bureau of Investigation, Report of Investigation, filed by Michael (Dave) Sadar, Jan. 12, 2001.

Autopsy reports on Carl, JoAnna, and Anthony Dutcher.

Reports filed by CBI Agent Michael (Dave) Sadar, Investigator James Howell, and Investigator Leonard Post, Jan. 4–5, 2001.

Chapter 4

Reports filed by Investigator Leonard Post and CBI Agent Michael (Dave) Sadar, Jan. 5–8, 2001.

Park County Sheriff's Office Continuation Sheet, filed by Bob Horn, dated Jan. 19, 2001, interview with Ty Dutcher.

Park County Sheriff's Office Continuation Sheet, filed by Bob Horn, dated Feb. 1, 2001, interview with James Dutcher.

Park County Sheriff's Office Continuation Sheet, name of filing officer indistinguishable, account of processing of Dutcher gunsmith shop/garage by CBI Agent James Crippin with assistance from Park County deputies and neighbor Alton Frantz, dated Jan. 5, 2001.

Chapter 5

Interviews with Leonard Post, Kathy Creech, Donna Grimes, and Charles Dutcher.
The Gazette, "A Nagging Little Detail," by Deedee Correll, Jan. 15, 2005.

Chapter 6

Multiple interviews with Donna Grimes.
Isaac Grimes's reports to the OARA recovered from computer hard drive.
Transcripts of multiple interviews with Isaac Grimes by investigators and attorneys.

Chapter 7

Interviews with multiple acquaintances of Simon Sue.
Court file, Simon Sue, list of items seized from E. Caramillo St. and E. Columbia St.
Interview with Glen Urban, Colorado Springs, Feb. 17, 2005.
Transcripts of multiple interviews with Isaac Grimes by investigators and attorneys.
Interview with Bonnie Matheny, Dec. 15, 2006.
Interviews with friends of Jon Matheny.

Interview with Cathie Cumming, mid-Dec. 2006.

Interview with Jess Brooke, Fort Collins, Aug. 8, 2005.

Investigators' reports filed by Michael (Dave) Sadar, Leonard Post, and James Howell on interviews conducted with Sue, Urban, Matheny, and Grimes at Palmer High School, Jan.–Feb. 2001.

Chapter 8

Transcript of Isaac Grimes's interrogation at Colorado Springs Police Department, Mar. 8, 2001.

Multiple interviews with Donna Grimes.

Chapter 9

Police report and search warrant affadavit, People's Exhibits 16 and 17.

Transcript of videotaped interview with Simon Sue at Colorado Springs Police Department, Mar. 8, 2001.

Chapter 10

Rocky Mountain News, "2 Arrested in Guffey Killings," by Dick Foster, Apr. 27, 2001.

Police report and transcript of recorded conversation between Glen Urban and Simon Sue.

Interview with Glen Urban, Feb. 17, 2005.

Glen Urban report, secured from computer hard drive, dated Feb. 10, 2001.

Report by Detective Richard Gysin, Colorado Springs Police Department, and transcript of recorded interview with Anthony Jacobs.

Chapter 11

Westword, "Welcome to America," by Alan Prendergast, June 23, 2005.

District Attorney's record of direct file petition with Judge Stanley Mayhew, Colorado Springs, Mar. 9, 2001.

The Gazette, "Palmer Students Arrested," by Raquel Rutledge and Eric Gorski, Mar. 10, 2001.

Multiple news accounts of Texas Seven arrests in Colorado Springs.

Interview with Kathy Creech, Sept. 2006.

The Gazette, "Neighbors Relieved but Still Take Precautions," by Eric Gorski, Mar. 10, 2001.

The Gazette, "Lawyer: Band Inspired Killings," by Bill Hethcock and Jeremy Meyer, Mar. 14, 2001.

Multiple interviews with Donna Grimes.

Interview with Bonnie Matheny, Dec. 15, 2006.

Chapter 12

Interview with Cathie Cumming, Dec. 2006.

Transcript of Glen Urban interview at Ed Farry's law office, Colorado Springs, Apr. 6, 2001.

Glen Urban report, secured from computer hard drive, dated Feb. 10, 2001.

Chapter 13

The Lever, Palmer High School student newspaper, May 2001, excerpted with permission of Anna Nussbaum.

Chapter 14

Interview with Leonard Post, Apr. 2006.

Photocopy of oath, People's Exhibit 14.

Transcript of Apr. 23, 2001, interview with Isaac Grimes, Fairplay District Attorney's Office.

The Gazette, "Slaying Defendant Accepts Offer," by Jeremy Meyer, May 1, 2001.

The Gazette, "Grimes Faces Prison at Early Age," by Bill Hethcock, May 20, 2001.

The Gazette, "Slain Son Remembered" by Jeremy Meyer, May 22, 2001.

Multiple newspaper accounts of Grimes's preliminary hearing and Sue's first court appearance.

The Gazette, "Park County Courthouse Fire Looks like Arson," by Bill McKeown, May 31, 2001.

Chapter 15

The Gazette, "Suspect Left Chilling Entry in Palmer's Yearbook," by Jeremy Meyer, June 1, 2001.

The Gazette, "Marching for Faith," by Danielle Nieves, June 1, 2001.

Multiple interviews with Donna Grimes.

Correspondence between Donna and Robin Grimes and Shaun Kaufman, reprinted with permission of Donna and Robin Grimes.

The Gazette, "Grimes Family Dismisses Attorney," by Jeremy Meyer, June 11, 2001.

The Gazette, "Suspect in Triple Slaying Asks for Move from Jail," Briefs, June 2001.

The Gazette, "Teen 'Brainwashed' in Killings," by Bill Hethcock, June 26, 2001.

Denver Rocky Mountain News, "Minister Seeks Clemency for Teen Triple-Murder Suspect," June 30, 2001.

Interview with Reverend Promise Lee, Aug. 27, 2001.

The Gazette, "New Attorney, New Deal?" by Bill Hethcock, June 26, 2001.

Photocopies of letters of support provided by Grimes family.

Letter to District Attorney Ed Rodgers by Pastor Keith Hedstrom, provided by Hedstrom.

Letter from Isaac Grimes, dated July 12, 2001, excerpted with permission of Grimes family.

Transcript of recorded telephone interview with Investigator D. J. Hannigan, June 25, 2001.

The Gazette, "Crash: Suspect's Son Was a Victim in Triple Slaying," by Bill Hethcock, July 31, 2001.

Chapter 16

The Gazette, "Jury to Deliberate in Carjacking," by Bill Hethcock, May 30, 2001.

The *Gazette,* "Boy, 13, Faces Charges in Shooting of Sister, 16," Aug. 26, 2001.

The Gazette, "Columbine Parent Arrested," Associated Press, June 13, 2001.

Interview with Glen Urban, Colorado Springs, Feb. 17, 2005.

The Gazette, "High-Profile Lawyer in Springs Barred from Practicing," by Jeremy Meyer, Oct. 12, 2001.

Information in this section comes from Dr. Frank Barron's extensive testimony before Judge Plotz at Isaac Grimes's sentencing hearing, Mar. 12, 2002.

Chapter 17

Investigator D. J. Hannigan's report, Oct. 18, 2001.

Investigator D. J. Hannigan's report, interview with Gabe and Simone Melchor, Oct. 18, 2001.

Photocopy of Jim Jones Summer Camp flyer.

Photocopy of Simon Sue biography evidence.

Isaac Grimes's plea hearing, Fremont County Courthouse, Oct. 2001.

Multiple interviews with Donna Grimes.

Chapter 18

Interview with Cathie Cumming and Glen Urban, Dec. 2006.

Multiple media accounts of the Colorado drought of 2002.

Letters from supporters of Isaac Grimes and the Grimes family, provided by the Grimes family.

Press conference with Robin and Donna Grimes at their home, Mar. 8, 2002.

Denver Post, "Parents Grieve for 16-year-old Inmate Son," by Erin Emery, Mar. 11, 2002.

The Gazette, "Calhan School Suspends Girl Who Had Guns, Bullets," Briefs, Mar. 2002.

The Gazette, "Boys in Adult Prisons," by Bill Hethcock, Mar. 10, 2002.

Sentencing hearing for Isaac Grimes, Park County Courthouse, Mar. 12, 2002.

Colorado Springs Independent, "Rough Justice: Isaac Grimes' Crime and Punishment," by Kathryn Eastburn, Mar. 26, 2002.

Chapter 19

Preliminary hearing for Simon Sue, Park County Courthouse, Mar. 19, 2002.

The Gazette, "Slaying Witness's Family Warned to Watch Safety," by Jeremy Meyer, Mar. 21, 2002.

Transcript of e-mail correspondence from Monty Gore, Park County undersheriff.

Multiple interviews with Donna Grimes, Cathie Cumming, Glen Urban, and Charles Dutcher.

The Gazette, "Teen Says He Had to Kill," by Jeremy Meyer, Apr. 10, 2002.

Isaac Grimes's letters to his family excerpted with permission of Donna and Robin Grimes.

Various media accounts of the Hayman fire, Summer 2002.

The Gazette, "Lawyer Switch Will Delay Trial in Guffey Slayings," by Bill Hethcock, Sept. 1, 2002.

The Gazette, "Triple Slaying Suspect Wants Case Dismissed," Metro Briefs, Oct. 16, 2002.

Trial of Jennifer Vandresar, El Paso County District Court, Nov. 18–26, 2002.

The Gazette, "Woman Guilty in Head-On Crash," by Bill Hethcock, Nov. 27, 2002.

The Gazette, "Judge Asked to Throw Out 'Confession,'" by Bill Hethcock, Nov. 23, 2002.

The Gazette, "Deaths Sent Life into Spiral," by Bill Hethcock, Nov. 25, 2002.

The Gazette, "Driver Not Responsible for Death, Defense Says," by Bill Hethcock, Nov. 20, 2006.

Chapter 20

Multiple interviews with Donna Grimes.

Colorado Department of Corrections Web site.

Plea hearing for Simon Sue, Park County Courthouse, Feb. 25, 2003.

Various media accounts of the Colorado blizzard of 2003.

Various media accounts of Operation Iraqi Freedom.

Sentencing hearing for Simon Sue, Park County Courthouse, Aug. 27, 2003.

Interview with Charles Dutcher, Aug. 27, 2003.

Chapter 21

The Gazette, "Last Ex-Student Accused in Triple Slaying Pleads Guilty," by Bill Hethcock, Oct. 8, 2003.

Sentencing hearing for Jon Matheny, Park County Courthouse, Dec. 1, 2003.

Chapter 22

"The Depressive and the Psychopath," by Dave Cullen, www.slate.com, Apr. 20, 2004.

E-mails from Maze Mom throughout 2004.

Web petition on Betrayed Innocence Web site.

Interview with Bonnie Matheny, Dec. 15, 2006.

The Gazette, "4 Soldiers Charged in Iraqi Death," by Tom Roeder, Oct. 5, 2004.

Letter from Isaac Grimes to Judge Kenneth Plotz, reprinted with permission of Robin and Donna Grimes.

Conversations with Dale Parrish and Robin and Donna Grimes.

Reconsideration hearing for Isaac Grimes, Park County Courthouse, Dec. 27, 2004.

Chapter 23

Interview with Charles and Rhonda Dutcher, Bear Trap Ranch, Jan. 2005.

Letter from Isaac Grimes to Dale Parrish, dated Feb. 16, 2005, reprinted with permission of Donna and Robin Grimes.

Reconsideration hearing for Simon Sue, Park County Courthouse, Feb. 28, 2005.

The Gazette, "Guilty Plea Must Stand in Guffey Murders," by Bill Hethcock, Mar. 1, 2005.

Colorado Court of Appeals decision, Oct. 13, 2005.

Denver Post, "Leniency Sought for Son's Killer," by Steve Lipsher, Feb. 6, 2006.

Second reconsideration hearing for Isaac Grimes, Park County Courthouse, Feb. 8, 2006.

Rocky Mountain News, "Judge Scoffs at Leniency for Man in Guffey Killings," by Dick Foster, Feb. 11, 2006.

The Flume, "Matheny Resentenced," by Cate Malek, Feb. 9, 2006.

Interview with Bonnie Matheny, Dec. 15, 2006.

Chapter 24

"Witnessing Nature's Recovery from the Hayman Fire," by Robert Yackel, www.coloradodiscoveries.com/articles/lostcreek.html.

Denver Post, "Rebirth of a Forest," by Dave Curtin, July 3, 2006.

Interview with Glen Urban, Feb. 17, 2005.

Interview with Leonard Post, Apr. 10, 2006.

The Flume, "Platte Canyon Shooting Summary," by Tom Locke and Cate Malek, www.theflume.com, Sept. 28, 2006.

Interview with Bonnie Matheny, Dec. 15, 2006.

The Gazette, "Death Notices," Sept. 7, 2006.

Interview with Donna Grimes, Jan. 2007.

Telephone interview with Kathy Creech, Jan. 2007.

Interview with Charles Dutcher, Jan. 2007.

Interview with Nadia Sue, 2007.

AUTHOR'S NOTE

I relied upon thousands of pages of police and court records, on direct observation, and on numerous interviews for the information in this book. Turning the story into a dramatic narrative, I re-created some scenes as they were related to me by others, or as they were related within the record. In doing so, I have tried to construct them as accurately as possible, though I am aware that one person's recollection is not necessarily the same as another's and that any reconstructed experience not directly witnessed will contain a certain amount of authorial supposition. Where accounts have differed or are not corroborated, I have attempted to provide appropriate attribution to individual points of view.

Full disclosure: Before I began writing this book, I participated as a community college teacher of English composition in a brief correspondence with Simon Sue, believing strongly in every prisoner's right to continue his or her education. At the time I was offered the opportunity to teach the class, I introduced myself to Mr. Sue and his mother as a journalist who had covered his case for a newspaper. I let them know that I would continue to attend court proceedings and write about the cases. None of our student-teacher correspondence, nor any insights gained as a result of class assignments, has been used in the book.

I have tried to represent all participants in these cases as they were represented or represented themselves in court, in the official record, and as they were recalled by friends and family. Any errors that remain after careful documentation and consultation and following superb editing are mine.